PARTICIPATORY COMPOSITION

Participatory Composition

Video Culture, Writing, and Electracy

SARAH J. ARROYO

Southern Illinois University Press
Carbondale

An earlier version of chapter 5 was published as
"Playing to the Tune of Electracy: From Post-Process
to a Pedagogy Otherwise," *JAC* 25.4 (2005): 683–715.

16 15 14 13   4 3 2 1

Library of Congress Cataloging-in-Publication Data
Arroyo, Sarah J., 1970–
Participatory Composition : Video Culture, Writing,
and Electracy / Sarah J. Arroyo.
    pages cm
Includes bibliographical references and index.
ISBN-13: 978-0-8093-3146-8 (pbk. : alk. paper)
ISBN-10: 0-8093-3146-2 (pbk. : alk. paper)
ISBN-13: 978-0-8093-3147-5 (ebook)
ISBN-10: 0-8093-3147-0 (ebook)
1. Online authorship. 2. Digital media. 3. Communi-
cation and technology. 4. Multimedia systems—De-
sign. I. Title.
PN171.O55A77 2013
302.23'1—dc23   2012047214

For Chris

CONTENTS

Acknowledgments ix

1. Introduction:
   Electracy, Videocy, and Participatory Composition 1

2. Recasting Subjectivity for Electracy:
   From Singularities to Tubers 29

3. The Question of Definition:
   Choric Invention and Participatory Composition 49

4. Who Speaks When Something Is Spoken?
   Playing Nice in Video Culture 77

5. Participatory Pedagogy:
   Merging Postprocess and Postpedagogy 101

6. Afterword:
   Productive Knowledge, Participatory Composition 119

Notes 141

Works Cited and Consulted 147

Index 163

ACKNOWLEDGMENTS

Several people deserve thanks for contributing to the making of this book. They include

Victor Vitanza, my dissertation chair, mentor, and friend, whose work inspired this book. Victor continues to inspire me in all areas of life. Gregory Ulmer, whose concept of electracy frames all aspects of my scholarship and teaching. Geoffrey Carter, who single-handedly helped propel my own thinking into video and participatory cultures, read the manuscript, provided extremely helpful feedback, and suggested the title "Participatory Composition." Robert Leston, Byron Hawk, and Thomas Rickert, who through many conversations inspired the evolution of my ideas connecting the theories we were all working with to video and participatory cultures. Eileen Klink, my department chair at California State University, Long Beach, who tirelessly supported me and advocated for my work. The College of Liberal Arts at CSULB and specifically former dean Gerry Riposa, for granting me a sabbatical in spring 2011, which gave me the sustained time to finally rework my ideas. Kristine Priddy at Southern Illinois University Press, who was a particularly patient, kind, and supportive editor. Bahareh Alaei, Cortney Kimoto (Smethurst), and Amy Loy, graduate students who have collaborated with me on this and other works; Mark Olague, Suzan Gridley, Luis Orozco, Linda Hua, Sarah Roussin, Teresa Troutman, and Noel Vincent, all former graduate students, whose ideas, projects, and participation helped form the concepts that shape this book. Without these smart and savvy students, I would not have been able to reconceptualize my arguments for video and participatory cultures.

And, finally, to Chris, the love of my life since way back when, who is my backbone. And to my babies, Jackson, Ashton, and Madeline, who all were brought into this life while I was working on this book. You are all three wise souls who teach me something new every day. My unbelievable, little family—Thank you.

PARTICIPATORY COMPOSITION

1. Introduction: Electracy, Videocy, and Participatory Composition

> All the practices used to conduct schooling are relative to the apparatus of literacy. In the history of human culture there are but three apparatuses: orality, literacy, and now electracy. We live in the moment of the emergence of electracy, comparable to the two principal moments of literacy (the Greece of Plato, and the Europe of Galileo).
>
> —Gregory Ulmer, "What Is Electracy?"

> I believe that the arrival of free online video may turn out to be just as significant a media development as the arrival of print. It is creating new global communities, granting their members both the means and the motivation to step up their skills and broaden their imaginations. It is unleashing an unprecedented wave of innovation in thousands of different disciplines: some trivial, some niche in the extreme, some central to solving humanity's problems. In short, it is boosting the net sum of global talent. It is helping the world get smarter.
>
> —Chris Anderson, "Film School: Why Online Video Is More Powerful than You Think"

Embed. Share. Comment. Like. Subscribe. Upload. Check in. The commands of our online world relentlessly prompt participation, encourage collaboration, and quite literally connect us in ways not possible even five years ago. This connectedness no doubt changes college writing courses in both form and content, thus creating a wide-open space for investigating new forms of writing and student participation. This book explores this dynamic space by arguing for a "participatory composition," inspired by the culture of online video sharing and framed through Gregory Ulmer's concept of *electracy*. Electracy can be compared to digital literacy but encompasses much more: a worldview for civic engagement, community building, and participation. For three decades, Ulmer has been predicting electracy's emergence, and he casts electracy as an "apparatus," a type of social machine that influences laws and conventions in a given historical era. *Participatory Composition* begins by exploring the apparatus of electracy in many of its manifestations while focusing on the participatory practices found in online video culture. Online video is becoming the prototypical experience of the Internet, and the culture it cultivates is both growing and already permeating the institutions of our daily lives. According to the *Cisco Visual Networking Index (VNI) Forecast, 2009–2014*, more than 91 percent of the web's global consumer traffic will be video by 2014. Surprisingly, Ulmer first envisioned electracy by way of analogue video in his 1989 book *Teletheory*, but he later changed the direction for electracy toward writing with hypertext in the 1990s. Thus, it will be my contention throughout *Participatory Composition* that we can again envision electracy through the lens of video: that writing practices are indeed shifting in the direction Ulmer has anticipated but with the added layer of sharing, networking, and participating that Ulmer could not entirely foresee. In *Teletheory*, Ulmer wrote, "The implication, and this is a premise, is that video permits the institutional *dissemination* of inventive thinking" (94; emphasis added), and while this has certainly been the case for the past several years, we can now add that video permits *participation* in inventive thinking. *Participatory Composition*, then, will cast electracy as the apparatus in which practices from video culture can be interrogated. As the framework for participatory composition, electracy "is to digital media what literacy is to alphabetic writing: an apparatus, or social machine, partly technological, partly institutional" (Ulmer, Introduction: "Electracy"). From this definition, we can see that electracy has a wide scope of influence. Writing, largely defined, is at the center of this scope of influence, and this book aims to interrogate the vast changes writing is undergoing within the larger context of the apparatus of electracy, participatory culture, and video culture. This wide framework creates the conditions for long-lasting disciplinary challenges to be addressed through a context framed by electracy, such as the construction of the writing subject, the role of definition in digital, malleable spaces, the question of authorship, and, of course, the creation of pedagogies for the electrate apparatus.

If the first purpose of this book is located in a general perspective in the sense that it merges the larger conceptions of participatory and video cultures with established practices for electracy, the second purpose takes a distinctly disciplinary perspective from within rhetoric and composition. D. Diane Davis argues that "the alliance between computers and composition [f]orces the posthumanist paradox into the writing classroom" (*Breaking Up* 249). That is, writing, in all of its manifestations, introduces a space where one doesn't "choose to write" but where, according to Cynthia Haynes, *"everything is writing"*(Haynes's "prosthetic rhetoric" qtd. in D. Davis, *Breaking Up* 250). In other words, the "posthumanist paradox" places writing at the center of human interaction, which makes it a cultural practice—not merely a tool for communicating thoughts—intertwined with identity construction, relationship building, and community involvement. The notion of "writing," then, plays a much larger, cultural role.

The general study of electronic spaces and composition is an extensive and expanding field of study that dates back to the early 1980s, exemplified by the early studies of the influences of word processing on student writing, such as David Dalton and Michael Hannafin's "The Effects of Word Processing on Written Composition" and Gail Hawisher's "Studies in Word Processing," to the nonlinear possibilities of hypertext for writing found in George Landow's and Jay David Bolter's work, and finally to interacting with students and teaching writing in online spaces as seen in Cynthia Haynes and Jan Rune Holmevik's *High Wired*. For nearly three decades, then, we have witnessed an explosion of scholarship interrogating technology and writing from several areas of study. From artists like Mark Amerika in "Expanding the Concept of Writing" and John Craig Freeman in "Imaging Place" to technical communication experts like Johndan Johnson-Eiola, rhetoricians like James Porter, and computers-and-composition gurus and prolific publishers like Hawisher and Cynthia Selfe, the amount of scholarship concerning technology and writing at large is impressive and dense. Much of the material interrogates specific problems and offers strategies for integrating technology into writing classes. Hawisher and Selfe's contribution in this regard cannot be overstated. Along with other collaborators over the years, Hawisher and Selfe have amassed an oeuvre of studies and gained recognition for their research in digital media and writing, which has significantly transformed the alliance between computers and composition.

Anne Frances Wysocki, Johndan Johnson-Eiola, Cynthia Selfe, and Geoffrey Sirc's *Writing New Media* remains an influential and highly useful text and offers concrete approaches for teaching composition with technology. More recently, J. Elizabeth Clark's "The Digital Imperative" shows how she refigured her composition course as an "emerging space for digital rhetoric" (27); Abby M. Dubisar and Jason Palmeri present strategies for teaching political video remix, and Cheryl Ball and James Kalmbach's collection *RAW: (Reading and Writing) New Media,* "builds on the first decade of work in new media research within English Studies" (*RAW* companion website) and offers many productive insights for the future of new media research. These works all serve as representative examples for how digital space continues to transform the teaching of composition, and I hope that *Participatory Composition's* specific focus on electracy and video culture will add another layer to this transformation.[1]

Many others have also contributed to the project of directly engaging the electrate apparatus in order to build a rhetoric for electracy, while not necessarily engaging composition pedagogy. Jeff Rice reminds us that scholarship for the electrate apparatus comes across "as both explanation and experiment" ("1963" 24). Accordingly, along with Ulmer, his former students have produced multiple works that engage with and perform electrate writing, and these works make up the network within which I place my book. These include Rice's *The Rhetoric of Cool*, Craig Saper's *Artificial Mythologies*, Michael Jarrett's *Drifting on a Read*, and Barry Mauer's "Lost Data, 2." Ulmer and his former students have also published *New Media/New Methods: The Academic Turn from Literacy to Electracy* (edited by Rice and Marcel O'Gorman), a collection associated with the "Florida School" of which they are a part. The self-named Florida School is intended to serve as "a form of pattern recognition, a strategy for organizing information in the otherwise overwhelming infoscape of new media studies and critical theory" (Rice and O'Gorman 7). Thus, while my work is not part of this act of self-naming, it can be seen as a link to and from it, or, perhaps, as a "friend" of it, as they suggest (7), along with many of my colleagues from the "Arlington School" whose work appears throughout this book. That is, my version of electrate writing, by way of "participatory composition," presents a version of what Rice and O'Gorman hope to accomplish with their own collection, since they write that *New Media/New Methods* "is meant to demonstrate as well how we have come to adopt Ulmer's notion of electracy, the consequent shift in meaning-making which follows—and integrates—orality and literacy" (5). Offering a version of electracy that dusts off Ulmer's earlier conception of "videocy" (from *Teletheory*), I'll update it with the practices associated with the culture of online video and put forth a viable practice for writing in the electrate apparatus.

Additionally, Lisa Gye's "Halflives, a MyStory," Gye and Darren Tofts's *Illogic of Sense: The Gregory L. Ulmer Remix*, and Talan Memmott's "Beyond Taxonomy" have all worked with electracy from an array of disciplinary perspectives and trajectories. In fact, Gye's article and accompanying MyStory have served as exceptional guides for students of electracy over the past several years. The sources I have cited represent only a fraction of the work these scholars have produced; each of them has taken electrate writing in their own direction, thereby creating less of an academic conversation and more of a complex network in which to place my own work. Finally, Collin

Brooke's *Lingua Fracta*, Thomas Rickert's *Acts of Enjoyment*, Byron Hawk's *A Counter-History of Composition*, Alexander Reid's *The Two Virtuals*, and Sidney Dobrin's *Postcomposition* also work alongside my effort from a disciplinary perspective. While they do not engage electracy specifically, they all call for a reconsideration of writing for the electrate apparatus, and they all present theories and practices for doing so, many of which I will build upon.

Participatory Composition is different in that it works with electracy by blending conceptions of video and participatory culture specifically to frame the book's central arguments, while making the arguments through a mix of scholarship in rhetoric and composition, continental theory, media studies, video sharing sites, and teaching situations. While I do not necessarily follow Rice, Saper, Mauer, and others by engaging in my own performance of electrate writing, I do present my arguments from a variety of perspectives while relying on exemplars from video culture, as well as creating accompanying videos that perform these arguments. Since electracy permeates all of the institutions of our lives, I hope that my focus on long-lasting theoretical questions in each chapter—the questions of subjectivity, definition, authorship, and pedagogy—combined with my research on electracy and video culture presents possibilities for electracy not yet articulated in existing works. This is not to say that what I do in this book is all that different from what has been done before; yet, I hope this layering of mixing emphasizes, first, that electracy is buzzing all around us; it is not something that we call up when we turn on our computers or mobile devices and shut down when we power them off. Rather, the cultural transformations, inspired by changes in technologies, reflect phenomena that reach us regardless of the presence of actual machines. Second, the behaviors and practices we see occurring in video culture, while not "new," present an unprecedented gateway for inquiry into the posthuman condition, and I hope to contribute to the growing number of studies doing so.

The Electrate Apparatus and Participatory Culture

Historically, electracy encompasses the second major shift in apparatus: the first was from orality to literacy, and now it's from literacy to electracy. According to Ulmer, electracy helps distinguish the "epochal possibility that what is at stake is not only different equipment but also different institutional practices and different subject formations from those we now inhabit" ("Foreword/Forward" xii). What Ulmer is suggesting here is that the apparatus of electracy impacts all areas of our lives—not just when we turn on our computers or mobile devices—and is creating a need to invent new practices for living in an electrate world. Of course Ulmer's articulation of the electrate apparatus calls upon the pioneering work of Walter Ong in

Orality and Literacy and Marshall McLuhan's in *Understanding Media* that
catapulted the study of the relationship between technology and humans to
the forefront. By making us aware of the impact of the move from orality
to literacy on human consciousness, Ong opened the door for future study
of language apparatuses. A statement made by Art Bingham in a review of
Orality and Literacy is quite pertinent. He reminds us that when discussing
our relationship with writing and print, Ong reveals that "our membership
in a society as completely committed to writing and print as ours has made
it necessary for [Ong] and others to describe primary orality in relation to
literacy. This necessity, he says, led to the use of such preposterous terms as
'oral literature.'" This statement connects directly to our present time when
we aim to describe the emergence of electracy and the electrate apparatus:
particularly with the use of such terms as "media literacy" or "electronic
literacy." Ulmer contends that we became "self-conscious about the nature
of the language apparatus only recently" ("Foreword/Forward" xi) and cites
Eric Havelock's *The Muse Learns to Write* as the best introduction to this
discovery. Ulmer suggests that Havelock and other grammatologists (histo-
rians of writing) "argued that we rediscovered the shift from orality to literacy precisely because we are moving out of literacy" (xi–xii). However, this
does not mean that electracy will surpass literacy; rather, electracy will work
alongside literacy and orality, as the apparatus continues in its emergence.

Similarly, at the 2005 annual meeting of the Conference on College Composition and Communication, Ulmer reiterated the importance of understanding the apparatus out of which our theories and practices emerge.
The apparatus, again, has to do with technologies, identity formations,
and institutions at work within a given time and place. Echoing Ong, Ulmer suggested that the aforementioned apparatus of print thus currently
drives how we think about and interact with our world in and out of the
academy, and, he suggested, is slowly being transformed (not eclipsed) by
the emergence of a new apparatus built around electracy. Ulmer reminded
us that electracy is often associated with electronic literacy; however, as
he was quick to point out, electracy has less to do with a new version of
literacy and more to do with a combination of the concepts of *electricity*
and *trace*. By combining the two terms, Ulmer echoes Derrida's idea that
the trace "is a rupture in metaphysics, a pattern of incongruities where the
metaphysical rubs up against the non-metaphysical" ("Jacques Derrida").
The trace of something does not appear as such, but the logic of it can be
exposed through a deconstructive intervention (*Of Grammatology* 65). Thus,
an engagement with the electric, or online, world necessarily leaves "traces"
of participation, and these traces, when juxtaposed, make up the electrate

experience. Both *electricity* and *trace* articulate the many societal features, logic, and metaphors we use to describe the electrate apparatus, which do not eclipse, but rather exist alongside the apparatus of print. Electracy emphasizes a multiplicity of meanings for any one concept, supports imagination, and encourages creativity and invention: all of which are traditionally not valued in a university environment built upon analytics. Ulmer called for us to become more aware of the emerging apparatus of electracy—which started with the invention of photography and continues today in the digital world—and encouraged us to intervene in its emergence. Our intervention will help invent and shape the new apparatus as it is unfolding, and Ulmer emphasized that we might intervene in the new apparatus best by helping to invent a rhetoric for electracy. The purpose of this book is to do just that: to intervene in the new apparatus by combining what we already know about electracy with the burgeoning culture of online video sharing, since, many of the practices manifesting in online video sharing sites reflect what Ulmer and others have been predicting for decades about the electrate apparatus.

Comparing the values and purposes for the three apparatuses is extremely useful, and the table allows us to see the different ways of seeing the world through the lenses of an oral, literate, and electrate apparatus. It is not difficult to find examples of how these schemas are playing out in the online and offline worlds. Practice, for example, is "entertainment" in electracy, and we only have to go as far as YouTube to see how entertainment has expanded from something people only consume in their leisure time to an entity with which people engage on a daily basis for any number of reasons, some educational and some not. One of the more obvious examples of this occurs with Khan Academy, a loosely organized educational enterprise created by Salman Khan. Khan began by assembling informal tutoring videos for his young cousin and posting them on YouTube, since they lived in different cities. Through the course of a year, Khan realized that his videos were more effective than face-to face tutoring for his cousin's learning, since she could watch and rewatch at her own pace, but the biggest phenomenon was that people all over the world starting watching the videos and writing Khan to thank him for finally getting them to understand math concepts they had been struggling with for years (Khanacademy). Today, the Khan Academy videos are being used in entire school districts and have been watched countless times by people around the world. This segues into the Internet as the "institution" in electracy, as school was the institution of literacy. School and Internet, in the case of the Khan Academy, are one and the same, but the difference lies in the structure of the school day and the sense of community in the schooling experience, as the basic curriculum has not changed. The Khan Academy is one of many instances of electrate practices being played out in the participatory realm. Most of the other distinctions on the table will be elaborated on in subsequent chapters of *Participatory Composition*, particularly the concepts for *axis* in chapter 4 and *ground* in chapter 3.

APPARATUS

	Orality	Literacy	Electracy
Practice	Religion	Science	Entertainment
Procedure	Ritual	Method	Style
Institution	Church	School	Internet
State of Mind	Faith	Knowledge	Fantasy
Behavior	Worship	Experiment	Play
Philosophy	Mythology	Epistemology	Aesthetics
Ground	God	Reason	Body
Ontology	Totem	Category	Chora
Mode	Narrative	Argument	Figure
Axis	Right/Wrong	True/False	Joy/Sadness

Source: Adapted from Ulmer, "Introduction: Electracy." Courtesy of Gregory Ulmer, professor of English, University of Florida.

Electracy thus creates a need for new theories about writing, reading, and thinking, about subjectivity, community, and representation: theories that will allow us to see how electracy creates new values and purposes for writing, conceptualizing identity, and forming communities. From the perspective of electracy, for instance, incrementally building an argument is not as important as building networks. From the perspective of electracy, entertainers are also teachers, and students are also archivists. From the perspective of electracy, shallow content juxtaposed with intellectual content is a rich learning experience. From the perspective of electracy, dynamic sites such as YouTube are a part of a complex network, creating communities by leaping out of their platforms and residing in countless digital spaces. Electracy and the electrate apparatus are changing the ways in which we conceptualize identity and community, build and maintain relationships, and learn both in and out of the university, and *Participatory Composition* will delve into these changes—by way of online video culture—in order to put forward a viable rhetoric for the electrate apparatus.

It goes without saying that the electrate apparatus can be easily coupled with the notion of "participatory culture," especially since both concepts have to do with the changing landscapes of learning. Participatory culture suggests a theory and practice that supports student learning in media environments; as Henry Jenkins et al. explain in *Confronting the Challenges of Participatory Culture,* participatory culture involves an "ecological approach, thinking about the interrelationships among different communication technologies, the cultural communities that grow up around them, and the activities they support" (7). The electrate apparatus thus reflects this type of environment and further supports its development. In an interview with Patricia Lange, Henry Jenkins defines participatory culture as

> a term that's used to describe spaces that are very open for individual contributions, where there is a supportive environment where people can learn and grow and share what they produce. So [it is] everything from video blogging and YouTube, the gaming world to fan fiction. . . . these are sites where people learn together, create together, grow together, communicate together outside of some of the rigid formal structures that shape school in its current form. . . . we throw ideas out into the world and we bring them back in an improved way because of our engagement with communities.
>
> (AnthroVlog "Participatory Cultures")

In this regard, participatory culture, as a networked site for learning, allows us to reenvision the image of learning: from skills in which individuals demonstrate competency to the act of creating, sharing, and developing complex networks around a given concept. Jenkins has been developing the concept of participatory culture for the past twenty-five years, so it is not unique to the online world. However, the quick development of the ability to create media content and share it online has catapulted the concept into the public realm. In a video discussing participatory culture and education, Jenkins states the following: "As reported by the Pew Center for Internet and American Life . . . 65 percent of American teens have produced media, and about a third of those teens have shared that media they produced with a community larger than friends and family, so there's a communication shift that's going on as more and more young people are becoming participants in their society" (edutopia). Given these numbers, and as an example supporting the Pew Center findings, we might see the provocative 2010 study "Academically Adrift" in a different light. The most stunning finding was that 32 percent of students surveyed reported that they have not written more than twenty pages in any of their college classes or ever read more than forty pages in a given week (Jaschilk). While this news might be appalling to some, it may reveal something other than low faculty expectations or student apathy: a blurring of page, screen, and participation in networked culture. This type of participation, which admittedly was not part of the study, is not counted in "pages" and might expose a gap between students' perceptions of learning and their actual practices. How, for example, would a student quantify watching and commenting on a video? Participating in social media sites? Adding and commenting on discussion posts? Using a search engine and sifting through Internet sites? Uploading media content? Creating a video? Remixing a video? And on and on. Since these practices are not in the realm of traditional learning, students most likely did not count them in their responses to questions that asked about time invested in studying or working on a particular course. By blending the larger notions of electracy and participatory cultures by way of video culture, I hope to offer a rich picture of how writing, in all of its manifestations, has expanded quite literally from the page to the network. One of the central aims of this book is to show how electracy and participatory culture work in tandem in our everyday lives. These terms and the conceptual connotations arising from them are particularly valuable, because they truly offer something different: not just an adjacent term to an existing concept. Similar to "oral literature," "media literacy" encourages critical reflection on media practices and is part of the literate apparatus. Participatory composition addresses the convergence of the visual, verbal, aural, and corporal by removing the hermeneutic requirement of analysis and instead advocating production and participation in every writing gesture, largely defined.

Resuscitating Videocy for the Participatory Realm

To link electracy and participatory culture to online video culture at large, we will look more closely at Ulmer's early conceptions of electracy in *Teletheory*, where he envisioned "video intelligence," or what he then called "videocy," as something enabled by the technological capabilities of video. Working out of Jack Goody, Ian Watt, Brian Street, and other literacy theorists of the 1970s and 1980s, Ulmer predicted that "video intelligence" would become a legitimate form of learning, and in contrast to analysis in literacy, invention would be the driving force behind "videocy." Ulmer writes: "Until now we could not institutionalize invention in the way that we have institutionalized analysis, because we simply lacked the prosthesis needed to democratize it" (94). As a prosthesis for invention, video served as the medium within which invention could finally stand at the forefront of writing and pedagogy: something scholars in composition were also arguing for at the time (see especially Crowley, *Methodical Memory*). This move is quite stunning, as Ulmer envisioned a much larger, cultural role for video, even though the only format available for widespread use at the time was VHS. In fact, it was quite a feat when Ulmer produced his "Mr. Mentality" VHS video, which is now uploaded to YouTube, as a spinoff of the 1951 *Mr. Wizard* television show in which kids visit a teacher and participate in a seemingly impossible experiment that they later find out they can accomplish at home themselves. Craig Saper's "The Felt Memory of YouTube" revisits "Mr. Mentality" to show how it brings new inventional strategies to the forefront by homing in on the "felt" of memories associated with traumatic experiences. Aside from Ulmer's own ruminations on "Mr. Mentality" and Saper's article, the inventive potential for video and videocy remains untapped.

Perhaps because of the technological limitations of producing analogue video, Ulmer moved toward hypertext in his 1994 book, *Heuretics*, especially since HTML code was so accessible. Many of us will remember how cumbersome working and teaching with VHS video was over the past three decades, so the possibilities afforded by hypertext offered a more viable technology for writing in electracy. With the arrival of online video, however, we can blend the vision of "videocy" articulated in *Teletheory* with the ease of linking, remixing, and repurposing that hypertext affords. *Heuretics* took the focus off of video and onto hypertext, but *Participatory Composition* brings video back, with the legacy of hypertext, since producing video is now a ubiquitous practice. Seeing "videocy" both in terms of electracy and participatory culture can bring back this vision to enhance what has already been articulated about the apparatus of electracy. Pre-dating his articulations about apparatus theory in terms of electracy, Ulmer writes, "Part of the project of teletheory is to imagine a different apparatus, beginning with a different technology. My assumption is that to inquire into the future of academic discourse in the age of a new technology, we must include the possibility of a change not only in technology, but also in the ideology of the subject and the forms of institutional practice" (21). Seeing this shift by way of television and video at first, Ulmer places the potential for the apparatus of "teletheory" in the ability to manipulate moving images.

It is not difficult to think of the many ways videocy works today: nearly every major site on the Internet has a video element, and video is literally embedded across most platforms online. From news organizations like the *New York Times* to social media sites like Facebook and Twitter, video not only gives us information but also invites participation, remixing, and repurposing. The videos we see on CNN.com, for example, are also on YouTube and sometimes countless other sites. News sites encourage people to upload video of events as they are happening, relying on the participatory nature of online video to create and spread the news.

Thus, in envisioning "teletheory" and by extension, "videocy," which are both precursors to electracy, Ulmer began to question how "theory," largely defined, worked in the age of television. Responding to a cultural outcry at the time lambasting the stultifying effects of television, seen especially in Jerry Mander's famous book, *Four Arguments for the Elimination of Television*, Ulmer argues:

> Against the "critics" of the new technology who charge it with being "uncritical" or incapable of representing critical cognition, teletheory offers this proposition: video can do the work of literacy, but no better than literacy can do the work of speech. It has its own features and capacities that are fully cognitive, whether or not they are "critical." The interest of teletheory is in defining these areas, and integrating them with the critical and rhetorical dimensions of academic discourse. (19)

Ulmer's vision for video speaks directly to the fact that video and "videocy" are part of a new apparatus that changes the way ideas and thoughts become institutionalized. According to Ulmer, Mander "reiterates some of the same objections to video that Plato made to chirography, with even stronger warnings about the disaster that awaits a civilization in which television is the dominant medium (part of the lesson of this example is this failure to distinguish between television and video). . . . As a medium video is inherently stupid, is anti-democratic, and is not reformable" (91). Ulmer's parenthetical statement about distinguishing between television and video is paramount, since it foreshadows the transformation of analogue video to the online video of today. Videocy, then, articulates a practice that aims to highlight working with image-events, and particularly producing moving images. To address the common misconception that video is inherently stupid, Ulmer realizes that "part of the argument of the apparatus is that ideology contributes to invention in part through the dreams and desires of a civilization. Mander joins in this line of thinking at least to suggest that video is a technology born of madness" (91–92). While the connection between video and madness deserves its own chapter and conjures up larger, philosophical debates, I point it out here to show that working with videocy illuminates the "joy/sadness" axis displayed in the table that shows the differences in the oral, literate, and electrate apparatuses. While it may be tempting to see video as only revolutionary and in a positive light, we also have to consider the "underbelly" of videocy that can lead to tragedy and ruined lives.

I wrote to Ulmer and asked him about his use of videocy" in *Teletheory*. He responded that he articulated the concept of videocy to counter the "literacy absolutists who think TV and entertainment in general destroy culture and thinking" (Ulmer, "RE: Question"). We can see Ulmer intuit his response to the "literacy absolutists" with a call for invention by way of video in every writing—or image—gesture. His response also aims to add complexity to something that is otherwise easily dismissed. Interestingly, when asked why he dropped "videocy" for "electracy," Ulmer replied that "videocy sounds too much like idiocy": a statement that is more crucial than ever in today's online video environment. Ulmer suggested that if he were to revisit videocy today, he would pursue the etymology of "idiocy," which leads to an articulation of a Cartesian *cogito,* a sense of self. While the project Ulmer suggests is beyond the scope of this book, it is still worthwhile to ruminate on the connection between videocy and idiocy, or, the "idiocy of videocy."

An example of "the idiocy of videocy" can be seen in a video posted by Alexandra Wallace, a student at UCLA, in March of 2011. Wallace's video, which she first posted on Facebook, is titled "Asians in the Library." The video shows Wallace talking to her webcam and complaining in a very condescending and racist manner about all of the "Asians" who crowd UCLA's library and living areas and who don't have "American manners." Needless to say, Wallace's video did not last long on Facebook, yet by the time she took it down, it had spread across the Internet, gained academic and mainstream media attention, and was reposted several times on YouTube. Within only a few hours, countless response videos and parodies appeared on YouTube, and news sites received commentary from academic bloggers like Anna Lau in *Psychology Today.* Wallace also quickly began receiving death threats. Within the mix of text comments, video responses, links to and from other sites, and professionally produced parodies such as Jimmy Wong's song "Ching Chong!," we see all aspects of video culture at work. Within the first week, the chancellor of UCLA even posted his own video in response to Wallace's video, as seen in "UCLA Chancellor Appalled by Student Video," and Wallace dropped out of UCLA ("Student Quits at UCLA over Rant"). Without going into much more about this story, I want to suggest that Wallace's efforts expose the "idiocy" of videocy. That is, she underestimated the ruthlessly public nature of video culture by thinking that only her "friends" would see her video. The joy of ranting and getting her frustrations out there was instantly replaced by the sadness of the wreckage that followed. We have only begun to understand the messiness involved in such a participatory blending of the public and private and the complexity involved in the idiocy of videocy. With Bahareh Alaei, I constructed a video exposing the idiocy of videocy through the Wallace case simply titled "The Idiocy of Videocy," which can be found here: http://youtu.be/6ozdBk2SGSo.

The Popcycle Revisited

While idiocy and videocy may be inexorably linked, it is possible to see their relationship through the lens of what Ulmer envisioned as the product of videocy, and by extension electracy: the genre of the MyStory. In *Teletheory*, however, Ulmer introduces the "popcycle," a heuristic for assembling the MyStory and discovering chance occurrences happening across all of the discourses of any person's life, which hold great inventional potential. He writes:

> Any one individual, as part of the oral life story, will possess a small set of images of wide scope, four or five at most, that constitute that individual's personal cosmology, and to which he or she is committed by desire and value. If method is important to problem-solving, the images of wide scope, with their emotional associations, are vital to the way the problem is represented in the first place. Such images organize the information into complex sets that direct the mapping or translation process of comprehension and learning, and finally of invention. (57)

By drawing on Roland Barthes's articulation of the "punctum of recognition" from *Camera Lucida* (to be discussed at length in chapter 3), Ulmer validates the emotional and visceral reactions we feel when looking at certain images or recalling certain events. Video, as a medium, allows image-events to be realized without having the burden of "putting into words" felt knowledge. Ulmer explains: "One purpose of teletheory is to make personal images accessible, receivable, by integrating the private and public dimensions of knowledge—invention and justification" (58). The discourses Ulmer places in the popcycle include: Family, Entertainment, and School. In later iterations of the popcycle, we see "discipline" (or career), church, and street (or community). Within each of these paradigms, the popcycle offers a heuristic for searching our own histories for uncanny connections that may well repeat themselves across the cycle enough for a writer to make something from them. In literacy, these connections would seem irrational, but for electracy they make sense if one regards the popcycle as Ulmer suggests as "learning how to *write* an intuition" (*Heuretics* 37). Also referred to as electronic or conductive logic—a form of logic that Ulmer suggests "supplements the established movements of inference between things and ideas" that we usually grasp through adductive, deductive, and inductive reasoning—Ulmer turns the popcycle into an entity that helps us become better attuned to our "unconscious thought" (*Heuretics* 127). While the aleatory procedures involved with such an approach to writing have often been regarded with some suspicion in the field of rhetoric and composition, such as in Janice Lauer's assessment of Ulmer in *Invention in Composition*, there are a great many works available online that suggest the popcycle strategy has been useful to people adapting Ulmer's ideas. I elaborate on the notion of aleatory procedures versus more traditional strategies for invention in chapter 3.

In any event, in Ulmer's first articulation of his own popcycle in *Teletheory*, he composed "Derrida at Little Big Horn," which Kevin Brooks explains like this:

> [Ulmer] tried to show (not exactly explain) how the French philosopher Jacques Derrida—who functions as Ulmer's academic star or hero—had been with him in Montana the whole time he had been growing up. . . . Ulmer comes to realize that his father's gravel and cement business, and particularly the process of sifting through sand, was a kind of lesson in being an academic, in sifting through texts to separate the fine grained and useful sand from the problematic but difficult to see larger chunks of rock. It just so happens that Derrida uses that metaphor in one of his essays. ("Lecture 1: Ulmer in Context")

These uncanny connections lead to discoveries that otherwise would not have been made. Ulmer uses a 1978 article by Howard Gruber, "Darwin's 'Tree of Nature' and other Images of Wide Scope," to develop his own conception of the importance of these images that guide our thinking throughout our lives. Ulmer cites Gruber's assertion that "An image is wide when it functions as a schema capable of assimilating to itself a wide range of perceptions, actions, ideas. This width depends in part on the metaphoric structure peculiar to the given image, in part on the intensity of the emotion which has been invested in it, that is, its value to the person (135). The wide image functions as a metaphor for the intersections of the popcycle and can be a driving force of invention. In explaining his own emblem, Byron Hawk writes: "For Ulmer, the emblem should cut across the discourses of the popcycle" ("Bystory"), that is, the emblem, or wide image is the thing that consistently repeats.

My own popcycle is based on the music of my childhood, since I have identified music played on the radio during the mid- and late 1970s as my image of wide scope, or emblem. After wrestling with this for some time, I realized that my own emblem is not static; I cannot identify one image for my emblem, which is uncanny in itself, since it adds a dynamic sense to the popcycle. My emblem is in motion; it is a video that consists of me listening to music on the radio while driving in the cars and school buses of my childhood. It started like this. I put my given name into the Internet anagram

server (Sarah Hazel Johnson) and one of the results was "raja shah zen solon."
This combination struck me in a few ways. First, I noticed the cross-cultural
connection to royalty: *raja* and *shah*, plus my name, *Sarah*, means "princess"
in Hebrew. I started pursuing this line but didn't get very far. So, I went to
solon, and this is where the minefield of connections started. I found out that
Ulmer, who I was studying at the time, discovered Solon, too, and connected
the ancient Greek tourist to his vision for a virtual consultancy for electracy,
the EmerAgency. The connection also resonated with me, since my first major in college was "Hospitality and Tourism," as I was drawn to the tourism
industry at the time. The theme of the tourist continued as I connected the
road trips of my childhood to my most resonant learning experiences; flee-
ing our small town in Minnesota for both vacations and excursions to the
Twin Cities, I discovered, shaped the way I not only envisioned the physical
landscape around me, but also the mental imagery associated with my own
developing literacy. Cars, roads, maps, and music continued to repeat for
me, and the theme of the "move" permeated my own popcycle. In contrast
to others' emblems that constitute one image, such as Byron Hawk's image of
a hawk simultaneously flying upward and flowing downward (Bystory), my
emblem is on the move. It is a video of a girl sitting with others in a moving
vehicle, looking out the window and listening to the radio. An image of this
scene would not be adequate, as it could neither support the movement of
the car and passing landscape nor capture the music from the radio. It could
not articulate the relationship between music and memory.

My emblem-as-video cuts across the popcycle as follows: *Family,* five of
us, then eventually seven of us, driving back and forth to the Twin Cities,
KDWB on the radio, 1970s top 40 songs playing, most notably "Real Love"
by the Doobie Brothers and "Afternoon Delight" by the Starland Vocal
Band. Dad drives everywhere: from road trips to California, Canada, and
New Orleans to just driving around town. We even get in the car to escape
summertime tornadoes. Chuck Mangione's "Feels So Good" plays while we
drive away from the menacing funnel cloud. *School:* riding on the school
bus through the snowy landscape, stopping at the junior high and high
school before finally getting to the elementary school. The bus driver also
has KDWB on (sometimes the local station, KLFD), and "Steal Away" by
Robbie Dupree is playing. The music is communal—no one has headphones
yet—so we all mouth the words of the song. *Entertainment:* sports are very
important to everyone in my family, and my parents have season tickets to
the University of Minnesota Gopher football games. The drive takes an hour
and a half and we go to every home game. Saturdays in the car, "Thunder
Island" by Jay Ferguson is playing. *Career:* Simply put, the moving image

of my popcycle evokes my relationship with my chosen field of rhetoric and composition: *contemplation in the presence of and alongside others while passing through the landscape.* Like Ulmer's description of Derrida at Little Big Horn, participatory practices, combined with various media, have always been with me. Perhaps we can now return to an unfinished analogy Ulmer started in *Teletheory* and, interestingly, one of the few place he uses the term *videocy*: Alphabetic literacy : criticism :: videocy: ——? (21). The question mark can be replaced with *invention*. Alphabetic literacy is to criticism as videocy is to invention.

My brief articulation of my own popcycle, while mostly based in the analogue days of the 1970s, shows how Ulmer's vision can be played out by adding to the requirement of choosing one emblem or one wide-image and envisioning it in terms of video. With Bahareh Alaei's help, I have created a series of three accompanying videos to perform this popcycle on the move entitled "Being Placed (Not!): 1970s Pop Music and the Cadence of Small Town Life": Parts1–3, and accessible at http://thechoricarcade.wordpress.com.

Teletheory's articulation of the popcycle and MyStory was followed by Ulmer's *Heuretics*, in which he again performs parts of his popcycle and composes a MyStory. In fact, the MyStory has been the quintessential genre for electracy since then. Ulmer's other prolific genre is the MEmorial, articulated at length in *Electronic Monuments*, which also encourages lateral associations, values chance occurrences, and uses seemingly irrational linkages to strategically blend public and private experiences in order to intervene in public problems, particularly the task of creating monuments for national disasters and catastrophic events. It goes without saying that the genres developed by Ulmer have made an impact. In effect, they have catapulted electracy into many composition courses, and scholars and students alike have amassed a valuable repository of exemplars over the past several years. The genres have also been extremely useful for composition scholars, as seen especially in Hawk's and Brooks's works; they allow fluid movement between public and private, observation and participation, and consumption and design. These facets have already been established and reworked by many who are also striving to intervene in electracy's emergence. However, it is no secret that Ulmer's work and these genres have been aligned with personal or expressive writing, especially in the sense of a return to the utopian sense of self-discovery, seen especially in Marcel O'Gorman's rendering of the MyStory as a form of "navel gazing" ("From Mystorian to Curmudgeon") and Brooks's paraphrase that the MyStory (and perhaps by extension the MEmorial) seems like "self-indulgent, new media expressivism to some skeptics" ("Exploring MEmorials").[2] Keeping in mind the exigency for bringing video and participatory cultures into the mix of already-established practices associated with electracy, I will take electracy and composition on another trajectory into video and participatory cultures, and, with participation as the key element, civic engagement and action is inevitable. That is not to say, however that social action will always be favorable; rather, on the contrary, electrate engagement encompasses the good, bad, and ugly of large-scale participation.

Electrate reasoning is crucial to the world of participatory culture and online video culture, and one of the central goals of this book is to add an overtly participatory element to the electrate work already in existence. Information in electracy is organized by image events, which exist outside the realm of rational analysis. In electracy, one does not critique media; one uses media to perform critique: critique and performance become symbiotic. By understanding the larger project of electracy, we see that electracy is not necessarily confined to Ulmer and his body of work. To tie electracy only to Ulmerian genres is to slight the cultural relevance inherent in the concept of the electrate apparatus. Ulmer's genres, which have produced amazing products already, represent a small piece of the work of electracy. If we follow Ulmer's definitions and explanations of electracy, we know that electracy is emerging and thus its rhetorics are emerging too. Video and participatory culture are integral to electracy, and likewise should be understood within its context.

Smashing Divisions: You, the Tube, and Participatory Composition

Linking electracy and video and participatory culture seems like a no-brainer, particularly after revisiting Ulmer's early articulations of electracy in *Teletheory* as *videocy*. After all, one of the central features of electracy includes making public moving images designed for eliciting participation, remixing, and reappropriation. The popcycle and MyStory invite collaboration and response by stirring up connections that would have otherwise not been made, and if we envision them as videos posted on YouTube, we can see how they would be instantly transformed. That is, if we go back to the articulation of my own popcycle and its accompanying videos, which are posted on YouTube, we will see that they gain the element of participation by having text comments underneath them, related videos to the side, and, potentially remixed versions of the videos posted in response. This is strikingly different from the MyStories currently out there that exist on their own platforms and are, for the most part, self-contained.

I must go back to the initial exigency for me to investigate the relationship between electracy and the burgeoning culture of video sharing. In

2008 while preparing for a CCCC presentation on YouTube, I stumbled on Alexandra Juhasz's now famous course at Pitzer College, Learning from YouTube. Juhasz has since taught the course several times, and published articles, blogs, videos, and a "video book" on the course (*Learning from YouTube*); all of these publications situate YouTube as haphazard, nonacademic, and pedestrian and conclude that YouTube as it stands today impedes serious learning. I immediately connected these assertions to some of the main features of the electrate apparatus, namely that the lateral associations encouraged by participating on YouTube do not impede learning; rather, they serve as the impetus for building networks of "learning" around particular concepts. Further, in the context of electracy, the layers of participation going on at any given moment on the site reflect the changing social and cultural dynamics of the site and present a rich space for learning.

Juhasz's article "Why Not (to) Teach on YouTube" laments that sites like YouTube smash the divisions that have traditionally held up a properly functioning classroom environment. These divisions include: public/private; aural/visual; body/digital; user/owner; entertainment/education; and control/chaos. "As these rigid binaries are dismantled," Juhasz claims, "the nature of teaching and learning shifts (I'd say for the worse)" (135). I certainly agree that these traditional binaries are blown apart on YouTube and other video sharing sites, but I don't think it's for the worse at all; rather, particularly on YouTube, where cultural phenomena develop so rapidly, dismantling rigid binaries accurately reflects the project of electracy and working in participatory culture. As I've already discussed, the most obvious split is between entertainment and education; in electracy, entertainment is the primary form of practice, thus recreating and remixing the relationship between education and entertainment. However, it is not enough to say that, in electracy, we "learn through entertainment"; rather, and as I will try to articulate, we become participants in the entertainment enterprise of learning while creating.

Why YouTube?

Most work on video cultures has been tied to YouTube, specifically, since YouTube has become synonymous with online video sharing. While other video hosting sites such as Vimeo, Tumblr, and Hulu have also gained momentum, YouTube remains the platform for video culture. As of this writing, YouTube boasts over 800 million monthly viewers, and many of these views originate somewhere else: "70 percent of YouTube traffic comes from outside the United States" ("Statistics"). Consequently, YouTube now features an "as seen on" link below some videos that shows where they originate. With this added feature, we can discover all the other places in which the video is located, thereby creating an instant "deck" of sites containing the video, each with its own rhetorical framework. For instance, I recently found out that one of my videos posted on YouTube has been embedded on a blog in Germany for several years; this video has also been formally published in the journal *Kairos* and has been linked to on some course syllabi. While my example is minor compared to some videos on YouTube that are re-posted and embedded thousands of times over, it shows how YouTube acts as the central platform for video hosting, even though it does not act as a traditional "center." While videos rarely stay on YouTube only, the platform is still the most widely sought after site for video upload, download, and participation.

One of the better sources for understanding the popularity of YouTube is *YouTube: Online Video and Participatory Culture* by Jean Burgess and Joshua Green. Burgess and Green delve into the culture inspired by YouTube by analyzing hundreds of YouTube videos and present a picture of the platform that allows us to peer into the inner workings of video culture as it stands today. Their work is at the forefront of studies that "attempt to tread YouTube in itself as an object of research" (6). "YouTubers" are those who participate in the site on all levels, and Burgess and Green suggest that YouTubers, and by extension those who participate in video sharing sites, approach these sites with their own purposes and aims and collectively shape YouTube as a dynamic cultural system: "YouTube is a site of participatory culture," they claim (vii). They even go on to suggest that "For YouTube, participatory culture is not a gimmick or a sideshow; it is absolutely core business" (6). The key point here is that, contrary to the site's tagline of "broadcast yourself," participants in YouTube experience success not because of the content they produce but because of "grounded knowledge of and effective participation within YouTube's communicative ecology" (56–57). Even "lurking" is a form of participation; Burgess and Green suggest that "one of the fundamental characteristics of co-creative environments like YouTube is that the participants are all at various times and to varying degrees audiences, producers, editors, distributors, and critics" (82). "Various times and to varying degrees" suggests that there are no predetermined roles or rules for interaction and participation on YouTube, and the "roles and rules" usually evolve and revolve around particular genres of videos, only to be reinvented again and again.

Thus, according to Burgess and Green, YouTube, as a cultural system, is better understood as a "continuum of cultural participation" (57). The continuum encompasses, they suggest, "the activities of not only content creators but also audiences and practices of participation, because the practices of audiencehood—quoting, favoriting, commenting, responding, sharing, and viewing—all leave traces, and therefore they all have effects on the common culture of YouTube as it evolves" (57). We can see videocy and electracy at work in that the video content on YouTube is just as important as the network—a network of creative practices—the content created within the various social network settings (58, 61). As a social network, YouTube connects people, but not in the formal and very structured way of other sites like Facebook.

Juhasz laments that YouTube studiously refuses the structures for community building, the hallmarks of web 2.0 (137). In electracy, however, technologies exist to create networks and not remain contained in one platform. This is why YouTube especially pushes the limits of how web 2.0 is currently conceived, since, the practices on YouTube rarely originate or remain on the site itself, despite its capacities as a social network. In agreement, Patricia Lange, in "Publicly Private and Privately Public: Social Networking on YouTube," found that "in addition to supporting social networks, video sharing practices helped create new connections and develop social networks" (367). Burgess and Green write that video sharing sites reflect technologies that are "expansible, adaptable, and malleable . . . and so preserving the potential for the technologies to be 'generative' of new or unexpected possibilities. Even the most usable and apparently simple technologies may offer creative possibilities that extend far beyond their most obvious, invited uses—possibilities most frequently realized (or even pioneered) by users, often to the surprise of the technology's designers" (64).

That YouTube represents technologies created for generative purposes lifts the division between control and chaos. In electracy, we become producers as we are consumers and inhabit these roles differently each time we engage with participatory sites. While "generating new and creative possibilities" may seem cliché, we actually see this happening as users figure out ways to re-create YouTube with their combined practices. What is at once controlled is also sent into chaos when, for example, comments, videos, or links pop up, thereby creating an instant network.

Networking and participation are central to electracy. YouTubers routinely branch out to other sites to enhance and supplement participation in YouTube, and their cross-registrations demonstrate that YouTubers, "as cultural agents, are not captive to YouTube's architecture" and also show "the permeability of YouTube as a system" (66). YouTubers move their identities and content among multiple sites and manipulate both to meet specific sites' communal conventions, which demonstrates another feature of electracy, especially the manipulation of content to meet a specific site's communal conventions. As I will explore in chapter 4, popular YouTubers intricately weave content, including videos, comments, remixes, and video responses, across the site, leaving traces of their identities in numerous places. Burgess and Green conclude that despite YouTube's technological limitations, the so-called YouTube community aims to "embed their video practice within networks of conversation"; they found that "their willingness to find ways to do this even if not supported to do so by the provided technology" was astounding (67). This practice is a key feature for participatory composition, as sharing and embedding are inherent in the practice.

We can thus see the conventions of participation found on YouTube continue to take shape by evolving on the site and adding to what Collin Brooke and Thomas Rickert have described as "information density" ("Being Delicious"). I consider Brooke and Rickert's essay in chapter 4 but mention it here to support the idea that participation drives the ever-changing social and technological dynamics of sites like YouTube. In fact, Burgess and Green suggest that "in order to operate effectively as a participant in the YouTube community, it is not possible simply to import learned conventions for creative practice, and the cultural competencies required to enact them, from elsewhere" (69). Rather, creative practices—remixed and remade with content from other sites—are consistently revised to fit the cultural moment in which YouTubers and YouTube as a cultural site find themselves.

If we return to three of Juhasz's divisions: Body/Digital; Control/Chaos; and Public/Private, we can see how smashing them productively reflects facets of the electrate apparatus. In electracy and likewise in video culture, these divisions are not opposites but instead work in tandem to reflect the shift in values at work. In the practice of video blogging (vlogging), for example, we see the body and digital working in tandem, and the result is a series of third options, which we see all over the site in the form of comments, video responses, and so on. That is, the former divisions merge to reflect a necessary blending of them for participatory culture. Lange studies practices on YouTube that specifically deal with the collapse of public and private space, and she concludes that most participants in video cultures offer some range of combining the public and private, hence her terms "publicly private and privately public." These terms indicate that no action in video culture can be seen as either private or public; instead, each level of participation offers a necessary public/private merge.

James Porter, in "Recovering Delivery for Digital Rhetoric," examines the idea of the body in digital space, especially since the body was once an important aspect of rhetorical delivery. While some people may think that, in a virtual space, the body disappears, Porter claims that the "body does not disappear in virtual space. It is certainly constructed differently, but it is there in all its non-virtual manifestations: gender, race, sexual preference, social class, age, etc." (212). He is dealing here with pictures or videos of people, and I think the vlog, used for so many purposes in video culture, stands out as an example of merging the body and digital, public and private, and control and chaos. Most vloggers come to the genre with neither experience nor script, and the resulting product provides an array of conventions with which to contend. Stunningly, "collaborative and remixed vlog entries were a very noticeable feature of the most popular content in [Burgess and Green's] survey" (65). Again, despite YouTube's interface not adequately supporting creating or remixing video on the site, vloggers continue to network to other sources to experiment with the genre of the vlog. The point I want to make has less to do with the content of particular vlogs and more to do with the bodily presences of the vloggers. In fact, most vloggers exert more bodily presence here than they do in a face-to-face situation, particularly if we take advantage of the technological capabilities of changing the timing and duration and remixing content, for example. (See chapter 4 for a discussion of particular vloggers at length.) These debates only begin the discussion of participatory composition and set the stage for each chapter to come. Participatory composition requires rapid remixing of identity formation, technical savvy, rhetorical skills, and participation in networks, all of which are necessary components of video culture. Thus, each chapter will include a manifestation of electracy from video culture to extend and connect these claims.

Participatory Subjects and "Three Countertheses" Redux

So what are we to do with [Vitanza's] radical critique of our field? The answer is easy: ignore it. And to a large extent, that's just what we've done. But I think that's a mistake. "Three Countertheses" is one of the most compelling critiques of composition in our literature—penetrating, perceptive, and on the whole, persuasive.
—Michael Carter, *Where Writing Begins*

Chapter 2 begins with a discussion of the rhetoric of empowerment to show how the idea of empowerment through critical reflection changes in electracy and particularly on YouTube, since YouTubers receive immediate and repeated response to their actions, thus continuously remaking subjectivity. I turn to Gilles Deleuze and Felix Guattari's concept of "desiring production" to articulate how subjectivity is continuously remade. Alex Reid suggests in "Exposing Assemblages" that "the externalization of the subject in the emergence of community, which is difficult and abstract in the print world, becomes more palpable and material in digital media networks," and this "externalization of the subject," Reid continues, "is even intensified by the shift from text into video." That shift plays a large role in this book's arguments; which is why I devote an entire chapter to the question of the writing subject for an electrate apparatus. I aim to create a complex notion of subjectivity for electracy and participatory composition that will serve as a framework that I will elaborate on in the subsequent chapters. A video produced by Bahareh Alaei accompanies chapter 2entitled "Choric Slam Tilt: Unpinning the Table," which can be located at: http://thechoricarcade.wordpress.com.

Chapters 3, 4, and 5 are organized around Vitanza's seminal article, "Three Countertheses: Or, a Critical In(ter)vention into Composition Theories and Pedagogies," written during a specific scholarly moment in rhetoric and composition—around 1991—when cultural studies, social epistemic rhetoric, and critical pedagogy were all gaining momentum and scholars were exploring the implications of postmodern theory for the still relatively new discipline; a time, as Hawk argues, when the pedagogical question inevitably evoked the social-epistemic question: "does this pedagogy seek to produce the proper political subject and corresponding critical text?" (*Counter-History* 207). Because of this timing, I am especially interested in the mood that the countertheses evoke today, since they were invented specifically as a direct response to these types of social-epistemic practices, which claimed to usurp prevailing notions of expressivist and cognitive rhetorics. Vitanza explains: "The countertheses are counterresponses to the strong *will* of the field of composition; they are conterresponses to (1) the will to systematize (the) language (of composing), (2) the will to be its author(ity), and (3) the will to teach it to students" (140–41). While Vitanza has amassed many more works since the publication of "Three Countertheses," his questions from that seminal essay serve as a very appropriate starting place for articulating participatory composition.

The countertheses did not advocate adding another category to the existing taxonomies; instead, through what is now considered a traumatic gesture, they worked to illuminate how creating categories at all excludes much of the potential available for writing, writing subjects, writing technologies, and writing communities. Rickert puts forth the notion that the countertheses initiated a trauma for Rhetoric and Composition and, years later, we are now in the midst of "the felt sense of crisis that necessitates a return to that traumatic event" (*Acts of Enjoyment* 9). This "felt sense," I contend, consists of the widespread emergence of the electrate apparatus and particularly the rise of video and participatory cultures. In fact, Hawk suggests that the "Internet opened the way for completely new social and pedagogical contexts" (*Counter-History* 207).

Accordingly, the countertheses served as both a critique of prevailing articulations of postmodern theory and composition and, almost paradoxically, a performance of integrating postmodern theory and composition. This notion—merging critique and performance—is very important for this book, since, by the end, I will have put forward a notion of "participatory pedagogy" that aims to do just that. Aside from Stephen Yarborough's book-length project *After Rhetoric,* and Michael Carter's book *Where Writing Begins,* there has been little interrogation or analysis of, or response to, Vitanza's scathing claims. Carter even suggests that the radical critique of the field in "Three Countertheses" has been systematically ignored (150, 230 n1). While Carter does go on to explicate and treat the countertheses, he does so from the vantage point of articulating a version of postmodernism: a "process postmodernism" that does not go far enough to create the changes Vitanza advocates.

Finally, returning to the countertheses and juxtaposing their contentions with the larger projects of electracy and video culture should push them toward what Hawk has called a "complex ecology" (*Counter-History* 224) for participatory composition, which is not another map, taxonomy, camp, or theory, but instead a series of live forces and forms that merge, converge, and change when practiced.

Chapter 3 was cowritten with Cortney Kimoto (Smethurst), MA graduate of California State University, Long Beach, whose research inspired the revised direction of the chapter. Her projects have served as catalysts that pushed my thinking toward connecting theories that I have been working with for over a decade to video culture. Chapter 3 is centered on the first proposition in the Gorgian trilemma and Vitanza's first counterthesis: nothing exists. "Nothing exists"—an ontological statement—is traditionally interpreted to mean that something is missing, *lacking;* if an essential or even contingent definition of objects is not possible, then there is no place to stand and thus achieve stasis, which, as a classical practice that remains relevant for inventional purposes, bestows a kind of status. In chapter 3, we unpack the question raised by Vitanza's first counterthesis, the question of definition, or What is *x*?, a question that allows us to examine the first of three theoretical constructs that serve as a framework for participatory composition. We pursue three ambitious goals: first, we connect the question of definition to stasis theory, which serves as the counterpart to choragraphy, Ulmer's method of invention that is based on the ancient conception of space, *chora*; second, we explore Barthes's and Ulmer's work on the punctum of recognition and seek to extend such work out into the participatory realm, eventually transitioning into a discussion of Brooke's recasting of invention as proairesis; third, after juxtaposing scholarship on chora with Deleuze and Guattari's dualisms for both spatiality and temporality, we turn to You-Tube as our exemplar for choric invention and conclude by exploring how a particular meme, with its complex folds of remix and reappropriation, illustrates how spreadable and undefinable media can influence participation as well as global collaboration, interaction, and communication. This meme, as well as the cultural phenomena arising around it, sets the theoretical concepts discussed in the chapter in motion in order to create a complex and rich picture of invention for the electrate apparatus. Finally, two videos accompany chapter 3. The first, titled "The Dancing Floor," (http://kairos .technorhetoric.net/17.2/topoi/vitanza-kuhn/arroyo_alaei.html), was produced by Bahareh Alaei. This video aims to present the concepts discussed in this chapter visually and perform the theories and examples articulated here. The second video, "Phoenix—Lisztomania—Long Beach/Bolsa Chica, CA Brat Pack Mashup" (http://youtu.be/Wg2AlNaoe1Y), produced by Kimoto, presents our own participation in the meme we describe in the chapter.

Chapter 4 treats the second Gorgian position and Vitanzan counterthesis: if something were to exist, it would not be knowable. A central question becomes, Who speaks when something is spoken? This chapter engages the question of mastery over knowledge. I interrogate the theoretical implications from this question and transfer these implications to video and participatory cultures. "Relinquishing the discourse of mastery" and developing a discourse of "speaking as a listener" will be central; and yet, as we see, "speaking as a listener" in video culture is quite complex and has proven to have both trivial and deep consequences in the online and off line worlds. The chapter first attempts to make a series of theoretical connections: from the deoedipalized subject to Vitanza's notion of "speaking as a listener"; from Lyotard's alternative to the Lacanian "discourse of the master"; and from pedagogical perspectives on these concepts such as Marshall Alcorn's "pedagogy of demand" and Kevin Porter's "pedagogy of severity," to Cynthia Haynes's stunning articulation of "postconflict pedagogy," I take a variety of twists and turns. Through it all, my goal is to apply these concepts to prevalent behavior found in participatory and video cultures in order to cast a wider net for the generative practices I advocate throughout the book. I also spend some time comparing the tenets from the second counterthesis with Thomas Kent's Davidsonian notion of "passing theories" and "hermeneutic guesswork" as well as Stephen Yarborough's pedagogical move toward "discourse studies," both of which are attempts to respond to the questions raised in the second counterthesis. This comparison will bring me to how the concept of community is both redefined under the premises of the second counterthesis and reinvented in video culture, especially when directly compared Kent's and Yarborough's explanations. I then extrapolate on how these theories come to life in video culture. While it may be tempting to see this blending of electrate and participatory practices as only celebratory, it is crucial to also explore a darker and more ruthless side of participatory culture that emerges when the distance between public and private behaviors quickly shrinks and the axis of "joy/sadness," articulated briefly in the discussion of videocy above, comes to light. I specifically turn to practices known online as "flaming" and "hating," which present Lyotard's listening game in a layered and complex manner and serve as a provocative complement to Haynes's call for a postconflict pedagogy.

Chapter 5 is centered on the third Gorgian position and Vitanzan counterthesis: if something can be knowable, it cannot be communicated. Thus, the third counterthesis also introduces the prevalence of the theory/practice split in rhetoric and composition, and I work with Vitanza's claim that there can only be "postpedagogy." Postpedagogy eliminates the idea of "turning" a theory into pedagogical practice, which has commonly been called the "pedagogical imperative" in rhetoric and composition. This responds to the question of "how to" teach something over which we can no longer claim authority, which I explored in chapter 4. I turn to both the first collection entitled *Post-Process Theory*, edited by Thomas Kent, and the follow-up collection aptly called *Beyond Postprocess*, edited by Sidney I. Dobrin, J. A. Rice, and Michael Vastola, to explore "turning" theories into practices, particularly since, in electracy, theories emerge as they are practiced. I first discuss Lee-Ann Kastman Breuch's essay "Post-Process Pedagogy" as a lasting exemplar of pedagogy as we currently envision it. I have seen Breuch's essay anthologized a number of times, and I know it has influenced many newcomers to the field. I then toggle between the first collection and the follow-up collection to see how, as Kent remarks, the "postprocess mindset" (Preface 16) works with and against electracy and participatory composition. As we will see, the follow-up collection certainly turns postprocess into something more like an ever-developing network.[3]

I then turn to the concept of heuretics, developed by Ulmer and extended by many scholars, combine it with the preceding discussions of participatory culture, electracy, and postprocess, and put forward the concept of "participatory pedagogy," appropriate for participatory composition, which Geof Carter first developed in our cowritten article "Tubing the Future:

YouTube U and Participatory Pedagogy in 2020." I further develop participatory pedagogy by discussing it in terms of Vitanza's third counterthesis
and the pedagogical imperative. Participatory pedagogy enacts the deoedipalized, ever-morphing writing subject (chapter 2), encourages *choric*
inventions and continuous remix (chapter 3), plays the listening game in
all its manifestations (chapter 4) and engages in both critique and performance (chapter 5) with each act of composition. The final section of that
chapter provides examples, or more accurately metaphors, for enacting a
participatory pedagogy.

Chapter 6 is an afterword wherein I offer snippets of student examples
engaging with participatory composition as well as commentary about the
process. While including examples may seem contradictory, I wanted to
show how students engage with the ideas presented throughout this book.
I also refer to my social networking site, electracy.ning.com, wherein many
more examples can be found. Both of the students represented in chapter 6
studied Ulmer, electracy, and participatory and video cultures in my grad-
uate-level seminar on digital rhetoric.

2. Recasting Subjectivity for Electracy: From Singularities to Tubers

Two specters are haunting the discipline of Writing Studies. Those specters are the unified subject and the hegemony of communitarian thinking. These specters come in the guise of process theory and ideology critique.

—Joe Marshall Hardin, "Putting Process into
Circulation: Textual Cosmopolitanism"

Yet critical pedagogy has been part of composition for nearly twenty years now. Is it fair to ask: At what point are you no longer blundering for a change? At what point are you simply blundering?

—Russell Durst, "Interchanges"

Doesn't she know people are making fun of her? She doesn't even know the words! Why is she doing this? She should stop making videos.

—students in a digital rhetoric seminar

In 2010, ToshBabyBoo's video—dedicated to her friends on the live video chat site Stickcam and posted on YouTube—circulated around the Internet and created an instant buzz. This video, which is over six minutes long, simply features ToshBabyBoo singing along to a popular song coming from her headphones, so we only hear her voice and not the music from the song. What turned the video into an Internet meme was ToshBabyBoo's unrelenting singing, mumbling, missing words of the song, and making up others with no seeming effort to improve. She also appears oblivious to the embarrassment her viewers vicariously feel for her. In effect, her video is the epitome of the rise of the amateur and what Alexandra Juhasz sees as the "shallow" content of YouTube that repels any type of serious learning ("Why Not (to) Teach on YouTube"). Yet, even though the video itself will most likely fall from popularity, I begin this chapter by referencing it because it offers a lasting exemplar for how subjectivity works in electracy.

Of course, we may think the subjectivity of ToshBabyBoo is more self-present and self-indulgent than ever before, since she assumes that people will want to watch her videos and become participants on her channel. And her assumptions are correct. Her videos receive numerous comments, ranging from the supportive to the extremely vile, and ToshBabyBoo keeps on posting. As Clay Shirky has pointed out, the subtle in-your-face style, or we might say, sheer bravado involved in posting a video like this might elicit us to wonder, who has the time (to be so self-centered) (*Cognitive Surplus*)? However, as both Henry Jenkins and Shirky rightfully argue, active participants on social sites believe their contributions—in any shape or form—matter to others ("Confronting the Challenges"; *Cognitive Surplus*), and this simple force is what drives YouTubers to continually post videos that, on the surface, appear to be damaging and embarrassing. This brings me to another point. I would argue that ToshBabyBoo's subjectivity is more accurately reflected in the idea of the singularity who is not separated from the community of singularities calling her subjectivity into appearance, rather than in traditional notions of self-indulgence. The comment that she should quit posting videos because they are wrecking her self-presence is not at all applicable, since the community itself is creating and re-creating her image. The issue of who is in control in this situation remains an issue. The interactions taking place on many sites continue to shift both the subjectivity of the YouTuber and the thousands of people who have contributed to the life of this video. This double whammy of communities of singularities, appearing to be self-present but actually becoming exposed through the actions of others' comments, remixes, and parodies, is certainly complex and deserves unpacking.

I begin with a discussion of the rhetoric of empowerment, so prevalent in and out of the field of rhetoric and composition. The idea of subjects-in-control who can change beliefs and actions based on critical reflection and act in their own best interests changes drastically in video culture, since the ideas of sharing and reciprocity (see Lange "Achieving Creative Integrity") drive action and cannot be separated from the subjects and the content themselves. In my discussion, I weave in theoretical elements about subjectivity from Gilles Deleuze and Felix Guattari and Giorgio Agamben, since they have been arguing for the idea of "singularities" for quite some time. I connect these ideas to specific practices in video culture, where "communities" rise up around videos, comments, and related material and remain, quite literally, alongside one another on the site, and I work through them in the context of the rhetoric of empowerment. I conclude with examples from participatory and video culture to show how subjectivity in electracy, which inherently works by way of participation, holds potential for cultural transformation in a merging of critique and performance.

From Subjects to Singularities to Tubers

Despite the extensive influence of critical pedagogical practices over the past several years, many scholars in and out of the field have in the past and are now again voicing concerns about the effectiveness of empowerment-oriented pedagogies as they are currently practiced in composition courses. As I have mentioned, one of the most important concepts to reconsider in electracy has to do with how we conceptualize the subjectivities and identities of writers. Even though the "death of the author" has been pronounced for decades and played out in digital spaces, composition pedagogy teaches that writers should maintain complete control and authority over their work. In "Tripping over Tropes: Of 'Passing' and Postmodern Subjectivity—What's in a Metaphor?" Karen Kopelson reflects on how we grapple with the question of subjectivity after modernity. She writes: "Teachers and scholars in rhetoric and composition studies have struggled for nearly two decades now with what is repeatedly referred to as the 'impasse of postmodern agency,' and/or the 'crisis' of postmodern subjectivity (see, for example Faigley [*Fragments*]; Jones ["Beyond"]; Trimbur ["Composition Studies"])" (435). Kopleson boldly brings the problem of the writing subject to the forefront, which, as I have mentioned, is the one of the most important conceptions that changes in a rhetoric for electracy. Richard Fulkerson's essay "Composition at the Turn of the Twenty-First Century" offers a follow-up taxonomy to his 1980 effort "Four Philosophies of Composition" and questions the shift of focus to changing subjectivity. Fulkerson reports that "judging from the scholarship of the past thirteen years, cultural studies has been the main movement in Composition studies, no surprise to readers of our leading journals" (659). Cultural studies, or empowerment-oriented approaches (which Fulkerson names CCS, or Critical/Cultural Studies) has as its aim, "not 'improved writing' but 'liberation' from dominant discourse" (660). Fulkerson worries about the shifted focus off of writing and onto student subjectivity, and sees no way out of the possibilities for indoctrination in CCS classes (665–66). Going much further, Thomas Rickert, in *Acts of Enjoyment: Rhetoric, Zizek, and the Return of the Subject*, offers a book-length response to the problems associated with empowerment-oriented pedagogies.[1] Rickert begins by acknowledging his own prior commitment to critical pedagogy and the ensuing disappointment he experienced after witnessing, again and again, the "fault line between knowledge and action" (2). Rickert explains the frustrating contradiction this way: "Why was it that knowledge about oppressive, unjust, or disadvantageous practices, combined with growing rhetorical savvy, led to . . . nothing, or at least nothing that I could see, beyond the ability to marshal such knowledge that became, once again, classroom exercises with little potential for productively impacting student lives?" (2). Rickert's question succinctly points to the major flaw of critical pedagogies: students—even after complying with assignments and writing fantastic papers critiquing ideological biases and unjust practices—retain cynical attitudes and behavior; their beliefs and actions do not significantly change. The result, then, in empowerment-oriented classrooms is no different from traditional classrooms: students comply with the assignments, "talk the talk" in class, and then continue behaving the same way despite their newfound knowledge of systematic oppression.

Marshall Alcorn has also argued against the formula that has sustained empowerment-oriented pedagogies. Refusing to reduce complex human behavior down to a matter of critical subjects exposing contradictions, critiquing them, and subsequently changing behavior, Alcorn insists on a practice viewing political thinking as that which reflects "the surface manifestations of a variety of values that are held most tenaciously at an unconscious libidinal level" (*Changing the Subject* 24). Thus, tapping into these deeply held political convictions is not as simple as teaching students to realize and rationalize both their ideological and bodily attachments; instead, Alcorn argues, "they strengthen the forms of defense against such attacks" (39), thereby producing either strong forms of resistance or encouraging, as Rickert points out, passive complacency. Using Rickert's and Alcorn's claims as starting places, this chapter will argue that, in electracy, the writing subject is reconceptualized, almost turned inside out and back again because of the constant interface with and melding of desire and the social. Gilles Deleuze and Felix Guattari famously told us long ago that "there is only desire and the social. Nothing else" (*Anti-Oedipus* 29), and we can see this almost literally materializing in video culture. According to Deleuze and Guattari, desire has absolutely nothing to do with "lack" or yearning for something that is missing. Instead, desire works as production: continuous making and remaking. Desire works not to create subjects but to create singularities. The uncoding of desire—territorialization, deterritorialization, reterritorialization—is a function embedded in the structure of the university or any other institutional power. By taking the focus off of *subjectivity* per se, Deleuze and Guattari move toward *singularities* in order to create *assemblages*: aleatory connections that happen among singularities brought together from several directions and discourses. Deleuze remarks that even if a person says, "'I desire this or that,' that person is

in the process of constructing an assemblage" (Stivale). Taking Deleuze's
description further, D. Diane Davis suggests that these connections and
constructions happen in "the space of the hole" (*Breaking Up* 46) between
de- and re-territorialization. This "between" space, this fissure, crack, and
void happens in the "flux of exploded identities" the "excess before re-dis-
tinction," where deterritorialization has occurred and reterritorialization
has not yet taken place. This flux and excess is precisely what makes electrate
writing possible. The goal is not to fill the apparent "gaps" (in someone's
learning or ideology, for example), but to remain in a constant state of
production, which moves desire out of the realm of the negative and allows
knowledge formerly excluded to emerge. Knowledge that happens in this
space of the hole can be extremely productive and innovative; we see this
in practice on sites such as YouTube where new knowledge emerges from
participants' re-creations, re-assemblages, and commentaries. Deterritori-
alized desire (yet to be reterritorialized) dismantles oppressive structures
and makes new assemblages: only to dismantle them and recombine them
perpetually. Thus, the reconceptualization of subjectivity serves as a driving force for the other theories and practices I will put forward, and I hope
to provide a complex notion of the writing subject that moves us toward
participatory and electrate writing.

Subjects as Singularities

> The idea of a de-oedipalized subjectivity is not especially new, but its
> characteristics, aesthetics, practices, and ethics are not fully explored.
> —Thomas Rickert, "'Hands Up, You're Free'"

In "'Hands Up, You're Free': Composition in a Post-Oedipal World," Rickert
aggressively questions the effectiveness of critical pedagogy as it is practiced
in composition and suggests, by way of Deleuze and Slavoj Zizek, that the
problem lies within the conflict arising between the current "post-" or "de-"
oedipalized subjects and the necessarily "oedipalized" subject of critical
pedagogy, who must learn to resist dominating forces in control. Deoedipalized subjects—socially networked "tubers"—appear to be carrying apathetic
attitudes toward politics, civic engagement, and varying forms of activism.
However, because they are not "attached" to authority—they are de-oedipalized—they cannot actively resist authority, institutional or otherwise.
Rather, they reflect participatory culture, where, as Jenkins et al. explain,
barriers for artistic expression and civic engagement are relatively low (*Confronting the Challenges* 5), thus enabling participation in many social realms
and platforms. Rickert argues that traditional, critical pedagogical practices
have neither "produced engaged, liberated students [nor] resulted in a slew

of good, politically engaged social critics" ("'Hands Up, You're Free'" 298).
Thus, relieving students of their unfounded assumptions does not guarantee
that they will change these assumptions and subsequently act for the good
of the collective; it does, for the most part, produce negative resistance in
students because they do not believe that their false assumptions are indeed
false and in need of critical change.[2] After engaging in extensive critique,
the subject would then—it is assumed—act in his/her own best interests.
Alcorn (*Changing the Subject*) and Sloterdijk (*Critique of Cynical Reason*)
have explained at length that people stick to their positions for anything
but rational reasons. It is assumed that employing the method of critique
through critical reflection will allow reason to guide emancipation from
dominant, oppressive forces in control. A major conflict occurs, however,
when students see and understand their supposed "mystified" attachment
to ideology in perfectly rational terms; this produces "enlightened false consciousness." Or, as Rickert articulates, they dutifully produce lengthy, written
cultural critiques resulting in no behavioral changes. These results (re)em-
phasize and reinforce their cynical and so-called indifferent subject status.

To help visualize the predicament Rickert points out, Davis and Greg
Ulmer provide vivid images of the notion the "self-present" composing
subject, reflecting Rickert's discussion above. I turn to these images, because
of the multiple possibilities they provide for a discussion on subjectivity
and video culture. Davis and Ulmer both cast their images to represent
students in a typical composition class. In "Finitude's Clamor; or, Notes
toward a Comunitarian Literacy," Davis makes an important distinction
regarding immanence: she first describes the transcendent "myth of immanence," which constitutes "a singular being driven by the notion that
he's equal to his signature, that he's a self-conscious self-presence who is
therefore *presentable*—and who presents himself via his own magnificent
inscription" (120). Calling upon Avital Ronell's discussion in *Stupidity*, Davis
refers to the collected letters of Gustave Flaubert, wherein he "details his
fascination with a certain inscription he encountered during his trip to the
Orient. Someone had carved the name THOMPSON in enormous lettering
on Pompey's column" (121; 120). Davis emphasizes that, despite recent re-
visions and reworkings, "a good bit of rhetoric and composition pedagogy
. . . hails students as Thompsons, reproducing the myth (in every student)
by pushing the figure of the self-present composing subject" and by using
the image of the "THOMPSON" to be "read allegorically as a causality of
the myth of human immanence" (121; 120). Hence, THOMPSON stands for
immanent, transcendent subjectivity: immanence that, as Agamben has
described, simply "remain[s], stay[s], dwell[s] within" (*Potentialities* 226).

Davis insists on turning away from the myth of the transcendental immanent subject; holding onto this myth makes it impossible to *hear* the communications of "post-oedipal," "whatever beings" occurring in the space between de- and re-territorialization. If they are heard, she says, they are hearable only as "noise" that must be reinscribed into rational communications systems. She explains, "sender-receiver theories of communication that push 'reasonable exchange,' that focus narrowly on 'speakers' and 'messages' tune out these ek-static communications" ("Finitude's Clamor" 133). "Sender-receiver" theories, such as those put forth by Thomas Kent (see Preface), argue that writers always write *from* some place, which I relate to *topos*: the grounded (location) on which to stand in order to speak or write. E. V. Walter calls this "Aristotle's doctrine of place [that] declares the separability of beings from places" (*Placeways* 205). This assumes that the writing subject and the place from which he/she stands can be separated and properly adjusted. Thus, while Kent's writers are always writing *from* some place, it is assumed that place and the writing subject are separable entities; in other words, the "miscommunication" that occurs between speaker and listener might be attributed to the place or ground from which each individual speaks. This notion is radically different in electracy, where the space of writing and the writer are intricately intertwined; we can no longer separate the writing spaces and writers. Rather, each act of writing is an identity performance, and subjectivity becomes the driving force behind composing; the writing subject and the space within which he or she dwells are symbiotic. Davis presents another useful metaphor for the self-present subject when she discusses "the morning mirror check" (*Breaking Up* 21). The morning mirror check provides an image for the "exscribed." During the ritual of the morning mirror check, she tells us, "twigs" of hair "just out of a frontal view" are not seen by the subject-in-control of his/her appearance who assumes that everything looks just fine. And it is precisely that sticking-up-twig of hair that shatters the "self-presence" of the subject: the twig *resists* and rebels. It shatters the "illusion of self-unity" (21), since it exists completely out of the subject's control. However, it still communicates, even though it is out of frontal view, and its communications are heard loud and clear.

Next, Ulmer relates his experience of stumbling into the University of Florida bookstore where he discovers a "row of Spirit Hands, giant, oversize, pulsating . . . index finger extended, inscribed GO GATORS on one side, with the logo of the university on the other . . . to permit the student fans to emphasize the gesture meaning 'We're number one!'" ("Spirit Hand" 142). The foam spirit hand serves as a reminder for how the overtly emphasized "#1" (inscribed on the index finger) is inevitably confused with the self-present "I" of the student/subject. He says, "The 'I' is ambiguous, as always, confused easily with me, Institution, or Number One" (149). Waving the spirit hand validates subject status. To locate his discussion, Ulmer cites several puns on the spirit hand, in writings and paintings, from Plato to the present, wherein the "hand" pointing represents the index, the signature of the subject, just like the Gator spirit hand with the school name inscribed in the index finger. A key example refers to Jacques Derrida's discussion of Martin Heidegger in "*Geschlecht II*: The Hand of Man According to Heidegger": Ulmer explains: "Heidegger says he prefers thinking a singular hand, as in handwriting, manuscripture, that is debased, depersonalized, and in which the distinctively human is lost when the writing is done with two hands, on a typewriter (148). With this link of the "one hand" to the "distinctively human" connects the two hands (or fingers) to the "posthuman": breaking out of the realm of the one giant hand ("I'm number one!") toward electracy, where multiple "hands" write together. Video culture merges these two images of the "hand": the one hand (maybe on a mobile device) and two hands (on a traditional keyboard) bring back the human element. Instead of scrawling "THOMPSON," the person would probably take a video of himself at the column, post it on YouTube, and see what emerges. In sum, Davis gives us the images of the THOMPSON and the unruly twig of hair, which both represent the myth of immanence, and Ulmer gives us the image of the waving spirit hand, the denotation for the "I" that is embedded within not only the university structure, but also in the literate apparatus. In participatory composition, we "crack up" both the THOMPSON and the spirit hand, for "cracking up" releases forces and intensities previously stifled and stopped up in the name of the oedipalized, self-present subject.

The figure of the "Whatever being," to which I have been referring, breaks up, cracks up both the images of the THOMPSON and the spirit hand. Like Deleuze and Guattari, who see positive aspects in deoedipalization, Agamben affirms the "deoedipalized" subject: the whatever being. This radical singularity—the whatever being—remains in a state of constant becoming. Agamben explains that the whatever "is neither generic nor individual" (*Coming Community* 27). Rather, whatever "adds to singularity . . . a threshold . . . a singularity plus an *empty space* can only be pure exteriority" (67; my emphasis). As a radical singularity, the whatever being exists only in relation to another whatever being. This description helps explain Agamben's attempt to do away with notions of "inside" and "outside" in terms of subjectivity and community. The "whatever" is always already situated alongside the other (see chapter 4 for a more detailed discussion of the whatever and community). Further, and now speaking particularly about subjectivity, Agamben claims that the "whatever singularity has no identity,

it is not determinate with respect to a concept, but neither is it simply in-
determinate; rather, it is determined only through its relation to an *idea*,
that is, to the totality of its possibilities" (67). As a potentiality, the whatever
singularity reflects the previous descriptions of postoedipal subjects, which
are not reliant on stable identifications in order to produce critical reflection and resistance.[3] In other words, whatever singularities do not identify
with essential qualities (race, gender, class, etc.); rather, whatever singularities occupy innumerable potentials and portals for invention. Hence, the
"whateverness" of the whatever being does not signify apathy; instead, it
offers a framework to think about how a conceptualization of subjectivity
might work when not occupying traditional subject positions and markers
of identity. I quote at length to show how the whatever singularity extends
the "postoedipal" world where subjects appear as "disinvested," apathetic,
and indifferent. Agamben allows us to see this in a positive manner, which
sheds some light on how writing works as desiring production.

Singularities as Tubers

> Through the language of critique and the rhetoric of empowerment,
> both critical pedagogy and postmodern pedagogy arguably seek to
> change the emotional constitution of the postmodern subject so as to
> produce either a democratic citizen who participates fully in public
> life or, more radically, a revolutionary subject who is capable of the
> kind of political struggle that will transform the world.
> —Lynn Worsham "Going Postal: Pedagogic
> Violence and the Schooling of Emotion"

In the same fashion as Davis and Ulmer, Lynn Worsham and Rickert have
pointed out that—despite the influence of various versions of postmodern
thought—by continually relying on an oedipalized, modernist conception of subjectivity, we continue to alienate students because they do not
change their actions after they have engaged in critical reflection: they remain THOMPSONS and spirit hands. By reconceptualizing the writing
subject in electracy and, by extension, participatory and video cultures,
we will be able to see our students not as apathetic and disengaged, but as
exemplars of our digital, YouTube moment. These students already have a
digital presence not necessarily tied to any centralized authority, already
write and produce content all the time in many different platforms, and
already see themselves as active participants in digital culture, as "tubers"
of the future. In electracy, critique is performed in a variety of ways and
not always hashed out from a distance. The subjectivity of the performer
changes, morphs, and identifies with the content of the critique only to

change again in the next performance. We see this phenomenon happening most frequently on sites where users create a particular user profile for a particular cause or purpose, as well as in sites as banal as *Yelp* or *Amazon* where the genre of the "review" influences behavior.

Deoedipalized subjects can still be transformed; in fact, social transformation occurs frequently in electracy, as we have seen in numerous examples. In the relation of "transformation" to "becoming," Deleuze and Guattari explain that "to become is not to progress or regress along a series. Above all, becoming does not occur in the imagination" (*Thousand Plateaus* 238). This last statement is crucial, for it might be tempting to envision the transformation of deoedipalized subjects as that which one simply "imagines." Hence, Deleuze and Guattari tell us, we can become multiplicities, "transformational multiplicities, not countable elements and ordered relations" (505). Thus, transformation of all sorts can and will occur, but, described as a becoming, it is neither predictable nor able to be systematized. Critique and performance thus occur simultaneously in an electrate transformation, which is most evident in the phenomena of Internet memes: viral content that is interactive and repurposed. Memes differ from traditional critique in that the goal is not to resolve a problem once and for all; rather, the goal is to create more content with which other users will connect and invest time in re-purposing, thus participating in spreading ideas and making them more complex. Inherent in memes, then, are both the acts of sharing and participation. Participants typically discover memes by way of *sharing rather than searching*, whether or not the sharing of a link, for example, is intended for certain users or not. The crucial concept here is that participants believe that their remixes and contributions actually matter and hold value for the loosely defined community of singularities that may emerge as a result of the meme. Shirky, in *Cognitive Surplus*, clarifies this point: "To participate is to act as if your presence matters, as if, when you see something or hear something, your response is part of the event" (21). This is so important for participatory composition, as the responses and the remixes created in response to an event that becomes viral are symbiotic with the event itself. In *Watching YouTube*, Michael Strangelove emphasizes this change when he reminds us that "the mass participation in online video making is already having an effect on the way events are recorded and remembered" (25). This is most evident in the 2011 spring uprisings in the Middle East, where protesters began forming networks online weeks before heading to the streets. I am in no place to comment extensively on these revolutions, yet I am certain the participation in digital culture that drove participation on the street will not be forgotten.

Taking somewhat of an unexpected turn, in the following section, I relate a story of an image that has lasting impact on my thinking about the predicament of the writing subject both in digital culture at large and within the discipline of rhetoric and composition. I have stubbornly held onto this image for several years, hoping to connect it somehow to my work with electracy and participatory cultures and I relate this story with the hope that it spawns connections. I will then show that not all practices in video culture reflect "tubing," or what I have been arguing by way of electracy. We will see that, while interesting, these practices replicate the methods for turning students into attuned, print-based cultural critics, thereby perpetuating the "myth of immanence" of the self-present, oedipalized subject. The importance of this discussion is to demonstrate how the conceptualization of the so-called oedipalized writing subject remains the largest hurdle to overcome when designing rhetorics for new media.

The U of Participation: Singularities on the Tube

I would think that there is great hope in questioning any and everything we do in the name of "cultural studies for composition." Is this not, after all what cultural studies is all about? Should we not, as theorists and teachers, engage in perpetual exchange of self-critique?
—Victor Vitanza, "The Wasteland Grows"

Let us now flash back to the election of 2004 for a moment, as this period marks a historical time when our country was extremely divisive, and many professors at universities and pundits from the general media placed a great amount of faith in critical pedagogical-like practices to open the country's eyes to the actions of the Bush administration. That is, during this period, the "self-present" subject, it was assumed, would see the inaccuracies, critique them, and elect someone else into office. Like many neighborhoods across America in the fall of 2004, mine displayed a variety of signs showing support for both candidates running in the presidential election. What caught my attention one day was a particular stop sign around the corner from my house. Sometime in late September, someone added a now well-known sticker—in the same lettering as STOP—that said BUSH. So, the revised sign read "STOP BUSH." I saw this simple defacement as an act of resistance not unlike the scrawling of THOMPSON mentioned earlier, but definitely unlike the THOMPSON, the subject did not leave his signature. Instead, remixing the stop sign by adding "BUSH" aimed to elicit participation. I can now see that this act was an offline version of an Internet meme: one in which participants altered STOP signs around the country in order to elicit political participation. The STOP BUSH meme, then, could be seen in varying capacities all over the

United States. During this time, my campus felt alive with political energy; students were busily registering to vote, and discussions in class reflected an interest in politics I hadn't encountered in some time. It seemed as if one of the aforementioned missions of critical pedagogy—to empower students to critique existing forces in control and make change based on that critique— was finally blossoming. It seemed as if students were finally extending this mission beyond the classroom and into the political arena.

And then the election happened.

Like an old record yanked off the turntable, the buzz evaporated. The familiar aura of cynicism, political mourning, and despair set in. Talk in class took on new topics completely, as if to avoid admitting that we had all been duped by our own political enthusiasm. People in the neighborhood took down their campaign signs in a stupor, and the hangover began. Slowly, former acts of resistance and calls for participation also began to vanish: stickers were scratched off, banners removed, and life as we knew it since 2000 resumed. All the talk, all the hype, all the public participation and celebrity endorsements did not change the actions of the majority of American voters. This excruciating contradiction stumped many of my colleagues and me; what went wrong, especially when so many rational and logical factors clearly pointed to the flaws in the current administration? Something else was certainly at work. Incidentally, not too long after the election, the STOP BUSH stop sign took on another curious transformation: someone had scratched off the "B" and "H" and revised it to flawlessly read "STOP US."

Since then I've stubbornly insisted that STOP US has something to teach us, particularly regarding the ways in which cultural studies, critical pedagogy, and the rhetoric of empowerment have been put to work in composition studies. "What went wrong" is precisely tied to Rickert's aforementioned "fault line" between knowledge and action. Now that the political climate has changed, I still think we can turn to the moment that elicited STOP US; STOP US may reflect the despair and/or cynicism students might feel when they *know better* (because they have engaged in critical reflection), but continue to practice behavior that is not in their own best interest. STOP US also asks us to reexamine our own practices; all other associations aside for the moment, I'd like to focus on "us" as intellectuals, as academics and teachers who serve as authority figures in institutions slowly losing their authoritative grip over deoedipalized students. How might the reconceptualization of the writing subject in electracy apply to us? How might we turn this command to "STOP" back on itself? Perhaps we can turn quickly to Geoffrey Sirc's comment in *English Composition as a Happening*. Sirc humorously suggests that "underlying Composition is not so much

Real-World Writing as Real-Wayne's World Writing: everything is under-scored with the parodic *Not!*" (213). Sirc's "Real-Wayne's World Writing" evokes Agamben's aforementioned whatever being. The "not" of the what-ever does not just indicate the opposite (negatively deconstruct) of what has been put forward; rather the "not" indicates a positive potential—what has yet to be invented (not a "no")—and a network of *potentialities* similar to what I have been arguing for. "Not!" moves the whatever out of compliance and onto the threshold of meaning. Agamben explains: "If every power is equally the power to be and the power to not-be, the passage to action can only come about by transporting (Aristotle says 'saving') in the act its own power to not-be" (*Coming Community* 36). Thus, every thought is always accompanied by "not," and, if considered in a parodic Wayne's World fash-ion, this "not" is not a refusal to act but an invitation to act.

Incidentally, after a year or so, the stop sign was transformed again. While faded from the sun, it morphed from STOP US to "STOP U." Both STOP US and STOP U can take us on another journey when recasting subjectivity in electracy. Similar to "US," "U" carries a multitude of connotations: from YOU to UNIVERSITY, we could take many trajectories. When everything else fades, we are left with the STOP U of participatory composition, and this is where I turn.

So far, I have introduced varying notions of subjectivity: deoedipaliza-tion, assemblages, or, the interplay between desire and the social (desiring production), the self-present THOMPSON and Spirit Hand, and the what-ever singularity, which aims to crack up both the THOMPSON and Spirit Hand, particularly in the context of empowerment-oriented rhetorics. I then presented a riff on the analog meme "STOP BUSH," which left us with the challenge of tarrying with STOP U. What I would like to do now is refer to examples from video and participatory cultures to highlight how subjec-tivity is recast in electracy. I will first articulate "STOP U" in terms of the example I referred to in the introduction having to do with the exigency for my beginning to connect video culture and electracy in the first place. This example is particularly telling, since it attempts to participate in Web 2.0 by way of static, cultural critique seeped in literate-only practices. It aptly demonstrates how using literate methods and conceptions of subjectivity in visual, digitally intermediated culture often backfires and produces cyn-ical, resistant results. In the fall semester of 2007, Alexandra Juhasz taught an entire course on YouTube at Pitzer College in Southern California. All assignments and course materials were posted on YouTube, and the course attracted national, mainstream media attention, from Fox News in particular. In an interview at the University of Southern California's 2007 24/7 DIY Video

Event reprinted on his blog, Henry Jenkins asked Juhasz about the goals for the course. She said that she "had decided that she wanted the course to primarily consider how Web 2.0 (in this case specifically YouTube) is radically altering the conditions of learning (what, where, when, how we have access to information)." She continues: "given that college students are rarely asked to consider the meta-questions of how they learn, on top of what they are learning, I thought it would be pedagogically useful for the form of the course to mirror YouTube's structure for learning—one of the primary [structures] being user or amateur led pedagogy" ("Learning from YouTube Part One"). The students thus came up with the content of the course and the learning outcomes. Jenkins explains that the course's critique of YouTube stems from the question of whether a participatory platform necessarily insures diverse, meaningful, or innovative content. Juhasz believes not. YouTube was singled out as a platform that, as Juhasz and her students concluded, cannot coexist with higher education because of the impossibility of carrying out traditional critique.

As both Jenkins and Juhasz remind us, Juhasz is very skeptical from the beginning about participatory culture in general; in fact, she states that she wanted to study YouTube because every time she went to the site, she was "seriously underwhelmed" with what she saw. This skepticism carried over to her students, which led to their conclusions that YouTube does not belong in higher education. Juhasz supports these conclusions by sketching out the following critiques. She begins: "by the mid-term, we could effectively artic- ulate what the site was <u>not doing</u> for us. Our main criticisms came around these four structural limitations: communication, community, research, and idea-building. We found the site to be inexcusably poor at

- finding pertinent materials: the paucity of its search function, currently managed by users who create the tags for <u>searching</u>, means it is difficult to thoroughly search the massive holdings of the site. For YouTube to work for academic learning, it needs some highly trained archivists and librarians to systematically sort, name, and index its materials.
- linking video, and ideas, so that concepts, <u>communities</u>, and conversa- tion can grow. It is a hallmark of the academic experience to carefully study, cite, and incrementally build an argument. This is impossible on YouTube.

The site is primarily organized around and effective at the entertainment of the individual. YouTube betters older entertainment models in that it is mobile, it is largely user-controlled, and much of its content is user-generated (although a significant amount is not, especially if you count user-generated content that simply replays, or recuts, or remakes corporate media without that DIY value of critique)." ("Learning from YouTube, Part One")

Similarly, Pitzer students say they can't learn from YouTube for the following reasons:

- Outsiders can post any unrestricted material on our page (users posted hundreds of unsolicited material on their page)
- Videos are not categorized in an easily understandable way
- All of our comments and discussions disappear within days, making it difficult to follow the progress of the class

The students continue: "YouTube is most known for videos that are humorous, silly, and reference pop culture. Material that is informative, political, artistic, and serious tends to go unnoticed on YouTube. It is no wonder that people cannot fathom a truly academic course based entirely on learning from YouTube. Our class will only be taken as seriously as YouTube itself is."

These remarks, surprisingly made by students, echo the goals of empowerment-oriented approaches as I have explicated above. They neither take into consideration the medium in which the practices take place nor the cultural system that YouTube reflects. First, Juhasz and her students believe that if something is not successful on YouTube (the aforementioned informative, political, artistic, and serious material), it has failed. They somehow missed the fact that YouTube is often the first place people go to find "informative, political, artistic, and serious trends." One of their main lines of study was popularity on YouTube, and they concluded that it is usually the frivolous that receives popularity (see dramatic chipmunk, sleepy cat, or Charlie Bit My Finger). Juhasz goes so far as to say that since popularity is a fundamental, organizing structure for YouTube, "searching for popularity leads to a kind of mediocrity of vision, mediocrity of form, mediocrity of content" ("MediaPraxis"). Thus, she contends, under the pull of popularity, the entire platform elicits mediocre work. She claims that since "YouTube is indebted to the logic of crowds [said Steve, the employee of YouTube that came to her class] . . . it creates a kind of insincere or ironic or glib relationship to culture and also one that's relatively immature and apolitical." Juhasz's critique is stinging; yet she cannot see beyond traditional conceptions of popularity as frivolous and unserious. While popularity is certainly an organizing structure on YouTube, it doesn't serve as the only catalyst that brings people to the site.

Yes, popularity means that many eyeballs have seen the material; they are popular because they take advantage of the medium of video sharing to make their "academic" arguments. They are also popular because they take advantage of the medium of video itself by creating work that is impossible to replicate either in print or in a face-to-face, live situation. In *YouTube: Online Video and Participatory Culture,* Jean Burgess and Joshua Green address this very issue when they boldly state:

> To understand YouTube's popular culture, it is not helpful to draw sharp distinctions between professional and amateur production, or between commercial and community practices. These distinctions are based in industrial logics more at home in the context of the broadcast media rather than an understanding of how people use media in their everyday lives, or a knowledge of how YouTube actually works as a cultural system. It is more helpful to shift from thinking about media production, distribution, and consumption to thinking about YouTube in terms of a continuum of cultural participation. (57)

Juhasz and her students think of YouTube only from the standpoint of media production, consumption, and distribution and do not see beyond the constraints placed on digital culture by industrial or print-based logics. Both Juhasz and her students admit that their videos are "bad"; in other words, they simply show participants talking to the camera while interspersing some text and audio. Also, the Pitzer students don't realize that "outside" attention to their channel gives it relevance outside of the context of their course; in other words, the content might not be used all together as the grand YouTube experiment, but various videos and responses are linked elsewhere, commented on, and responded to. Pitzer students' materials are all over YouTube and elsewhere. They have created a network well beyond their original intention: a network in which they fail to see value, despite its reflection of participatory culture.

Mainstream media coverage of Juhasz's course helps solidify a notion that describes YouTube more like a Web 1.0 site: static and self-serving, and a distinctive object of study. The communities created by YouTube only sometimes originate in YouTube and usually don't stay in YouTube. Communities spring up and often vanish, but many times they continue off the site. They are not usually sustainable in the traditional way and cannot be closed, despite features on the platform such as establishing a channel devoted to a specific theme. Juhasz and her students assume that, in order to learn something, we must be part of a closed community made up of participants who are privy to a course's content. Juhasz's skepticism and Jenkins's lauding of participatory culture echo the old debates between those who believe critical pedagogy is at the heart of all learning and those who don't. Juhasz and her students concluded that YouTube is not a platform for learning but is instead a platform for entertainment (and mediocre at that), particularly for individuals. It follows, then, that the platform for entertainment can be endlessly critiqued, just as Hollywood films have been critiqued for decades, but it cannot be participated in. The ironic thing is that the students actually became part of the medium itself; because of mainstream news coverage and media scrutiny, students themselves were implicated. They had become the course and thus did not have the critical distance necessary to critique. This was frustrating for the students and professor, since they could not point to a static page and say "this is what we are doing." Rather, many of their videos went viral, many of their comments were buried among outsider comments, and it became impossible to locate the course in a static space. This phenomenon describes the process of doing academic work in video culture, where composers blend the academic with entertainment and use the same practices to engage with both. Yet, we see that, when using practices created in and for the literate apparatus, we only experience frustration and heightened cynicism.

Ulmer argues that the institution of entertainment contains the same set of practices in electracy that schooling holds for literacy. In other words, if we accept that a shift toward electracy is taking place, then we see that entertainment and learning should not be separated (Ulmer, "Toward Electracy"). From the perspective of electracy, YouTube is part of a more complex network, creating communities by branching out of its platform and residing in countless spaces. Juhasz says that YouTube's user-driven cataloguing and tagging procedures make it severely unreliable and even suggests that expert archivists take over the cataloguing duties. In electracy, cataloguing and tagging are important skills with which content contributors engage. While Google may be exploring a way to put some "order into the chaos of YouTube" (Chmielewski), these practices remain a central part of content producing and eliciting participation and thus make them part of the writing itself.

If we look at YouTube from the perspective of electracy, then it cannot be seen as simply entertainment for the individual; rather, and as I articulated in chapter 1, we can see forms of videocy occurring. Videocy and electracy demand networking; in dynamic sites, and especially in YouTube, isolation is not possible. Speaking about the microblogging platform Twitter, which allows users to post small "tweets", and answering the claim that these platforms only make us more individualistic, Clive Thompson suggests "the real appeal of Twitter is almost the inverse of narcissism. It's practically collectivist—you're creating a shared understanding larger than yourself." This contrasts sharply with Juhasz and her students who claim that YouTube promotes only entertainment for the individual; in fact, the whole goal of the site is to create any number of communities, and students who are inherent players in participatory culture will already understand this. Assignments uploaded to YouTube and other sites take on lives of their own, merging and morphing with the comments, responses, and related videos left alongside them; students who participate in participatory communities on their own do so for all sorts of reasons, and we can do a better job of creating the conditions for these communities to come into existence and hold relevance for academic learning.

We might recall that controlling writing, and by extension traces of subjectivity left all over sites like YouTube, is difficult at best in electracy. Davis insists that "[writing] is not an I-dentity booster but an I-dentity buster, an exposure" ("Finitude's Clamor" 138). Seeing writing as an "identity buster" (written by whatever singularities) is very different from using writing to critique, reflect, act, and change beliefs and actions. In electracy, critique moves from "what does it mean?" to "how does it work?" By asking how something works, we can never know (nor would we desire to know) for sure what something represents, or means for certain, but we will always experience its force, intensity, and production. I now turn to the video-culture-specific genre of the video blog (vlog), which, best shows subjectivity as singularity, and which is a fitting example for Davis's assertions about writing as an "identity buster."

It is important to note Burgess and Green's revelation that "vlog entries dominated the sample [of YouTube videos they researched], making up nearly 40 percent of the videos coded Most Discussed and just over a quarter of the videos coded Most Responded" (94). The practice of vlogging, then, is not only wildly popular, but it also helps build the "YouTube community." We can perhaps see ToshBabyBoo's subjectivity as singularity in a new light. If YouTube is merely "entertainment for the individual," then ToshBabyBoo's legendary vlogs would have remained in her relatively small community of "friends" on Stickcam. However, because she so boldly posts videos again and again that seem to be damaging to her self-presence, we can only see this act of "writing" as identity-busting. All of the comments and related material on her videos bring forth her singularity, which, as we can see when looking at the videos on her channel, makes and remakes her image each time. The practice of vlogging in general is so rich with examples like ToshBabyBoo, and it is not the purpose of this chapter to delve into many of them. However, I would like to close the chapter with a short discussion of vlogging in order to demonstrate how the practice first shows whatever singularities are in action and second offers an alternative to the aforementioned predicament of engagement in empowerment-oriented rhetorics. I can make the general assertion that most vloggers are deoedipalized in one way or another. Since deoedipalization relies on the concept of not being tied to an institution of authority, vloggers vlog for any number of reasons. Patricia Lange has conducted lengthy ethnographic studies on the practice of vlogging, and in "The Vulnerable Video Blogger" argues that the practice of vlogging is not part of a "self-indulgent, solipsistic obsession. Rather, it provides a means to connect with others and raise awareness in ways that are less overt than acts such as public marches but are nevertheless quite important. Video bloggers acknowledge that the video image, rather than text alone, promotes a key connection" (5). While Lange's perspective is clearly anthropological, her work is invaluable in that it gives us a glimpse into a practice and ensuing community of singularities that not only hint at Davis's notion of exposure, but place exposure and identity busting front and center. Building on Lange's work with vulnerability, Ryan Omizo writes, "by demonstrating vulnerability through the disclosure of personal, intimate, if sometimes mundane details, vloggers can forge relationships with other like-minded viewers, and these connections, when nurtured and mobilized, can lead to social change" ("Vulnerable Video"). Omizo admits that Lange's conclusion is sweeping. Thus, his asks, "Left unexamined is the question of why video presentations of vulnerability prove so motivating to an audience? How do these intimate but mediated moments foster communities of attention and action when other instances of vulnerability—for example, a homeless man panhandling on a street corner—arouse disdain and foreclosures of sociability?" I find these questions intriguing and perhaps a melding of the aforementioned STOP US and STOP U, and while I won't go into the psychological research to which Omizo turns, I will say that vlogging as a practice opens up a network of so many possibilities when looking subjectivity as singularity. Lange suggests vlogs move us precisely because we see something in the vlogger that calls up associations in our own bodies, which then triggers our response.

Exploring this idea further, in another essay on vlogging, "Videos of Affinity on YouTube," Lange follows vloggers who do nothing extraordinary, but who happen to have a significant number of subscribers, comments, and video responses. These videos range from YouTuber "Panda" simply drinking tea to "Ryan" showing his new hairstyle (78–81). While Lange discusses these videos in terms of "affinity" for these types of videos, and describes them as videos that "typically interest delineated groups of people who "wish to participate and remain connected socially in some way to the video maker" (73), I contend that they are more than that. In effect, vlogging videos of "doing nothing" expose Deleuze and Guattari's aforementioned folding of desire and the social: one cannot be separated from the other, particularly since all vlogs are posted with the sole purpose of gaining views. Vlogging videos are thus inherently social and not simply examples of self-present, self-interested narcissists. Rather, in a gesture of radical exposure, vloggers' unruly "twigs of hair" move to frontal view and take on the form of comments, video responses, and remixes.

Bonnie Kyburz's movie "Status Update" both provides a fitting complement to the discussion of vlogging in general and an appropriate coda for this chapter. In the film, Kyburz asks a fairly simple question regarding the genre of the text-based status update on Facebook: why aren't more people updating their statuses with video? She reminds us that the technology is there, that is, mobile devices and webcams make updating one's status with video a piece of cake. The myth of the status update is "the notion of the egocentric narcissist endlessly tweeting." Kyburz's film "worries with this myth by playing with the following possibility: In articulating the mundane (what we often find in status updates), we activate our desire for simple communion." While I would take Kyburz's assertion a bit further than "simple communion" and include exposure to a community of singularities, I see the video status update as much more appropriate than the text-based update for a number of reasons.

Most notably, however, unlike the manipulation of text, video remixes and comments literally remake our image, our so-called self-present subjectivity right before our eyes. Kyburz adds to this when she ruminates on why the textual status update still prevails over the more "exposed" video status update. She writes: "That is to say, for many status updaters, it may seem that sharing the mundane through the relatively static imagistic register of words in a box honors a stable, performing self rather than the richly multimodal, cinematically mediated sublime." By bringing the body into the status update, the "static-ness" of the status is lifted, and suddenly, the space of the update is just as important as both the singularity doing the update and the update itself. I will elaborate on the space of the update in chapter 3, but here we can see that it serves as a fitting illustration of melding desire and the social, permutating subjectivity, and leaving the same sort of trace of becoming as the practice of vlogging. Kyburz concludes, "for those who contributed their video updates to my project, it seems that a kind of emergent desire . . . has compelled them to play." Kyburz's words suggest a desire that is reluctant at best, but after "playing," after letting go of the idea that one's image will be critiqued, the fear of self-presence lifts and participatory subjectivity takes over. The simple act of posting a video status update encapsulates the goals of this chapter with performance, participation, and production at the forefront.

3. The Question of Definition: Choric Invention and Participatory Composition

> What is X? . . . is a question that excludes and purges. What do I want, wanting to know? . . . What is it to know (to no)? This contrary question allows me to interrogate the What is X? question . . . By saying No, we would purchase our identity. Know ourselves. By purifying the world, we would exclude that which, in our different opinions, threatens our identity.
>
> —Victor Vitanza, *Negation, Subjectivity, and the History of Rhetoric*

> *Chora* is the spacing which is the condition for everything to take place, for everything to be inscribed. . . . Everything inscribed in it erases itself immediately, while remaining in it.
>
> —Jacques Derrida, qtd. in Gregory Ulmer,
> *Heuretics: The Logic of Invention*

Vitanza's first counterthesis raises the question of definition, or What is *x*?, and this chapter examines this first of three theoretical constructs that create a framework for electrate and participatory practices. These three constructs are based on the countertheses and include: the question of definition (What is *x*?), the question of authorship (Who speaks when something is spoken?), and the question of pedagogy (How is knowledge communicated?). Examining the first counterthesis, we will link the question of definition to the classical practice of stasis theory that serves as the counterpart to choragraphy: Ulmer's method of invention that comes out of the ancient conception of space, or *chora*. Choragraphy is another way to describe "choric" invention. On the way from *stasis* to *chora*, however, we will revisit the forces animating our recasting of *chora* as an inventional practice, namely Barthes's punctum of recognition, Ulmer's reappropriation

---

This chapter was cowritten by Cortney Kimoto (Smethurst), a graduate of the English rhetoric and composition M.A. program at California State University, Long Beach, and a certified technical and professional writer.

of the punctum, and Collin Brooke's concept of *proairesis*, in order to offer a complex and rich picture of invention for the electrate apparatus.

Thus, this chapter has three ambitious goals. First, beginning with the question of definition, we will revisit the doctrine of stasis theory, a commonplace inventional strategy that is pedagogically familiar. Sharon Crowley and Debra Hawhee suggest that the questions of conjecture, definition, quality, and procedure posed by stasis theory generate *copia*, an abundance of language wherein one might generate arguments or figures for any situation. Second, after exploring Barthes's and Ulmer's work on the punctum of recognition, we will extend their concepts into the participatory realm and then transition into a discussion of Brooke's recasting of invention as *proairesis*, a postcritical approach to invention that he aligns with Ulmer's "process of conduction" (*Heuretics* 85). Our discussion of Brooke's notion of *proairesis* acts as a relay toward our investigation of *chora* that we juxtapose with Deleuze and Guattari's dualisms for both spatiality and temporality. Displacing binaries through the generative logic of the *and* complicates traditional efforts to arrest movement to achieve stasis and propels us into a discussion of online video and participatory cultures through which we can see the aforementioned theoretical concepts in action. Finally, we turn to YouTube as our exemplar for *choric* invention and conclude by explaining how a particular meme, with its folds of remix and reappropriation, illustrates how spreadable (and undefinable) media can influence participation as well as global collaboration, interaction, and communication. Online video sharing sites and the cultural phenomena arising throughout them serve as striking exemplars of the theoretical concepts discussed in this chapter, especially since, as reported in chapter 1, more than 91 percent of the web's global consumer traffic will be video by 2014, according to the *Cisco Visual Networking Index (VNI) Forecast, 2009-2014*. These numbers indicate that video sharing and the participatory practices that are a necessary part of video culture will continue to rise. The purpose of this chapter will be to look forward by looking back: back to the age-old question of definition as it pertains to the electrate and participatory context in which we find ourselves. Combining these elements together, we hope, will create a dynamic picture of invention.

The Question of Definition: From *Stasis* to *Chora*

The central tenets of the first counterthesis are extremely important for rhetoric and composition wherein what constitutes the discipline's object of study is continuously under contention.[1] That said, however, this chapter is concerned with how the question of definition relates to practices of rhetorical invention as well as the generation of knowledge in digitally mediated environments and, particularly, in a digital culture pervaded by video. The first counterthesis

> (de)centers on the age-old issue of whether knowledge can be legitimized or grounded either on some universal, ontogenetic theory (that is, on some universal law, or *physis*) or rhetorically on consensus theory (that is, homology, or local *nomoi*). The first counterthesis, which is contrary to such knowledge, is informed by the Gorgian proposition "Nothing [of essence] exists." (Vitanza, "Three Countertheses" 145)

The first counterthesis is a counterresponse to the practice of systematizing discussions about the object of study in rhetoric and composition. Vitanza explains that the first counterthesis suggests two possible conclusions for its relevance to composition: "either that there can no longer be or that ethically, micropolitically, there should not be any foundational principle or covering law or ontogenetic model for composition theory and pedagogy" (148). This was and still is traumatic for the discipline (see Rickert, *Acts of Enjoyment* 9); Vitanza tells us in the first counterthesis that with any and all attempts to control, map, and construct models in the name of language, we will witness language turning "against the models that are constructed in its name" (148). Following up on this crucial point, in *Negation, Subjectivity, and the History of Rhetoric*, Vitanza warns: "Wherever there is a system (totality, unity), there is the trace of the excluded" (4). This is one of the most provocative yet pressing notions for our discussion: asking what something is, in order to define and set up boundaries, undoubtedly excludes and purges that which it is not. This purging, which creates a hole in order to re-create a new whole, deflects that which it has excluded. Vitanza emphasizes, "if what has been excluded is deflected, it eternally returns. Therefore, it is present in its absence" (15). The "hole" created by the excluded is indeed an active receptacle, a space of generation and constant reinvention, as opposed to a seemingly empty container. The practice of building boundaries and providing final answers to the question, What is *x*? creates specters of the excluded.[2] Similarly, Ulmer explains the necessity of addressing these specters that generate new content. He suggests, "the one who invents is the one who is able to turn ghosts into agents" ("I Untied the Camera of Tastes" 578).

The question, What is *x*? has been appropriated by many in the field when working specifically with rhetorical invention. As James Berlin describes in *Rhetoric, Poetics, and Cultures,* a central tenet of social-epistemic rhetoric concerns uncovering and identifying contradictions (binary constructions) present in society. The practice of uncovering and identifying binary structures is linked to the doctrine of *stasis*: finding a place on which to stand and generate arguments. *Stasis* theory, although from the Classical tradition, remains relevant for inventional purposes in most of the prevailing epistemologies of writing in use today. We do not refute or renounce *stasis* theory, but rather read the residue of what it has been asking writers to do for centuries. In other words, we hope to affirm the knowledge that *stasis* theory necessarily excludes. In his translation of Aristotle's *Rhetoric*, George Kennedy suggests the following regarding the theory's history:

> Much of what Aristotle discusses in [Chapter 15: "Ways of Meeting a Prejudicial Attack; the question at Issue"] was later absorbed into *stasis* theory, the technique of determining the question at issue in a trial . . . This subject was first organized systematically by Hermagoras of Tenos in the second century B.C. and supplies the major theoretical basis for inventional theory in the Rhetoric for Herennius and rhetorical writings of Cicero, Quintilian, Hernogenes, and later authorities. (265)

Because Aristotle himself did not systematize what later became *stasis* theory, Kennedy suggests that he "does not seem to have realized the fundamental rhetorical importance of determining the question at issue" (265–66). Through Kennedy, we can see that determining the question at issue did not always necessarily involve a systematic series of questions to answer. While we do not intend to recover the lost origin of the doctrine of *stasis*, we do find it interesting that perhaps the ambiguity of what Aristotle "did not do" (since most of the other sections of *Rhetoric* are divided into several categories) carries some significance. *Stasis* involves defining something to the greatest extent. Yet, although the process of determining the point of *stasis*, or of eliminating that which does not belong, is important for forensic discourse, such a process is highly ambiguous and arbitrary. As we will see, Roland Barthes plays off of this ambiguity, which, he contends, allows access to that which cannot be articulated in language. In addition, Thomas Conley suggests that the "curricular innovation" of *stasis* theory (which was primarily used as questions for debate in a trial or to clarify wording of the law) is one of the most, *if not the most significant events* of rhetorical invention (32, 33, emphasis added). Conley's suggestion helps explain Kennedy's later assertion that Aristotle's "failure to treat stasis as a part of invention and to create a technical terminology to describe it is probably why *The Rhetoric* was rather little studied" (Aristotle 265). Therefore, it would follow that a systematization of the ambiguous parts of *Rhetoric*, most notably how to invent places to stand, motivated people to read and use it for pedagogical purposes.

Perhaps because of the historical significance attached to stasis theory, discussions about it abound in scholarly articles and composition textbooks in our field, thereby attesting to its longevity and applicability to practices of rhetorical invention. Along with the aforementioned popular textbook by Crowley and Hawhee, *Ancient Rhetorics for Contemporary Students*, we turn to two more examples that we feel are important for our discussion. First, Janice Lauer, when discussing Michael Carter's article "Stasis and Kairos," argues that stasis is a "method for identifying the issue at hand and also for leading rhetors to the topoi appropriate to it" (*Invention in Rhetoric and Composition* 184); she explains that stasis classifies issues as questions of fact, definition, quality, and procedure and thus reduces the possibility of confusion and noise. "Leading to the topics" will be an important contrast to our casting of chora. Second, while dated, Virginia Anderson's article "Confrontational Teaching and Rhetorical Practice" is extremely useful for illustrating how stasis theory is connected to empowerment-oriented rhetorics. Anderson argues that instructors, especially those who espouse critical pedagogy, should rely heavily on stasis theory for inventional purposes.[3] Doing so, according to Anderson, allows instructors to evade opposition from the subsequent "resistant" students who feel that they must conform to their instructor's own political views, while still allowing students to become aware and critical of their own cultural biases.[4] Stasis theory, Anderson claims, represents not the instructor's politics, but "Western tradition" (211). Therefore, students will not resist the questions posed to them, since "Western tradition" is asking them; instead, they will systematically answer the questions, thereby realizing that "beliefs they have taken for granted do not look so obvious to everyone" (211). Stasis theory is pedagogically favorable, and it forces students to take a stand. Stasis theory affords systematized short-cuts for "how to invent" and is not usually seen as an area of contention in the field. In other words, its "status" is typically considered "obvious" to anyone seeking to invent ideas. Stasis theory provides a systematic guide for "how to" invent written arguments and assumes that answering the question, What is *x*? will be no problem for writers.

However, we argue that if writers begin by tossing out anything that feels irrational or irrelevant, their writing reproduces what has already been predetermined by social codes. Vitanza, in the first counterthesis, helps explain this. If we ask students to discover their arguments by way of answering the questions of stasis theory, they will not "discover" anything at all. He writes, "what appears to be writing as discovery is only—unbeknown to its unselfconscious mystified self—writing that uncovers what has already been predetermined by the modes, or the social codes, of production and representation" (150). Thus, students will likely replicate the very discourses that they aim to complicate.

From Punctum to *Proairesis*

We now explore what is deflected in the name of defining things to achieve stasis. Both Barthes's work with third meanings, particularly in his text *Camera Lucida*, and Ulmer's appropriation of Barthes provide access to this deflected residue, to what has been systematically pushed aside by asking and subsequently answering "What is *x*?" In addition, Collin Brooke's recasting of invention as *proairesis* will illustrate an alternative that, again, does not dismiss stasis theory but reappropriates it. Ulmer describes Barthes as ultimately searching for these deflections: the "undefinable," the "inaccessible." He writes:

> Much of Barthes's work in the last decade of his life consisted of the development of a methodology—a procedure or operation—that would provide access to the third meaning. . . . Barthes addresses a level of reality that exists at the limits of knowledge excluded from the extant codes of both opinion and science. This is the level of the third meaning—the obtuse, the oblique, the novelesque, the filmic, the biographeme. ("Barthes's Body of Knowledge" 224)

Barthes finds this access in photographs and film stills that produce obtuse, third meanings. These third meanings do not so much destroy as subvert traditional forms of interpretation (Barthes, "The Third Meaning" 64) and are usually experienced as feelings or emotions that arise instantaneously when in contact with photographs or images. Barthes believes that the photographic image contains a message without a code, making verbal articulation impossible. While Barthes develops his theory in relation to still images, we will remotivate it in relation, as well as in application, to online video, which inevitably adds a participatory element (to be discussed shortly). First, however, we will spend some time with Barthes's reading of photographs in *Camera Lucida*, sparking a passage toward the question of definition and its role in participatory culture.

Barthes is troubled by the question, What is *x*? in relation to pictographic representation. His journey is triggered by the tremendous desire to know

if something exists (What is *x*?), which is the first question of stasis theory. However, this question is complex, and Barthes eventually discovers
that the confusion and ambiguity resulting from his desire to know if
something exists is actually what he has been looking for all along. In fact,
Ulmer describes the writing that Barthes exemplifies as "that of a writer
who 'catches' language from another text the way something catches fire,
ignites" ("Barthes's Body of Knowledge" 222).

Barthes's desire drives him to "learn at all costs what a photograph is 'in
itself'" (*Camera Lucida* 3). The (overwhelming) question he poses to himself is "does it exist?" However, the first question of stasis theory cannot be
answered; it simply cannot be determined. Barthes reports, "I wasn't sure
if photography existed [or] that it had a 'genus' of its own . . . photography
is unclassifiable" (3–4). Therefore, not only the first, but also the second
question of stasis theory remains unanswered; they simply cannot be determined. Barthes believes that the photograph's infinite reproduction of
that which has happened only once produces its ambiguity and singularity,
its ability to evade classification. Frustrated by attempting to define photography in general, Barthes turns to the photograph in particular. He feels
suppressed by the "voice of knowledge," which continuously urges him to
dismiss/deflect/exclude what is disturbing him about the photograph and
to return to something that can be codified, grounded in representation
and rationality.

This disturbance or disorder, initiated by the inability to define and revealed by the desire to write about photography, suddenly "corresponded
to a discomfort [he] had always suffered from: the uneasiness of being a
subject torn between two languages, one expressive, the other critical" (8).
He focuses on why some photographs "wound" him, or evoke a corporeal
reaction, while others are just "there." We have explicated Barthes's di-
lemma in detail to show the complexities that arise from simply asking,
"is it?" Barthes, for an instant, attempts to follow procedure or, perhaps,
protocol: defining what "is" to the audience to establish the point of stasis.
However, what Barthes finds, by resisting protocol and following his body,
is that arriving at a definition is the very thing that suppresses desire. In
other words, standing still is not an option, and he cannot simply ignore the
immense internal agitation he feels while looking at certain photographs.
He cannot *not move*, or shift ground as he investigates his desire to write.
There is no place to "stand."

The principle of adventure allows Barthes to "make photography exist"
(19). The adventure is neither mapped nor planned; it happens in a flash
that can be neither predicted nor apprehended in such a way as to establish

a firm ground upon which to build an argument. Suddenly, and with no comprehensible warning, certain photographs become animated. Barthes explains that the adventure works both ways: the photograph reaches and animates him just as he animates the photograph. This is a wonderful explanation of the participatory experience we undergo when interacting with images and video online, and we will elaborate on this connection shortly. However, Barthes calls the participatory experience "a *wound*: I see, I feel, hence I notice, I observe, and I think" (21). Curiously, the wound includes the co-presence of two discontinuous elements: an experience that calls for a third conception to complicate, as well as to break out of, the otherwise clear demarcations of a binary structure. Barthes searches his own lexicon to describe that adventure, that certain co-presence in the photographs that wound him, but his language (French) makes it impossible. Instead, Barthes chooses two Latin terms, *studium* and *punctum*, to describe the experience of interacting with photographs.

Barthes looks at a photograph of a war-torn street in Nicaragua. He notices the copresence of soldiers and nuns walking down a deserted street, claiming that the photograph does not please, interest, or intrigue him. "It simply existed (for me)" (23), he writes. Hence, what he feels about this and several other photographs "derives from an average affect, almost from a certain training. . . . it is culturally that I participate in the figures, the faces, the gestures, the settings, the actions" (27). Culturally coded reactions and interests constitute the *studium*: predictable, *inert* responses that stand still, frozen in stasis. Barthes continues: "To recognize the *studium* is inevitably to encounter the photographer's intentions, to enter into harmony with them, to approve or disprove of them, but always to understand them, . . . for culture (from which the *studium* derives is a contract arrived at between creators and consumers" (27–28). Barthes's notion in regard to culture as a contract is extremely important to note; for this contract between creators and consumers is what achieves stasis. Hence, to arrive at the *studium* is to arrive at stasis: to understand what has been produced and to share that understanding with a common culture.

The second concept, the *punctum*, cannot be separated from the *studium*; it is neither better nor worse than the *studium*, but the punctum breaks through, interrupts, and disrupts the *studium*. The element that "rises from the scene, shoots out of it like an arrow and pierces me" (26), becomes, Barthes explains, the punctum. It is a wound, a prick, a mark made by a pointed instrument, and the wound comes by way of a detail. However, the detail is usually not present because of the photographer's intentions; the person looking at the photograph feels the detail and is overcome by it. The sting of the punctum cannot be articulated by something that can be defined. Another of Barthes's photographs shows a blind gypsy violinist somewhere in central Europe being led by a boy. In contrast to his reaction of the first photograph, Barthes experiences a punctum with this one: the texture of the dirt road stings him. This "wound," the texture of the road, gives him the "certainty" of being in central Europe. Here is where Barthes realizes the utter significance of the punctum. He recognizes, with his "whole body," the "straggling villages" he passed through in Hungary and Rumania long ago (45). The punctum provides access to the unrepresentable by breaking out of the banality of both the *studium* and definition. The punctum of recognition emerges from the body, instigating disruption and disturbance, a sort of disorder. Each disruption sets in motion a network of associations, which can then be paralogically linked. Stasis theory only concerns the *studium*: There is no wound, since the stasis questions reproduce cultural conventions and, thus, strengthen the contract between creators and consumers.

The concept of the punctum is important for reenvisioning the question of definition for the electrate apparatus, since it provides access to knowledge residing in the body. Although Barthes acknowledges that the punctum of recognition gives access to the third meaning, he continues a Modernist theory working out of the dialectic of tragedy: one acts, one suffers (through the wound), one learns. We especially see this at work in the second half of *Camera Lucida* as Barthes mourns for his mother's death. This is why we turn to Ulmer's rereading of Barthes in "Barthes's Body of Knowledge," an essay read by few yet one that remains central for the question of definition and electracy. In this essay, Ulmer discovers a way to evade Barthes's mourning for what is not, and thus moves out of the negative mode of critique. Ulmer understands the punctum experience as a moment for connection, for conduction to occur, rather than a moment for mourning. Ulmer explains that the punctum "represents an alternative to the conception of knowledge that underlies normal academic writing. . . . . the primary quality of Barthes's approach is its renunciation of the notion of knowledge as a mastery over the object known" (224). Ulmer's description of the punctum of recognition connects invention with discovering patterns in an aleatory manner. The punctums that arise, Ulmer suggests, will identify works that are "events," works that evoke a bodily, emotional response and sting one into an "awareness of reality" (228). These works are linked, but not contained, in a set and are invented from accidental occurrences. Ulmer explains: "The past moments thus rescued [by way of the punctum] are not a spectacle for nostalgia, but tools for opening the present" (*Teletheory* 112). This assertion, "tools for opening the present," is crucial when discussing the question of definition, since these past moments are not to be defined or mourned; rather, they are celebrated as triggers that set future linkages *in motion*.

As previously discussed, one of the main goals of this chapter is to extend Barthes's and Ulmer's important work by involving it with the participatory realm. Such involvement is necessary since even Ulmer's former students have critiqued the personal aspects of these inventional practices by aligning them, for example, with "navel gazing" that "produce[s] work no more innovative than the self-exploratory essays encouraged in freshman composition classes" (O'Gorman 1). Recall Ulmer's postulation that "what literacy is to the analytical mind, electracy is to the affective body: a prosthesis that enhances and augments a natural or organic human potential" (qtd. in Ulmer, "Chora Collaborations"). No doubt one may oppose this somewhat cyborgian notion of a virtual prosthesis; yet, as Alex Reid suggests in his essay "Exposing Assemblages," "the externalization of the subject in the emergence of community, which is difficult and abstract in the print world, becomes more palpable and material in digital media networks." Moreover, Reid adds, "this palpability is even intensified by the shift from text into video." In other words, if we move the discussion from static images to moving images, the means with which videographers communicate throughout online video and participatory cultures, we not only recognize a sharing of relations, but upon such recognition see and, more importantly, *feel* the making of meaning. In fact, according to Clay Shirky, such "sharing makes the making better" (qtd. in "Storytelling"). Jean Burgess and Joshua Green, in *YouTube: Online Video and Participatory Culture*, also attest to the generative nature of video sharing. Indeed, they emphasize that participation is a crucial requirement in the YouTube architecture, an architecture that "has never functioned as a closed system" (66) and thus encourages, and almost demands, sharing and repurposing.

Given this shift toward participation, which we argue gained momentum with the rise of video and participatory cultures, we turn to Brooke's recasting of the classical rhetorical canons in *Lingua Fracta: Toward a Rhetoric of New Media* and call particular attention to his term for encapsulating the changing role for invention in digital culture: *proairesis*, an open-ended mode of invention. Brooke explores the possibilities of a proairetic interface, which contrasts with modes of hermeneutic invention that seek resolutions, closures, and stopping points. While navigating the possibilities of *a* proairetic interface, Brooke draws heavily on Roland Barthes's distinction between readerly/writerly texts in *S/Z* (1975), which he suggests opens a "transition from literary/textual object to interface" (63). Proairesis unsettles *and* moves us to respond. It is a practice that evades stasis. The goal is not to respond by defining that which unsettles us, but rather to encompass both critique and performance in a remix or reappropriation. As Casey Boyle suggests in a review of *Lingua Fracta*, Brooke offers an approach to new media invention that "generates without a set end, deferring endlessly any sense of resolution." Proairetic invention is less concerned with achieving stasis and more interested in creating points of departure from which future inventions will traverse and take place. We see proairesis occurring in video culture with videographers creating, re-creating, and commenting on videos with virtually no original content, thereby complicating traditional notions of invention.

An example of proairesis is a popular video composed of shared clips depicting several celebrations from across the globe after Landon Donovan, a player on the U.S. World Cup soccer team, scored a dramatic game-winning goal against Algeria during the 2010 World Cup. One clip showed a young man celebrating by running up and down a flight of stairs in his house. While this example is not new or unique, it represents a transformation of the traditional genre of the "home movie" into something that reveals cultural patterns and norms through the banality of "home" life that operates differently from staged filming. In video culture, proairesis aims to provoke, reel in, and generate responses and editing by (multiple) viewers, both in textual and video formats. As Brooke says, proairesis is "contingent on the present moment, [and] the constantly changing conditions to which it responds" (*Lingua Fracta* 77).

Brooke aligns his postcritical approach to online invention with a "process of conduction," a process that Ulmer outlines in *Heuretics* through "a space (*chora*) for experimentation that is the counterpart to analysis and interpretation" (Brooke, *Lingua Fracta* 85). As Brooke notes from Ulmer's *Teletheory*, the affix or combining form *duction* is "shared by the fields of logic and electricity" and it allows for a "description of a reasoning or generative procedure" (85). Electrate reasoning is neither the finalization of form nor a linear procedure to a predetermined end; rather, it is a process of exposure, an experience of *now-time*, during which one—in being-*with* or connected—*feels* "the form-taking of concepts as they pre-articulate thoughts/feelings" (Manning 5). In short, electrate reasoning works proairetically, creating conditions for innovations to emerge. While Brooke characterizes proairetic invention with discrete sets of technologies and social networks, like Flickr, Wikipedia, Google Reader, and Zoom Clouds, we believe that online video culture relies on *proairetic* invention *and* electrate reasoning, both of which expose the question of definition to spaces of participation where strict boundaries of belonging, such as "inside" and "outside," blur and thus necessitate movement. According to José Gil, "the meaning of movement is the very movement of meaning" (qtd. in Manning 28). Once again, however, now in reference to online video and participatory cultures, standing still is not an option. Instead of getting things "set" for an argument (stasis), proairesis aims to unsettle stability. What is *x*?, then, is reworked, repurposed, and remixed to ask, What is the productive potential for *x*?

Video and participatory cultures provide new ways of eliciting participation, encouraging remix, and writing the punctum: welcoming the disruptions instead of systematically excluding them. We can see that this process does not reflect *on* but reflects *in*, thus creating possibilities for that which cannot be expressed in language to move to the forefront. In the final section of this chapter, we will offer examples of what is expressed in the language of online video and participatory cultures, which, as a language of popular culture, is understood through sharing, or being-*with*, relations of exteriority. We now turn to the *chora*, the "active receptacle" that provides the methodology for this rediscovery.

The Holey Space of *Chora*

As deployed in the work of Julia Kristeva, Jacques Derrida, and Gregory Ulmer, the chora transforms our senses of beginning, creation, and invention by placing them concretely within material environments, informational spaces, and affective (or bodily) registers. . . . By refocusing on what falls outside discourse proper, like emotion or the chora itself, or redistributing rhetorical agency across a network of human or nonhuman agents, these writers suggest we can (and should) reapproach the inventional question Plato wrestles with in the *Timaeus*, which is how to move from static ideas to vital activity, from the speculative theory of the *Republic* to a dynamic, vital Athens. The chora, brought forward into our age, stands to radically reconfigure our understanding of rhetorical space.

—Thomas Rickert, "Toward the Chora"

In "Toward the Chora," Rickert revisits the work of Plato, Kristeva, Derrida, and Ulmer to present chora as a complex ecology for rhetorical invention. Rickert explores how contemporary work on the chora argues that there are no delimitations between *inside* and *outside* and that inventional practices are not linear methods with which to establish a discursive place where topics emerge and develop, but rather involve being "immersed in, negotiating, and harnessing complex ecologies of systems and information" (253). Rickert's effort explicates chora from its pre-Platonic connection to both a "dance" and a "dancing floor" (254), and traces the concept through the following: Kristeva's semiotic chora as a "particular form of beginning, one [Rickert] would like to describe as 'invention *inventing* itself'" (262–63), and Derrida's idea that choric "invention may inhabit a paradoxical or impossible place within rhetoric, precisely because of its always-ongoing withdrawal" (265). Working heuretically through the chora, Ulmer "makes of the *chōra* an inventional methodology" (269) and can then "theorize *and* practice how this seeming inconsistency or paradox [the chora] is actually productive" (270). Therefore, despite the apparent impossibility of the chora, in terms of its necessitating becomings or *inventios* through generative withdrawal, Rickert explains, "The impossibility has nothing to do with what we can *do* with choric invention except the one, self-reflexive exception: what is impossible is that a discourse of representation can capture invention" (270). In other words, representation can delineate particular paths, like stasis theory, that one may follow with intent to invent. "But," as Rickert acknowledges, "the impossible emerges when we try to equate this with invention itself" (270).

Inspired by the question of definition, we have thus far devoted the majority of this chapter to tracing a theoretical circuit leading to chora, and we will now build on Rickert's theoretical precedent and unpack the perspective of other researchers who have worked with chora in various capacities (see especially Rice, *The Rhetoric of Cool*; Saper, *Artificial Mythologies*; and Jarrett, *Drifting on a Read*) to create possibilities for "choric," rather than "topic," invention. Rickert makes a point that is crucial for our effort to restore movement to invention and, specifically, to definition. He writes, "one thing choric invention provides us with is a way to put invention itself back into question, not as a metaphysical problem (a la 'What is invention?' with 'invention' being defined as a category with X number of characteristics), but as an inventional problem" ("Toward the *Chōra*" 262–63). This lifts invention out of the practice of accessing *topoi* and into the practice of making, or, in other words, of nonstatic generation.

Chora is an indeterminable space between being and becoming that, being neither intelligible nor sensible, evades conceptualization and must be "grasped" by some sort of sensuous or, as Plato describes, "bastard" reasoning (qtd. in Walter 136). Like Rickert, we also turn to Ulmer's casting of chora in *Heuretics*. Using the chora, Ulmer attempts to reason by means of intuition, chance, and pictographic representations: that which usually gets excluded in what we know as "academic writing." Unlike a literate, heuristic method (such as stasis theory), wherein a set of procedures directs one's path to varying outcomes, this aleatory method attempts to grasp that which cannot be articulated in language and is realized through the methodology of choragraphy: "a way of gathering dispersed information into an unstable set held together by a pattern that is the trace of understanding or learning" (213). Choragraphy does not offer a set of preestablished procedures; it creates a network in which to *feel* an invention that is both sparked by a punctum and remembered by the body. The chora, Ulmer explains, is "most resistant to interpretation (hermeneutics)" (63) since it relies on analogy and chance. However, it is important to keep in mind that choragraphy is not simply coincidence; rather, it asks one to be attuned to occurrences that do not fit into general, hierarchical methodologies and to make something from such occurrences.

E. V. Walter, who Ulmer turns to, explains that Greek writers used the words *topos* and *chora* to differentiate certain typical features in the experience of places, and he first locates this distinction in the opening lines of *Oedipus at Colonus*. Here, Walter acknowledges, we hear Antigone referring to the place that she and Oedipus presently rest as *"choros"*: a *holy* place. Later, when Oedipus speaks about where he must die, he uses both terms: *"topos* stands for the mere location or the container of the sacred *choros,* the grave" (Walter 120). The "holey" space of the chora, according to Walter, is also very sacred: "holy," the place where the literal remains of the dead "remain." Ulmer explains that we might "think [of place] before [it] was split into topos and chora," à la the dancing floor that Rickert points out when tracing pre-Platonic understandings of chora. Accordingly, Walter "distinguishes [chora] from topos by noting that the former term names a 'grounded' mode of thought that was available in Plato but that has been buried" (70). The chora is a generative space where inventions appear and disappear, leaving only traces, without becoming grounded. Byron Hawk explains that Ulmer "conflates the binary of chora as space and topos as place. Rather than chora as metaphysical space and topos as literal place, Ulmer sees the chora as cultural space that emerges between metaphysical space and physical space" ("Hyperrhetoric" 75). We see a direct connection between Hawk's assertion and Deleuze and Guattari's treatment of smooth, striated, and holey space. We suggest that their discussion, both in general and in very specific regard to their third term "holey space," complements the concepts we have explicated above as well as adds another layer of complexity to the notion of chora and the question of definition.

We might recall that Deleuze and Guattari work from what Reid, citing Vitanza, has called "third interval wayves" (Reid, *Two Virtuals* 190; cf. Vitanza "Abandoned to Writing" para 4), which resist stasis and champion the ebb and flow created by choric invention. Stuart Moulthrop, one of the first scholars to study electronic media and its relation to theory and practice in English studies, connects Deleuze and Guattari's notions of spatiality to the changing culture of digitized writing. Academic writing as we know it is traditionally invented from striated space: the "domain of routine, specification, sequence, and causality." It manifests itself in "hierarchical and rule-intensive cultures . . . like the university," and "the occupants of striated space are the champions of order—defenders of logos" ("Rhizome and Resistance" 303). One invents measurable arguments from existing places through striated space. Smooth space, on the other hand, is dynamic, understood "in terms of transformations instead of essence" (303). Ulmer explains that its "'logic' is associational [and] organized as a network" (*Heuretics* 34). Thus, our momentary location is less important than our continuing movement or line of flight. Moulthrop continues, "this space is by definition a structure for what does not yet exist. It propagates in a matrix of breaks, jumps . . . smooth space is an occasion; Deleuze and Guattari call it a becoming" (303). In smooth space, movement occurs and cannot be controlled or resisted in the traditional sense; rather, we charge into the very thing we are trying to resist. Ulmer remarks that the task will be "to build, in place of a single argument, a structure of possibilities" (*Heuretics* 34; cf. Bolter 119; see also chapter 5). Using a combination of Moulthrop's and Ulmer's descriptions of smooth and striated space, we see a crucial point regarding Deleuze and Guattari's dualisms: smooth space is not an alternative (good) to striated space (bad). Instead, as Deleuze and Guattari explain more than once, there must be binaries, but these binaries do not exist in opposition, wherein one is privileged over another. Instead of creating only two possibilities, their dualisms fold into each other and restore the flow of desiring production to create countless becomings, lines of flight, and assemblages: desiring production that is possible in the "hole" before deterritorialization occurs. Such becomings are what allow for the possibility of a cultural praxis to emerge. Folding avoids stasis and (Aristotle's notion of) grounding; therefore, everything becomes re/included. This has been thoroughly explained by, among others, Barthes, Deleuze and Guattari, and Agamben, however, it may nevertheless be tempting to read the smooth and the striated as traditional binary oppositions: a reading that excludes and deflects holey (choric) space.

The processes of smoothing and striating, their passages and combinations, happen persistently. There is no finality for smoothing and striating space: no "whole" or One to ever reach. This is also very different from simply affirming kairotic eruptions from smooth space: eruptions that may initially appear to reverse dominant, oppressive striations. The movement and energy changing along smooth spaces spark striation again only to unfold smooth space and then striated space again and again. John Rajchman describes this generative process: "[Deleuze] speaks of 'disparation' that does not divide space into distinct parts, but rather so disperses or scatters it to allow the chance for something new to emerge" (Deleuze Connections 55). This process shows that liberation will not happen by simply engaging in a negative deconstruction. Hence, the third term, holey space, provides the passage, a place where both the smooth and the striated meet and the third meaning can be accessed. As intensities residing in the "cracks," the third meaning can only be felt. Once felt, a mood is produced that remains in a constant state of generation; the mood, when felt, links elsewhere, but never stops. Thus, unlike "Aristotle's doctrine of place," we must affirm the dwelling space where the mood is felt; it cannot be separated from the third meaning, because it is in its composition. Deleuze and Guattari remind us, "Nothing is ever done with: smooth space allows itself to be striated and striated space reimparts a smooth space, with potentially very different values, scope, and signs. Perhaps we must say that all progress is made by and in striated space and all becoming occurs in smooth space" (Thousand Plateaus 486). However, progress and becoming are not separate opposable entities. Even the striated space of the university gives rise to smooth spaces that might be linked to moments of invention: becomings that happen in smooth spaces are striated, then those striations are smoothed, creating perpetual movement among/between intensities. Becomings happen perpetually, yet are usually dismissed (excluded) for not fitting in the realm of what can be deciphered through rationality and the dominant structures in place. Deleuze and Guattari tell us that we can become multiplicities, "transformational multiplicities, not countable elements and ordered relations" (505). Thus, transformation can and will occur, but described as a becoming, it is neither predictable nor systematizable. Transformational multiplicities might be seen as "holes" in smooth/striated space through which invention takes place. Holey space becomes invented and reinvented, persistently "flowing out," never to be filled up.

This notion of holey space differs from viewing cracks, fissures, and holes as simply gaps needing to be filled or demystified in order to resist dominant ideologies: a view remaining in the negative with one seeing such holes as indicating a sort of *lack* in one's learning or ideology, and thus yearning for what is supposedly missing. Holes instead are seen as affirmative responses. D. Diane Davis's explanation in *Breaking Up [at] Totality* is paramount: "But lack theories are negations that assume holes in the whole: affirmative responses, on the other hand, assume a wild and overwhelming excess of 'parts' that will never make a 'whole': there can be no final One, no final Totalization, and therefore no lack" (57). Hence, dominant ideologies will be resisted by affirming the intensities that reappear through the cracks, and then reassembling them into new combinations through remix and reappropriation.

Circling back to Hawk, we want to highlight his assertion that, through choragraphy, "invention becomes something neither unconscious nor conscious. It becomes attentive—a way of being-in-the-world, a way of becoming" ("Hyperrhetoric" 88). The chorographer captures (through a series of punctums) and arranges "memories that float between the cultural and the personal": that which resides in the chora, the space between de- and re-territorialization. Hence, invention brings what the body knows intuitively into awareness. Practice within the chora, then, will be understood, as Ulmer explains, "in the order of making, of generating. And it must be transferable, exchangeable, without generalization, conducted from one particular to another" (*Heuretics* 67).

The chora affirms the singularity and potentiality of the whatever being. Vitanza refers to the chora as the "chora (us)" to show that, in electracy, acts of production require "Total Collaboration" ("Shaping Force"); hence, when working with the chora, there is no such concept as the individual writing subject who invents arguments, or, as Chris Anderson identifies in reference to online video culture, of "the lone genius having a eureka moment that changes the world" ("How YouTube Is Driving Innovation"). The chora cannot be apprehended by reason. According to Walter, the chora is "a knowledge that must be 'grasped' [with one's entire body, not just his or her hands] because it cannot be conceived and it cannot be perceived" (122). It is neither in the rules of rational thought nor a product of sensory experience, "but something else: a curious, spurious mode of grasping reality" (122). Material for invention exists everywhere, so it must be evoked rather than found or uncovered. Recall Ulmer's suggestion that when one invents using choragraphy, he or she is able to turn "ghosts into agents" ("I Untied the Camera of Tastes" 578): not securing ownership or mourning for the lost, but calling for perpetual movement. Thus, the chora, the space where "grasping" takes place, cannot be separated from that which is grasped;

Rickert explains it in this way: "Such invention takes place in material and affective situations that in turn create us" ("Toward the *Chōra*" 263).

Interestingly, and similar to the aforementioned practice of stasis theory, "what's there" and "what's not there" are also important for choragraphy. The difference lies precisely *when* "what's there" becomes known. First of all, in regard to stasis theory, "what's there" becomes known when the subject critically "reads" his or her world and identifies definitions and contradictions. For choragraphy, however, "what's there" becomes known once something is felt by the body and caught in the chora through a network of "'punceptual' rather than conceptual" linkages (Ulmer, *Heuretics* 228). Inventing through the chora affirms what the body might "know," instead of simply casting memories and knowledge in the body as emotional feelings that the rational person would dismiss as irrelevant to serious work. Ulmer warns: "one of the difficulties in grasping chora is that, being neither intelligible nor sensible, it has to be approached by extended analogies. Analogy is inherently ambiguous" (67). We have come back to the inherent ambiguity of invention. Thus, in practice, and in the space of the chora, the inventor will experience punctums of recognition, third meanings that "arise out of the particular way memory stores information in 'emotional sets,' gathering ideas into categories classified not in terms of logical properties but common feelings" (142). The moods and memories recovered then link elsewhere through an unfolding and rhizomatic network of associations. They become moments, events, celebrations, and collaboration during which inventions then "catch" and come into appearance.

Describing how one's movement through a choric space can spawn a network of associations, Ulmer looks to the aborigines who, as nomads moving through their space, conducted "a sort of cognitive map or allegory or mystory . . . a collective story in which the culture and civilization and landscape that the people moved through were one in the same" ("Ulmer Tapes" 4.04). In his own discussion of aboriginal dreamtime or "the Dreaming," Walter argues that the aborigines "cannot separate their way of feeling from their way of thinking about places. The Dreaming," he continues, "grasps the nature of place holistically as a unified location of forms, powers, and feelings" (139). Walter explains that this sort of dreaming, or holistic, corporeal experience of an in-between space, necessitates "an exceptional mode of perception—dreaming with our eyes open" (123). As a kind of dream logic, or as Ulmer describes in *Heuretics*, a "dream time relay," (39), and as we mentioned earlier, choragraphy is not a process through which one reflects *on* what he or she sees, but rather a process through which one reflects *in*. Reflecting in necessitates experiencing all possibilities as events rather than found topics for invention.

Choragraphy as a process through which one reflects *in* rather than *on*, brings us to Deleuze and Guattari's temporal dualism between *chronos* and *kairos*: The former is quantitative, whereas the latter is qualitative and thus subversive to control and dominance. Prior to exploring this temporal dualism, however, we stress that kairos not be privileged over chronos as various versions of postmodern rhetorics might do; rather, we align ourselves with Brooke's notion of a posthuman rhetoric that "finds room for both [chronos and kairos]" ("Forgetting to Be [Post] Human" 790–91). Though, finding room for both necessitates that we move to Deleuze and Guattari's third term for a temporality: *haecceity*. That said, recall that Deleuze and Guattari are not concerned with "finding room" for different conditions of space or time; rather, analogous to how they describe smooth and striated spaces, they describe chronos and kairos as happening, instantaneously, in a perpetual refolding fold. Deleuze and Guattari attribute the origin of haecceity to Duns Scotus, who, as they write, "created the word and concept from *haec*, 'this thing.'" However, they also call attention to how haecceity is sometimes written "ecceity," which adding rather than detracting from one's understanding of the term, "suggests a mode of individuation that is distinct from that of a thing or a subject" (*Thousand Plateaus* 540–41 n33). In other words, similar to the other third terms, haecceity resides outside subject-object relations within which singularities are thought to exist only in relation to other singularities. In the *Dialogues*, Deleuze argues that there are "no more subjects, but dynamic individuations without subjects, which constitute collective assemblages . . . Nothing becomes subjective but *haecceities take shape according to the compositions of non-subjective powers and effects*" (qtd. in *Deleuze Dictionary* 274, emphasis added). Considering how haecceities take shape, as well as recalling Walter's description of "the dreaming" as that which "grasps the nature of place holistically as a unified location of forms, powers, and feelings" (139), we may now explore the connection between choragraphy and Deleuze and Guattari's dualism of time; for it is the act of *grasping*, touching, or linking to the *hole* (chora) that sparks the formation of haecceities. In fact, as previously mentioned, Walter explains that chora necessitates "an exceptional mode of perception," because the "illegitimate reasoning" (123) by which the nature of chora must be grasped elicits "a wider experience of clutching or holding that does not stop with the hands but sometimes involves the entire body" (133). Therefore, working in tandem with chora, haecceities mark the potentiality of becoming along each composition or, rather, each felt assemblage of relations. Again, haecceities do not generate subjects; instead, they generate the conditions for the possibility of a becoming to occur. Deleuze and Guattari warn that "it should not be thought that a haecceity consists simply of a décor or backdrop that situates subjects, or of appendages that hold people and things to the ground" (262). Alternatively, they describe haecceity as follows: "Haecceity, fog, glare. A haecceity has neither beginning nor end, origin nor destination: it is always in the middle. It is a rhizome . . . [ceasing] to be subjects to become events, in assemblages that are inseparable from an hour, a season, an atmosphere, an air, a life" (*Thousand Plateaus* 263, 262). Deleuze and Guattari's idea of haecceity as fog or glare, a kind of visual obstruction, reinforces what Walter deems "an exceptional mode of perception" (123). In fact, according to Ulmer, because chora is "generation and may only be known by a feeling or affect . . . you have to work with it *darkly*" ("Electracy: Writing to Avatar"). In short, one must work through being-*with* relations of exteriority or, in other words, assemblages.

Similar to Davis's "ek-static" communications, haecceities are *only heard* and *only hearable* without predetermined, totalizing structures in place (such as Freud's "Oedipus," critical pedagogy, stasis theory, etc.). This transitions the goal of defining things from wanting precise answers to enacting a sort of timelessness, or, as Davis has suggested elsewhere, "glimpsing what lies between . . . toward interstanding the in-between of the 'seeing' and the 'not-seeing'" (Ballif, Davis, and Mountford 587). The in-between remains at the threshold and often occurs in the fog. To elaborate, this in-between or "outside" is not a beyond; rather, it is a *threshold* or conduit of pure exposure along which bodies, through relations of *touching*, experience the emergence of otherwise unknown capacities and the shaping of new assemblages. Thus, it comes as no surprise that Deleuze and Guattari affirm the necessity of the fog, the timelessness of haecceity. Losing oneself in the fog, however, is not aimless drifting. Davis, by way of Martin Heidegger, refers to the fog as the abyss: the placeless place where the ground falls off and becomes lacking, therefore producing a longing for its "bottom." She contends, "what makes the abyss agonizing is one's unanswered desire to hit bottom so that one might start building one's way back up and out" (*Breaking Up* 76). However, there is no way out, yet there is no trap. This abyss is where we reside; it is not a place on which to stand or out of which to emerge, but the chora, the "hole" that cannot be separated from life itself.

Our juxtaposition of the scholarship on chora with Deleuze and Guattari's discussions of spatiality and temporality allows us to see how categorization and definition, particularly by way of constructing binary oppositions, are conceptualized in the electrate apparatus. Deleuze and Guattari show us that there is no way to escape dualisms without resorting to a negative deconstruction and thus suggest turning to the fold: that which, like holey space, gives rise to third terms and creates multiple possibilities for invention and production. Since this concept has been reinterpreted by other postmodern theorists, and reworked again and again, we want to wrestle with how the debate over dualistic invention has changed (or not) in the electrate apparatus.

Electrate Reasoning: The Logic of the "And"

We begin with an exemplar of the sort of dualisms Deleuze and Guattari work to avoid by quickly turning to the later work of Berlin, wherein he aligns himself with Teresa Ebert and others who advocate a "resistant-postmodernism" in direct opposition to "ludic postmodernism." Berlin, as well as other scholars adding to the many debates regarding postmodern issues in the late 1990s, may not come across as destructive; however, resistant postmodernism nevertheless argues intently against the "merely ludic," thus closing down conversation and allowing Berlin to continue arguing for the "possibility of individuality and agency" (*Rhetorics, Poetics, and Cultures* 108) within a "postmodern" framework.

We can now connect this debate from the late 1990s to online video culture in order to illustrate how postmodern debates, despite insistence of their being "old hat" (which Rickert dispels in *Acts of Enjoyment*), are remixed in reference to, as well as throughout, the online world. For example, in regard to online video and participatory cultures, Alexandra Juhasz constructs five binary oppositions in "Why Not (to) Teach on YouTube" in order to argue, as well as to perhaps satisfy her persistent skepticism, that YouTube is not an ideal site for higher, disciplinary learning: aural/visual, body/digital, user/owner, entertainment/education, and control/chaos. In other words, comparable to how Berlin favors a predetermined postmodern framework within which individuals can make and remake their "contingent narratives" through a series of interactions with the social, economic, and political forces surrounding them, Juhasz clearly favors a predetermined university framework within which "experts" (i.e., professors) and "experts-in-training" (i.e., students) build knowledge in the "disciplined space" of the college classroom (139). Of course, such disciplined space, exemplary of Deleuze and Guattari's striated space, appears in opposition to the open, or smooth, space of YouTube; yet, again and as Deleuze and Guattari argue, "the [two] spaces can happen simultaneously" (*Thousand Plateaus* 475). As Tamsin Lorraine explains, "Deleuze and Guattari are interested not in substituting one conception of space with another, but rather in how forces striate space and how at the same time it develops other forces that emit smooth space" (qtd. in *The Deleuze Dictionary* 256). Because of the tendency to polarize epistemologies and theories, we argue that Deleuze and Guattari's treatment of binary constructions is extremely productive for thinking about electrate writing and participatory culture.

By displacing binaries, electrate reasoning "functions not in terms of matched *pairs* (signifier/signifieds) but of [external] *couplers* or *couplings*" (Ulmer, "Object of Post-Criticism" 102). Furthermore, such exterior relations—linking by means of "the conjunction, 'and ... and ... and ...'"—do not impose binaries by which the space between is "a localizable relation going from one thing to the other and back again," but rather spark "a perpendicular direction, a transversal movement that sweeps one and the other away" (Deleuze and Guattari, *Thousand Plateaus* 25). Rajchman explains the importance of these *connections* in Deleuze's thought, which is known as the logic of the "and." Rather than draw up boundaries by asking what something "is," the logic of the "and" keeps the question going, much like the rhizomatic network of associations created through choric invention. "We must thus make connections. But this pragmatism—this And—is not an instrumentalism, and it supposes another sense of machine. It is not determined by given outcomes, not based in predictive expertise. On the contrary, its motto is 'not to predict, but to remain attentive to the unknown knocking at the door'" (7). The "unknown" remains at the threshold, not to cross over into the realm of analysis, but to stay there and work at the level of production. Rajchman explains that "connection requires a style of thought that puts experimentation before ontology, 'And' before 'Is'" (6), which, he contends, makes it a form of pragmatism. Recall Rickert's understanding of choric invention as that which "put[s] invention itself back into question ... as an inventional [rather than metaphysical] problem" (262–63). In other words, Rickert does not ask what invention "is," but rather reanimates invention and, particularly, its relationship to definition. Moreover, returning to Rajchman's understanding of connection as "a form of pragmatism," Rajchman explains, "the principle of such a pragmatism is posed in the first sentences of *A Thousand Plateaus*, where Deleuze and Guattari declare that multiplicity, more than a matter of logic, is something *one must make or do*, and learn by making or doing ... We must always *make* connections, since they are not already given" (6).

The emphasis on making is crucial, for the connections created cannot ever be known in advance; however, they can be discovered through associational or "And" logic. Rajchman tells us, "Making connections involves a logic of a peculiar sort. Outside established identities, divisions, and determinations, logical and syntactical as well as pragmatic, it has often been assumed that there is only chaos, anarchy, undifferentiation, or 'absurdity'" (8). Rajchman's characterization of Deleuzian connections as pragmatism is different from the "ludic" label often imposed on such connections. For instance, we may imagine these connections in terms of the hyperlink, which Dave Weinberger identifies as "a new type of punctuation": "The old types of punctuation tell you where to stop, [whereas the] hyperlink encourages you, beckons you, to continue" ("The Virtual Revolution"). Thus, electrate reasoning is movement, or, more specifically, the performance of meaning through the touching of external relations that map a space in movement.

In the first counterthesis, and coinciding with this act of mapping space in a movement, Vitanza (by way of Lyotard) advocates *paralogy*, wherein the central focus is to "'bear witness to differends' . . . that is, to bear witness to the unintelligible or to disputes or differences of opinion that are systematically disallowed by the dominant language game of homological science and are therefore 'silenced'" ("Three Countertheses" 146 cf. Lyotard *The Differend* 13). In other words, it is necessary to link, but not how to link (147), which is another way to describe the logic of the "and." The notion of paralogy reinforces what has already been said about proairesis, chora, haecceities, and "total collaboration." We see all of the theoretical contentions from this chapter playing out, quite literally, on video sharing sites, and we wish to conclude by providing an exemplar that we hope resonates into the next chapter, where video and participatory cultures will be the focal point for tarrying with the second counterthesis.

Tubes and Tubing: Archive and Choric Remixing of the Question of Definition

YouTube serves as our exemplar for choric invention. In an essay I cowrote with Geoffrey Carter, we characterized YouTube as "an ever-changing and growing networked ecology" upon which "Tubers" (i.e., participants) drift and reinvent meaning "through the re-purposing of . . . rhizomatic Tubes" (i.e., videos) (1). Analogous to the way in which chora is *spacing*, YouTube is *tubing* as it incites connection and networking, and we put forward "tubing" as the participatory practice of YouTube. Burgess and Green argue that one of the "fundamental characteristics of co-creative environments like YouTube is that the participants are all at various times and to varying degrees audiences, producers, editors, distributors, and critics" (82). Even lurking entails participation, since doing so contributes to the rise in view counts for videos, and material users upload and write on the site is inherently participatory. Although YouTube is commonly understood in terms of the relative value of individual videos, Ryan Skinnell argues that the impact of a single video or even several videos "must be considered in light of the accumulative effect of collecting millions of user-generated videos together—YouTube's archive" (2). Skinnell does acknowledge that YouTube's archive replicates traditional features of archives, such as finding aids, organizational strategies, and permissions; however, rather than limit his investigation of YouTube's archive to such definitive features, Skinnell explores the archive as "a revolution in the role of archives": Whereas archives have traditionally been limited to materials privileged and preserved by archivists, YouTube's archive is "generated and predominantly adjudicated by the community of users" (2). Therefore, one is invited to view YouTube's archive as what Alex Reid calls "a communitarian video network" (10), or, as mentioned earlier in relation to my perspective and Geof Carter's, an "ecology": "the interrelationship [or spacing] between any system and its environment" ("ecology," *OED*, 3rd ed., def. n. 1c). In addition, Henry Jenkins argues, "Video is a tool that allows us to reflect on ourselves and on our environment. And that's a foundation for social empowerment" ("Storytelling" pt. 2). While such views of YouTube's archive reasonably lead some scholars, like Rick Prelinger, to suggest that YouTube is not really an archive (268), the same views lead others, like Pelle Snickars, to argue that YouTube is "an important archival media phenomenon . . . [that] offers completely new ways of thinking about both storage and the distribution of information" (294). One such way of thinking then is to posit YouTube's archive as chora: an in-between space in which the process of withdrawal perpetuates traces, as opposed to cultural objects with assigned conditions of belonging, that appear and disappear through "the touching of tubes."

To understand YouTube's archive as chora is to celebrate accessibility and, thus, disrupt the role of traditional archives to keep content *contained*. This notion of containment, however, precedes archival tradition, linking back to "Aristotle's assimilation of *chōra* to space and matter" (Rickert, "Toward the *Chōra*" 253). As Walter explains, "Aristotle . . . restricts place to its physique. In his way of thinking, *topos* [the concept under which he subsumed chora to signify 'pure position' (120)] does not represent a great metaphysical principle but merely stands for the inert container of experience . . . and *chora* means the room or capacity of the container" (121). In contrast to Aristotle's early effort to ground chora, as well as to the value bestowed upon topic invention, Ulmer explains that "the writer using choragraphy as a rhetoric of invention will store and retrieve information from premises or places formulated not as abstract containers, as in the tradition of *topos*, but by means of . . . spacing" (*Heuretics* 73). That said, however, one may argue that YouTube, with its reputation as a digital *repository* for users' *broadcasts*, is little more than an online container for disconnected tubes to amass and collide. For instance, in implicit opposition to the notion of "the touching of tubes," Juhasz claims, in her video-book *Learning from YouTube*, that "YouTube promotes empty and endless collisions isolated from culture, history, context, author, or intention. Collision without consciousness." However, to claim that YouTube is defined by unconscious collisions that occur *within and of itself* is to see YouTube as "a container." Through this description, Juhasz asserts distinctions between online and offline: the former, a location, defined apart from the individual, in which to store bits of information that entertain more than inform. Her notion of containment privileges *topos* over *chora* and thus ignores the potentials of YouTube as a choric archive where communication happens through the proairetic touching of tubes.

The "touching of tubes" can be understood through Deleuze and Guattari's description of machinic assemblages. They explain: "There are not individual statements, there never are. Every statement is the product of a machinic assemblage, in other words, of collective agents (i.e., multiplicities) of enunciation" (*Thousand Plateaus* 37). For example, not only do the capacities of tubes emerge through relations of exteriority within YouTube's ecological network, but such capacities also continue to emerge as Tubers, "not captive to YouTube's architecture" (Burgess and Green 66), link tubes across the web. According to Henry Jenkins, "YouTube represents a shift away from an era of stickiness (where the goal was to attract and hold spectators on your site, like a roach motel) and towards an era where the highest value is in spreadability" (qtd. in Skinnell 7). Therefore, YouTube's archive is not so much a "place" as it is a choric space, folding time and space in and out of the platform. In other words, tubers communicate through YouTube's archive by moving meaning, whether by creating their own tubes, commenting on tubes, remixing tubes, or by sharing tubes on YouTube and through the web.

Lisztomania: Remixing Spatiality and Temporality

We conclude with a video meme that began as an homage to 1980s high school films, consisting of a simple mash-up of dance scenes merged with a current pop hit from the band Phoenix, entitled "Lisztomania." In the original mash-up, the user "avoidantconsumer" shuffled dance scenes from an assortment of John Hughes's brat-pack films to make a music video for the hit song. The video was subsequently taken down by YouTube for copyright violation (see vinimzoTube, 2010); however, another user has since reposted avoidantconsumer's remix (see jaimedelaguilayrei, 2009). According to Julian Sanchez, a Washington-based writer and journalist, this original mash-up is an example of "stage one remix," which involves "individuals using our shared culture as a kind of language to communicate something to an audience." Stage one remixing often creates the conditions for proairetic invention and electrate reasoning to occur.

What is most pertinent to this chapter, to the question of definition, and to choric invention, however, is what Sanchez calls "stage two remix" or "social remix": a process whereby one remix inspires interested participants to invent similar remixes that contain nuanced content and thus divergent lines of communication. The first social remix in the Lisztomania meme responds to avoidantconsumer's original "Lisztomania" video-remix. It features a group of friends in Brooklyn, New York, who filmed and shared their own live-action, brat-pack dance scene, mimicking the dance moves from Hughes's 1980s films while on top of a building. The video, titled "phoenix—lisztomania *brooklyn brat pack mash up*" (thepinkbismuth, 2009) not only remixes the dance moves and sequencing of the original, but it also offers sweeping views of the New York City skyline and portrays the group of people as if they are friends, New Yorkers, modern day brat-packers, and lisztomania all merged together. With over 400,000 views, this social remix has elicited countless others, all spotlighting a specific geographic location (from San Fancisco to Rio de Janiero, Winnipeg, Manila, and Versailles, to name just a few), a specific group, ranging from families to friends to individuals, and the same (yet very much repurposed) dance moves from Hughes's 1980s iconic films. Importantly, however, each group's social remix both responds to previous remixes and creates proairetic openings for other remixes to be made, and some morph into entirely new situations (i.e., in a bedroom or local convenience store) to add to the burgeoning network. "Lisztomania" is also a term describing "Liszt fever," an affliction dating back to the 1840s that triggered intense levels of hysteria in fans of composer Franz Liszt. Each remix is posted as a video response to another Lisztomania video, and they inherently work with one another: not as a dialogue, but as an invitation for innovation and creativity. According to Sanchez, this "social remix," involving relationships among all of the versions, "isn't just about someone doing something alone in his basement": rather, the practice "becomes an act of social [and participatory creativity].

And it's just not that it yields a different kind of product in the end; it's that, potentially, it changes how we relate to each other.". In other words, Sanchez argues that these remixes mediate people's relationships with each other, and he explains that the brat-pack characters are used as a "template for performing the social reality of each group." The result is that these videos become platforms for "articulating the similarities and differences in the groups' social and physical worlds."

This meme does not stop with the act of social remixing. The group of friends from the Brooklyn version not only had the opportunity to meet with Glassnote Entertainment Group (i.e., Phoenix's record producer), but Lawrence Lessig used the meme to describe how, in response to their becoming platforms for social interaction, the videos have challenged copyright laws in a new way, considering that the premise of the remixes lies in commercial material and the "original" remix was removed (Lessig). Lessig claims that the Lisztomania videos highlight how both the commercial culture and the culture of Internet sharing are merged to encourage innovation. The Lisztomania videos are prime examples of spreadable media, which defy definition, since their goals inherently include both social remix, potential innovation, and cultural intervention. In writing about the cultural potential of online videos, Chris Anderson points out that in video and, particularly, in meme culture, "ideas spawn from earlier ideas, bouncing from person to person and being reshaped as they go" ("Film School" 115). The brat-pack phoenix Lisztomania meme, with its complex layers of remix and reappropriation, certainly shows Anderson's assertion in action, as its global reach illuminates how spreadable (and undefinable) media can influence not only participation, but world-wide collaboration, interaction, and communication. These videos also have the potential to serve as a platform to expose cultural differences and not-so-sunny events occurring in specific locations. Participating in this meme invites investigation into local geographies and cultures, which serves as critique and performance to expand the network already in existence.

Finally, not only does the prompt renewal of avoidantconsumer's original mash-up illustrate participants' readiness to respond to actions that contradict the ephemeral values of their coming communities. but it also speaks loudly of such values as one can see from the two currently "highest rated comments" written below the re-posted video: "haha! suck it WMG!" (from nCorelli); and, "Thank you for posting this again. It really sucks the original got taken down for copyright reasons, but I'm glad it's been reuploaded :)" (from yukinkoicy). Although one may consider these brief comments to be informal offenses, they ultimately reveal a popular—not to mention, *obtuse*—sentiment shared among participants in the growing global online video community. With that, we now turn to chapter 4, where mild to extremely severe comments like those revealed above will be central to the chapter's theoretical underpinnings.

4. Who Speaks When Something Is Spoken?
Playing Nice in Video Culture

> And in this game one speaks only inasmuch as one listens, that is, one speaks as a listener and not as an author.
> —Jean-François Lyotard, *Just Gaming*

> And the question is how to write as auditors rather than orators.
> —Cynthia Haynes, "Postconflict Pedagogy:
> Writing in the Stream of Hearing"

> But the purposes and meanings of *YouTube* as a cultural system are also collectively co-created by users. Through their many activities—uploading, viewing, discussing, and collaboration—the *YouTube* community forms a network of creative practice.
> —Burgess and Green, *YouTube: Online
> Video and Participatory Culture*

In the spring of 2010, a YouTuber who went by the moniker "peachofmeat" posted a video in which he revealed that he had just pulled off the YouTube scam of the century by manipulating Facebook fan pages. To grasp the severity of the scam, we must first understand the importance of "subscribers" to any one YouTube user. As both Burgess and Green and Alexandra Juhasz have pointed out, achieving popularity on YouTube catapults particular users into YouTube fame, and to achieve popularity, users must not only accumulate numbers of views on their videos, but they must also work to accumulate subscribers. The gesture of subscribing sets in motion a sort of loyalty, or, as Patricia Lange has reported, an obligation for reciprocity, which is known as "sub for sub" ("Achieving Creative Integrity"). The act of subscribing, then, is something prolific YouTubers hold as almost a sacred move; it notifies users any time their subscriptions have been active on YouTube, and it creates what they call the "YouTube Community," which distinguishes the site from other video sharing sites (TheWillofDC). Peachofmeat intruded on this sacred practice by creating a subscribing scam, which he built from a loophole on Facebook fan pages. He invited users to become a fan on Facebook of very clever and enticing topics, such as "the best way to break up with your girlfriend or boyfriend." When users clicked on the link to become a fan, they were asked to first confirm and then click two more times; the second click asked them to make sure they were logged into their YouTube accounts, and the third click, unbeknownst to them, both made them a fan of the item on Facebook as well as a subscriber to peachofmeat's YouTube channel (see TheWillofDC).

On the surface, this scam may seem like just another juvenile hacking prank; however, the fallout from this move was fierce, mainly because of the video peachofmeat posted that explained what he had done, which is a cardinal breach of ethics in the so-called YouTube community. Popular YouTubers like TheWillofDC and KalebNation found out that peachofmeat achieved over 100,000 subscribers in twenty-four hours. This catapulted him into YouTube's coveted list of "top 100," and yet, as these Tubers discovered, he had only posted two videos, and his videos received only a minimal number of views. TheWillofDC explained that what peachofmeat did was "perfectly legal" in terms of YouTube's rules, yet, his antics exposed the limits of obligatory ethical behavior that was formerly taken for granted among the prolific Tubers. If he had not blatantly discussed his scam, people may not have even paid attention, as JTOTokay claims when he says that, if peachofmeat had simply "posted an impressive video" after gaining all of those subscribers, his breach of ethics on YouTube may have been forgotten. However, because peachofmeat did not attempt to engage his subscribers by uploading content in which they may be interested and instead posted a video boasting about what he had done, he instantly became demonized.

While this controversy could warrant its own chapter, it will set the stage for this chapter in two ways. First, in his video response aimed directly at peachofmeat, KalebNation screamed: "YOU are not TUBING!" This utterance lambastes peachofmeat for not caring about contributing anything to the other members, not engaging in the unspoken convention of reciprocity, and not working at all to build a reputation and engage with other YouTubers. "YOU are not TUBING!" directly places the practice of "tubing" at the center of the YouTube community, and it thus has spawned my own thinking about how the theoretical question "Who speaks when something is spoken?" plays out in video culture. Second, as argued by TheWillofDC and JTOTokay, peachofmeat's scam destroyed what was once a sense of trust among users, since he did "not earn those people watching [his] videos and then subscribing" (TheWillofDC). They both claim that inflating subscriber numbers renders the act of subscribing meaningless and hurts those Tubers who are abiding by the unspoken rules and "earning" subscribers. In fact, JTOTokay claims that the act of subscribing now doesn't really mean anything anymore, and Tubers will have to find other ways to earn credibility. To other users who have taken advantage of the Facebook fan page scam, TheWillofDC pleads for them to "contribute to the debate on whether or not they think this is good or bad for the community." This invitation is a perfect segue into the main goals for this chapter, which will bring together theories and practices centered on the question, "Who speaks when something is spoken?"

This chapter takes up the second counterthesis in Vitanza's "Three Countertheses: or, A Critical In(ter)vention into Composition Theories and Pedagogies," which, in a broad sense engages the question of mastery over knowledge. I will interrogate the theoretical implications of this question and transfer these implications to video and participatory cultures. "Relinquishing the discourse of mastery" and developing a discourse of "speaking as a listener" will be central; and yet, as we will see, "speaking as a listener" in video culture is quite complex and has proven to have both trivial and deep consequences in the online and the offline worlds, as we saw with the peachofmeat scandal. These consequences range from instant celebrity and the building of loyal and reciprocal relationships to complete destruction, "flaming," and "hating," which can quite literally ruin lives. Thus, as we will see, this chapter will explore the darker, more unsettling elements of electracy and participatory cultures, which adds another layer of complexity to the project. If we recall the table in chapter 1, we can note that the "axis" of electracy ranges from joy to sadness, rather than from truth to falsehood. We will see how joy and sadness serve as the emotional conduit for interrogating the question of who speaks raised by the second counterthesis. It will also be important to call up arguments about video culture addressed in chapter 3, particularly where we treated the concept of proairesis. Recall that we stated that proairesis in video culture aims to provoke us, reel us in, and generate response and editing by (multiple) viewers, both in textual and video formats. As Collin Brooke says, proairesis is "contingent on the present moment, [and] the constantly changing conditions to which it responds" (*Lingua Fracta* 77). However, this is not to say that these unsettling elements should be tamed; rather, as this chapter will argue, we can explore them as part of the coming rhetoric for the electrate apparatus.

It is also important to call up the notion of the deoedipalized subject, which I explicated at length in chapter 2. Again, as Thomas Rickert and Lynn Worsham explain, deoedipalized subjects are not "attached" to authority—

they are deoedipalized—and therefore cannot actively resist authority, institutional or otherwise. As we will see, in video sites like YouTube, deoedipalized subjects reign despite Google's efforts to create a platform with boundaries and regulations. In fact, in "The YouTube Gaze," Virginia Kuhn, citing Yochai Benkler's declaration that, in a "networked information economy," people are not inhibited by something like an "alien bureaucracy" (Benkler 137), makes the following assertion:

> In the case of YouTube, however, this "alien bureaucracy" is, in fact, present; it is increasingly cumbersome, multifaceted and oppressive. Although the standards of practice are implied to be community based, YouTube deploys automated identification software to police content on behalf of media conglomerates such as NBC Universal, Warner Brothers Music Group and Viacom. Disabled video notices are rampant and often uncontestable.

We thus have a double-bind on YouTube: both the dream of a platform unencumbered by authoritative, bureaucratic rules and regulations and a reality of those very regulations employed in a phantom and accusatory fashion. If YouTube is a "continuum for cultural participation" (Burgess and Green 57), then the question of "who speaks" within a platform with seemingly random "rules" becomes paramount.

In the context of the previous, brief introduction to the complexities involved when taking on the question posed by the second counterthesis, "who speaks when something is spoken?" this chapter will first attempt to make a series of theoretical connections. From the deoedipalized subject to Vitanza's notion of "speaking as a listener"; from Lyotard's alternative to the Lacanian "discourse of the master"; and from pedagogical perspectives on these concepts, such as Marshall Alcorn's "pedagogy of demand" and Kevin Porter's "pedagogy of severity" to Cynthia Haynes's stunning articulation of "postconflict pedagogy," we will take a variety of twists and turns. Through it all, my goal will be to apply these concepts to prevalent behavior found in participatory and video cultures in order to cast a wider net for the generative practices I have been advocating. If in chapter 3 we described the massive archive of material on YouTube as a site of choric invention, in this chapter, I will explore the more sinister side of things, calling up sites in which anonymity and the lack of an archive reign supreme (e.g., 4chan) and where the question of who speaks is more important than ever.

Thus, I begin with the second counterthesis and the major theories associated with it. I then spend some time comparing the tenets from the second counterthesis with Thomas Kent's Davidsonian notion of "passing theories" and "hermeneutic guesswork" as well as Stephen Yarbrough's pedagogical move toward "discourse studies," both of which are attempts to respond to the questions raised in the second counterthesis. I turn to Kent and Yarbrough to add a disciplinary perspective: one that, as Collin Brooke and Thomas Rickert point out in their essay treating postprocess theory, presents a "one-sided view of language as hermeneutic . . . with its inability to see the constitutive role of technology and environment" (253). This comparison will bring me to the concept of community as both redefined under the premises of the second counterthesis and reinvented in video culture, especially when directly compared to how Kent and Yarbrough explain it. I will then turn to the theories discussed above to argue how they come to life in video culture.

The Language Game: Breaking and Making the Rules

The second counterthesis, Vitanza explains, "centers on the Neitzschean-Freudian question Who speaks when something is spoken? (It's a question of author[ship])" ("Three Countertheses" 152). Vitanza tells us that in the "humanist tradition," human beings speak; but that to Lyotard "human beings do not speak, they are spoken" (152). The notion of being spoken is complicated and has been dealt with by many others throughout Western philosophy.[1] However, for the purposes of the second counterthesis as well as for this chapter, Lyotard's thinking on "being spoken" will be the central focus. Vitanza explains further:

(It becomes somewhat clear that this second counterthesis is locally informed by the second Gorgian position that if anything exists, it cannot [should not/ought not to] be known). The best way to understand this notion of being spoken is to place it, at least initially, in a larger framework of Lyotard's view of language games or pragmatics, which he locates within the exclusive categories of either addresser or addressee.

(152; cf. Lyotard, *Just Gaming* 38)

Vitanza suggests that Lyotard's three pragmatics might also be seen as "indirect counterstatements" to the Kinneavy model of the communications triangle (see *Theory of Discourse*). Alcorn also relates back to Kinneavy's model (his four discourses) but instead equates the four forms of discourse (persuasive, informative, literary, expressive) with Lacan's four discourses (master, hysteric, university, analyst). This is important for understanding how desire is always implicated in the question, "Who speaks when something is spoken?"[2] I will quote Vitanza's summary of Lyotard's three pragmatics, articulated in *Just Gaming*, at length, and then in the following pages expand on the third pragmatic, "speaking as a listener," and show how it comes to life in electracy through video culture.

1. The addresser, as in control of language, as its author(ity). (This pragmatic is grounded in the presuppositions of philosophical discourse; it is the "Parmenides game.")
2. The addressee, as in obligation to listen and, therefore, not in control of language. (This pragmatic is grounded in the "theological" Judaic tradition and is the "Moses game.").
3. The addressee, as in the addressee without an addresser, or a receiver without a sender. (This last pragmatic is situated in a postmodern countertradition, which Lyotard calls the "Pagan game.") ("Three Countertheses" 152; see *Just Gaming* 38–39)

The first pragmatic grants control to the speaker, and the second to the (necessarily obligated) listener; thus, Vitanza and Lyotard favor the third. The third pragmatic explains language as a listening game. In this listening game:

> No one may be the authority. . . . it is a game without an author. In the same way the speculative game of the West is a game without a listener, because the only listener tolerated by the speculative philosopher is the disciple. Well, what is a disciple? Someone who can become an author, who will be able to take the master's place. This is the only person to whom the master speaks.
>
> (*Just Gaming* 71–72)

Instead of being a "disciple" to an author in order to someday take that author's (master's) place, one listens in order to become another listener, never to become, finally, the next master. This is important because, as a listener, inquiries would always remain open, which allows for knowledge previously excluded to emerge. The position of the sender must, according to Lyotard's discussion, remain empty. This listening game, Vitanza suggests, is a turn against language as a speaking game: the language of philosophy and "traditional-modern composition theories, whose goals have been to control/master language and knowledge" (153). The importance of speaking as a listener, however, becomes evident when we distinguish between Lyotard's second and third pragmatics, since the second denotes a passive listening and the third requires activity. However, by "active" I do not mean to suggest that the listener listens only to reinscribe the other's utterances; rather, the activity involved in the third pragmatic involves the generation of new thought and the grafting of new connections.

The obligation in the listening game is to remain a listener, but not with the expectation of total submission or of the promise of someday becoming a speaker (master). Vitanza explains that Lyotard "has placed the speaker-writer (encoder) in a situation of non-authority; for the speaker (of the traditional communications triangle) can only be a speaker now by virtue of having been, more so, a listener (decoder, reader)" (154).

Fittingly, in a video-lecture for the European Graduate School (EGS), Vitanza uses an example from the 1973 Robert De Niro film *Bang the Drum Slowly* to illustrate these concepts (egsvideo). I discuss it here because it offers an image to which to return in the latter sections when I apply the listening game's effects on video culture. Vitanza recalls the scenes in the film when De Niro's character and his friends play a card game called TEGWAR (The Exciting Game without Any Rules). To play TEGWAR the characters literally make up the rules as they go, and they rely on an amalgamation of "rules" and conventions that they have learned from participating in their local environments, ranging from fishing to baseball to simple arithmetic. The rules for TEGWAR, in this regard, are not determined in advanced, but pieced together as the game progresses: invented, in a choric fashion, depending on a variety of cultural factors. No one person determines the rules in advance of the game; rather, each player "listens" to the others and generates the game based not on winning, but on the act of playing itself. Yet, each player carries the potential to shift the conditions of the game. When the game is over, the rules for the particular session are discarded, only to be remixed and reinvented the next time around. By turning to the TEGWAR game, Vitanza, and by extension, this chapter, shows the listening game in action. There is no anarchy. Instead, the game is all about listening and generating the rules of possibility.

Playing Out the Listening Game: From Speaker to Tourist

In this attempt to treat the second counterthesis in terms of the entire discipline, we now turn to two scholars who have worked with conceptions of the listening game: Thomas Kent and Stephen Yarbrough. These two versions are important contrasts to the main arguments of this chapter and also provide some scholarly context to which I will come back when discussing interactions, behaviors, and attempts at listening in video culture. First, Kent explains that writing occurs among "individuals at specific historical moments and in specific [albeit ever-changing] relationships with others" (*Post-Process Theory* 2). Following Donald Davidson, Kent argues that we all possess a cohesive set of beliefs—or "prior" theories—"from which we start in order to communicate with others" (4); since no two people hold the same prior theories, then "what really matters is how people employ their prior theories in action" to create what Davidson calls "passing theories" (4; cf. Davidson "Nice Derangement"). Thus, our passing theory is what we employ in communication situations. In revisiting these same assertions, Byron Hawk clarifies: "In short, Kent's notion of postprocess theory relies on the dialectical 'give and take' of hermeneutic guesses among humans in particular situations involving human communication" ("Reassembling Postprocess" 120). These assertions respond to Kent's claim that there can never be one process to master for speaking or writing. However, by constructing passing theories and hermeneutic guesses, and in the context of Vitanza and Lyotard, we are reinscribing what is being said and thus resembling (albeit temporarily) the speaker in Lyotard's first pragmatic. Thus, Kent's writing subject would use writing for the means of communicating successfully. Although he clearly states that the process by which people write and communicate cannot be captured and generalized, Kent only deals with the first two of Lyotard's communications pragmatics, thereby constructing a binary or a dialectical relationship between the speaker and the listener: a relationship that exchanges authority while both speaker and listener construct passing theories. Thus, Kent's assumptions rely on an addresser and an addressee who align "utterances with the utterances of others" in "uncodifiable moves" (3). This alliance is what, according to Kent, makes communication successful. Hence, all communications involve interpretation; communication is never an entirely passive process and therefore relies on the shifting and passing of authority from speaker to listener. What we will see, however, is that in video culture, this dialectical passing of authority and construction of passing theories is quite destructive and, in that regard, requires a third option to emerge that breaks out of the hermeneutic requirement of one speaking as an authority.

Second, Yarbrough in *After Rhetoric* (a text that specifically treats Vitanza's three countertheses), provides a response to Vitanza and Kent who, as I have suggested, both call into question the authoritative position of the speaker, albeit in very different ways. Taking a pedagogical turn, one of Yarbrough's central arguments is that the required composition course should be done away with, because it is predicated on a view of language that is no longer relevant: "language serves as a medium between ourselves and the world" and thus people can be taught "how to write" (217). Yarbrough then turns to Vitanza and claims that, through the second counterthesis, Vitanza's position is that "all language is mediated through 'language games,' which cannot be foundationally unified" (218). What comes from this explanation is that, according to Kent, we cannot teach composition, and according to Vitanza, "we can but we should not teach it" (219).[3] While I will take this claim up more extensively in chapter 5, I want to focus on Yarbrough's assertion that both Vitanza and Kent "retain the view that language is a medium between ourselves and the world" (221).

With Vitanza's second counterthesis, and contrary to Yarbrough's claims, language is not "represented" as a medium between our world and ourselves. Rather, as D. Diane Davis has also suggested, language is not in the speaker's control (see "Finitude's Clamor"). Additionally, the language game of which Vitanza speaks blurs the distance between speaker and listener so that both remain alongside one another: in an adjacent relationship rather than a dialectical one. Yarbrough explains: "modes of listening [such as those described by Vitanza] do not posit in advance what another's words should mean or how that meaning should be expressed" (226). While this appears to match what has been said in the second counterthesis, we can see that it does not, perhaps because Yarbrough couples Vitanza's "mode of listening" with Davidson's notion of "radical interpretation," which he describes as follows: "Unpredictable utterances always point toward conditions of which we are not aware. Others may very well be wrong about some of the things they say, but unless we believe them initially, we will never know what it is about the way things are that prevented us from predicting their errors" (7). Now, this statement suggests that, as speakers, even if we suspend authority temporarily, we still act as the judge for the listener's utterances. We are still looking for errors and judging if the other's words are right or wrong: looking to see if the other's utterances match our interpretive guesswork. Thus, there is still the possibility of "getting it right" the next time through prediction, meaning that the speaker, through aligning his/her guesses, can ultimately control the communication. Again, we see that this resembles Lyotard's first and second pragmatic: either as a (dominant) speaker or an (obligated) listener, taking turns of being in control.

However, the second counterthesis suggests that predicting utterances is not and should not be the goal of listening; for a prediction will serve only as a reinscription (or in Deleuze and Guattari's terms a reterritorialization) of the "master" in control. Yarbrough admits that "perhaps such counter-games [as Vitanza advocates] occasionally come in handy when the writer believes his reader will insist upon imposing the rules of an alien game upon his discourse" (226), a statement that replicates everything I've already stated above and adds another layer. Recall Vitanza's TEGWAR example from *Bang the Drum Slowly*, where "alien games" help create the rules for the game. The notion of an "alien" game as something that exists outside the players becomes problematic when attempting to interact in wide-open, social spaces of the digital world, where interacting with alien games is the norm. The same can be said for Kuhn's aforementioned description of YouTube's inherent "alien bureaucracy" within which Tubers must navigate and interact on a daily basis. Yarbrough continues by arguing: "language games do not constitute situations even though they sometimes attempt to organize them" (226). If language games do not constitute situations, then they are simply at the disposal of the speaker/writer in control. Similarly, Michael Carter, when explicating Vitanza's second counterthesis, suggests that "Such gaming [as described in the second counterthesis] undermines the will to knowledge, as well as the will to mastery that supports the teaching of writing. If teaching writing is defined by the will to be its author(ity), then writing should not be taught" (163). What Carter seems to be arguing here is that, if we accept the concept of relinquishing the discourse of mastery, then we should not teach writing at all. On the contrary, however, "teaching" language games is extremely necessary in our networked world, where, as Brooke and Rickert state, "we, too are transformed" (248), which indicates that movement never slows down enough for mastery; yet, this does not mean that learning does not occur. I would argue that learning and teaching in this manner produces more possibilities for writing and more productive knowledge. Brooke and Rickert also forward the notion that "we must take seriously that in Web 2.0 space [and I would add, especially in video culture] the intuition that we are not who (we think) we are in analog spaces" (248). I will return to this crucial statement shortly in order to connect all such notions to video culture.

Yarbrough's and Carter's statements about language games become problematic when thinking about the role of authoritative forces; as the second counterthesis shows, the "listening game" cannot be simply enacted by the will of the "individual" speaker, writer, or content producer. Rather, in the listening game, there is no authority, no One in control, and therefore beliefs cannot be extracted from the situations in which they occur. This is better understood in the context of working in electrate, social spaces; as Brooke and Rickert argue, in social and dynamic online spaces (like YouTube, for example), "one's own activities register immediately, contributing to the shifting patterns and overall density of information directly, and in ways that impact the information environment itself" (252). In that regard, so-called alien games become the norm, since the very space—and rules—of the game are in constant flux.

To further highlight these crucial differences between Vitanza's and Yarbrough's notions of communication (and listening in particular), we can turn to Davis, who suggests that Kent's (and I would add Yarbrough's as well) theories of the communicative interaction also explain his version of how (contra to the popular notion of discourse communities) communities are created. Davis argues, "Kent proposes a 'community' that takes place (only) in the here and now of communicative interaction, which brings subjects into being, each time, in the instant of interpretation or understanding that makes it possible" ("Finitude's Clamor" 126). Thus, successful communication, or, when passing theories intersect or "triangulate," creates communities rather than the other way around. Recall that the listening game blurs the distance between speaker and listener so that both speaker and listener remain alongside one another: adjacent and not in a dialectical relationship that uses language as a medium. Thus, the listening game does not engage in a give and take in which speaker and listener "translate" each other's words into their own (self)same (127). Rather, through the listening game, our finitude is exposed. As Jean-Luc Nancy explains, "Finitude co-appears or compears . . . the finite being always presents itself 'together' . . . for finitude always presents itself in being-in-common . . . The compearance of singular beings—or of the singularity of being—keeps open a space, a spacing within immanence" (28, 58).[4] Hence, finitude creates community, but not a community based on interpretation; rather, community turns toward the incomprehensibilities that singularities share. To elaborate, this is a threshold or conduit of pure exposure along which bodies, through relations of touching, experience the emergence of otherwise unknown capacities and, thus, the shaping of new assemblages. Therefore, Nancy suggests, community "means, consequently, that there is no singular being without another singular being" (28). This is important, since "singularity" should not be confused with "individual." As (whatever) singularities (see chapter 2), what creates community, what we share, is our finitude: the potential to be exposed. Davis calls this, contrary to interpretation, "communitarian reading," proceeding with "excessive hospitality, welcoming the incomprehensible Other in a posture of extreme humility" ("Finitude's Clamor" 138). This is yet another way to describe Lyotard's third pragmatic, except it exposes how community is possible when speaking as a listener: a community that, as Agamben has shown, is always coming into presence (see Coming Community). This is in contrast to Yarbrough, who claims that any education should not derive from a unified conception of the world; rather the goal should be aiming "toward a unified conception" (241). The community of listeners who speak as listeners is neither unified nor aiming toward unification. Rather, this community remains in a nascent state.

As a fitting segue into the next section, I turn to Ulmer who argues that we "approach knowledge from the side of not knowing what it is, from the side of the one who is learning, not from that of the one who already knows" (*Teletheory* 106). Thus, in Ulmer's view, there are no "masters" of knowledge; one is always on the side of the listener, perpetually inventing instead of only reproducing knowledge. In a clever and conductive meta-phor, these listeners move from the position of the master to the position of the "tourist": traveling becomes the subject of writing instead of knowing. Ulmer calls the experience of tourism "Solonism," after the Ancient theo-rist-tourist, Solon. He explains:

> Solon is credited with being at once the first tourist and the first theorist. E. V. Walter noted that Herodotus described Solon's visit to the ruler of Lydia as being for reasons that included *theoria*: Originally *theoria* meant seeing the sights, seeing for yourself, and getting a worldview. The first theorists were tourists—the wise men who traveled to inspect the obvious world.
>
> (*Heuretics* 120; qtd. in Walter, *Placeways* 18)

But Solon did not just see the sites. He dwelled in them and listened to them and recounted them in stories and poems. Apparently, however, one of Solon's most famous stories, the story of Atlantis, did not survive through him. In fact, Ulmer tells us that Solon had indeed heard about the story of Atlantis, "but it didn't survive through him. He, unlike Socrates, did not want to be a master" (75). Thus, the "memory" of Atlantis was "forgotten" in the official memory of the state, and it was up to those who heard Solon's tales to reinvent them through each retelling.

You Are Declared: Listening with Tubes in Our Ears

> YouTube is a hybrid media ecology where many participatory cultures come together, and it's precisely because there are tensions between participatory cultures, and because it's open to a public much larger than these participatory cultures, that you start to see hating and conflict.
> —Henry Jenkins, quoted in AnthroVlog, "Participatory Cultures"

> Language and technology are constitutive and transformative.
> —Collin Brooke and Thomas Rickert, "Being Delicious"

So far, this chapter has explicated the second counterthesis and the theories associated with it. I have pointed out competing theories put forward by Kent and Yarbrough, and I have shown how the idea of "speaking as listener" brings up different scenarios for both writing and forming communities, particularly in dynamic, online environments. What I would like to do now is focus on how these theoretical contentions about speaking as a listener

and community play out in video and participatory cultures, starting with
the recollection of KalebNations's cry, "YOU are not TUBING!" First, however, let us recall Brooke and Rickert's assertion that "we are not (who we
think) we are in analog spaces" (248), while I take a brief moment to point
out a very specific scene in Milan Kundera's novel *Immortality*. I take this
unsuspected turn because this scene has guided my own thinking about
the listening game and our participation in it for over a decade, and especially juxtaposed with the accusation "YOU are not TUBING!," it provides
fodder for how we might think about behaviors and experiences in video
culture—and particularly with the practice of commenting on a specific
Tuber's video logs (vlogs)—since we are exposed to our own image more
so than ever before. In fact, on YouTube, vloggers are more than exposed
to their own images: their images are made and remade in front of them
through the dynamics of others' participation.

Kundera's story explains what happens when people rely too heavily
on their self-presence to guide their interactions with others. Kundera's
characters are never in control of their subjectivity and are thus most often
misunderstood, therefore having to deal with the contrast between their
self-perceived images and the images that arise through exposure to others.
Ultimately, Kundera shows people's images are not something on which they
can reflect and over which they can control. Rather, one's image becomes
what others describe, resulting in a perpetual fold, a constant remix, of the
personal and social. Kundera does not grant his characters the self-present
subjectivity to control their lives, even though they might think they are
in complete control. I will cite just one scene from the novel to help make
the point that confronting finitude, or, rather, confronting our own image
in the eyes of others, adds a wound, similar to the punctum of recognition
discussed in chapter 3, but different in that it completely shatters any guise
of mastery and control in the language game. In the tradition of the video
clip, I hope the images conjured from this scene resonate with and mix in
with the theories that I have been discussing throughout this chapter and
continue to do so for the remainder.

While walking with his friend Paul, the character Bernard, who has quite
an elevated image of himself, suddenly bumps into a stranger. This complete
stranger looks at Bernard and abruptly shouts that he is "a complete ass,"
while handing him a diploma with the declaration, "You are hereby declared
a complete ass" boldly printed on it. After initially wanting to cry out as a
victim of an attack, Bernard then "realized there was absolutely nothing
[he] could do" (125). With his image shattered, and his self-present sense of
subjectivity disrupted, Bernard did nothing but *shake the stranger's hand*;

his instinctive reaction was *not* to resist the stranger or interrogate him, but to agree with him, to say "yes" to him: to dive into the very thing he is supposed to resist.

I want to link this scene to what Deleuze and Guattari call "incorporeal transformations," theoretical constructs that give images to thoughts. They write, "the incorporeal transformation is recognizable by its instantaneousness, its immediacy, by the simultaneity of the statement expressing the transformation and the effect the transformation produces" (*Thousand Plateaus* 81). They use the example of the statement, "you are no longer a child" (81), to show how a declaration (having nothing to do with the body/action) "inserts itself" into bodies' actions and passions. The body is the same, yet the "child" then becomes transformed: previous actions change, self-reflexivity enacts those actions that "a child no longer does." The body becomes a "body image"; in other words, incorporeal transformations create a notion of "what the body (image) is" rather than "how the body works." Declarations such as "you are no longer a child," "you are a complete ass," etc., create the image and require action. This declaration thus ruptures Bernard's image and prompts Paul to comment: "when a person is declared an ass, he begins to act like an ass" (125). Bernard's instantaneous transformation into a "complete ass" will take over his image, for Kundera tells us that Paul realizes from now on, "he would never again think of him as Bernard but only as a complete ass and nothing else" (126).

It is not difficult to see how Bernard's predicament of being declared a complete ass translates directly into the practice of commenting on videos and participating in video culture. In fact, each time I read comments on videos that resemble these types of declarative statements—especially on vlogs, where hateful comments are most prevalent—I conjure up the image of the stranger handing the official-looking diploma to Bernard. This corporeal gesture is played out again and again in the online world, and it may as well be in the offline world as well, as the wound and the incorporeal transformation are the same. We can find examples galore on YouTube of wounded Tubers, responding to these instances of incorporeal transformation, or adding images to thoughts, again and again. This declarative practice is known online as "flaming" or "hating," and is more prevalent than ever, particularly on YouTube, as Peter J. Moor's 2008 study, "Flaming on YouTube," concludes. Patricia Lange explains that "A 'hater' is generally defined as a person who leaves unnecessarily harsh criticism on a video, often using stereotypical phrases containing images of homophobia, racism, sexism, and violence or death, as in the stock phrase, 'go die'" ("(Mis) Conceptions" 94). On flaming, Moor suggests that a flame constitutes a general sense of hostility rather than the use of profanity. However, Lange suggests that the definition of a flame is less important than examining "the interplay between flames and flame claims" ("What Is Your Claim to Flame?"). Lange's statement about the interplay between flames is more relevant for this chapter, since, I argue, flames cannot be separated from the network (or community) of which they are a part.

Lange has developed a body of work dedicated to interrogating the genre of the video comment from an ethnographic perspective (see especially "Achieving Creative Integrity") and points out that the practice of posting severe or hateful comments has been studied from a variety of disciplinary perspectives ("(Mis)Conceptions" 95). Flaming and hating are complex behaviors, and it is not the purpose of this chapter to delve into the psychological and anthropological research of these practices; rather, I turn to them to illustrate what happens when authority figures, the "speakers in control" are absent and the traveler has taken their place: when the listening game is in full force and the "interplay" of flames is "out there" to which everyone can bear witness. The metaphor of the traveler is so fitting to Tubers and the practice of Tubing, since they move from site to site, leaving traces of their visits. Their communities rise up around videos, comments, and related material and remain, quite literally, alongside one another on the site. Recall Nancy's explanation that I paraphrased earlier regarding how community turns toward the incomprehensibilities that singularities share. This difficult concept explains the interactions going on in some hating situations more accurately than Kent's claim of community based on interpretation.

A discussion of one Tuber's complex network of videos, most of which attempt to engage his haters and flamers on YouTube, helps exemplify the statements made above about community and the listening game. I will link this exchange to three practices—the pedagogy of severity, the pedagogy of demand, and postconflict pedagogy—in order to merge what occurs in video culture at large with a more specific disciplinary perspective. In the spring of 2010, a graduate student in one of my seminars assembled a five-minute video mash-up consisting of various YouTube vloggers responding to the "haters" who had left comments on their videos (MissSarah537). After watching the video in class, we literally heard most, if not all, of the popular expressions of profanity and discrimination, and I distinctly remember the dazed looks on students' faces after the video stopped. Especially for the people who had never been exposed to hating on YouTube, "Haterz be hatin' on dis" packed a serious punch. We saw Tubers from all walks of life reading the hateful comments they had received and responding—some calmly, some erratically, and some with a sense of humor—to each and every one of them. What surprised us most was that, despite the severity of the hateful comments, many of which included no less than death threats, the Tubers continued to engage with and listen to their so-called enemies. Not once did they attempt to engage in a tit-for-tat or assume authority over their YouTube channels; rather, they created responses, which spawned more comments, more responses, and so on. This practice—offensive, yes, but violent, no—was quite surprising. One Tuber featured in the video mash-up who particularly caught my eye was "CopperCab," a red-haired teenager who is known on YouTube for screaming into the camera while vlogging (as evidenced by his video titles and video descriptions that are written in all caps), especially to the haters who post comments on his videos calling him a "ginger," a derogatory term for red-heads. I then watched the whole video from CopperCab aptly titled "ATTENTION HATERS!!" as well as the many videos and other materials associated with it, and what I found turned out to be extremely pertinent to this chapter.

As of February 2013, just over two years after it was posted, "ATTENTION HATERS!!" had nearly 6 million views, numerous parodies, (including one on the television show *South Park*), dance and techno remixes, and thousands of comments and video responses that keep on appearing. Like TheWillofDC and KalebNation, to which I referred earlier, CopperCab is adamant about maintaining some sense of ethics in the community of vloggers on YouTube to which he, as well as other Tubers, are loyal: that is, creating a sense of "tubing" by which legitimate Tubers abide. Though, included in the notion of "tubing" (and especially for CopperCab) is hating, and he calls out the "trolls" or, in other words, the haters who simply focus on appearance (notably his red hair and weight) rather than the actual content of his videos or the contributions that he makes to other Tubers (i.e., "sub for sub" and other reciprocal practices associated with the perceived obligation to the community). After "ATTENTION HATERS!!"arrived, CopperCab's motive for vlogging morphed into responding to "trolls," who simply kept on posting hateful comments on his videos to stir up controversy and keep the network growing. As it turns out, this Tuber's image is literally created before our eyes, through his many videos and the related material posted by haters and supporters alike. CopperCab is like Kundera's Bernard on steroids, as he has been "declared" a "complete ass" so to speak hundreds, if not thousands, of times. However, what is notable about CopperCab's YouTube presence in "ATTENTION HATERS!!" is that he both resists and "shakes the hand" of one hater, embarrassingly (for my purposes, at least) yet appropriately known as "IshatOnU." I will share an excerpt directed at IshatOnU from "ATTENTION HATERS!!" and then continue with the commentary. CopperCab says,

I don't know where y'all get the idea that you can just go hatin' on people whenever you want, and they'll cower down. I won't cower down. I'll keep making videos. YOU GOT THAT? IshatOnU, kinda being mean, but he made some valid statements . . . he wants me to post a video, why gingers are so good. Well you know what, IshatOnU, I'll make that video for you, bro, I'll make that video. And for all the haters out there, who say I can't make a f***** video, and tell me I'm fat and all that, I DON'T CARE WHAT YOU SAY! I DON'T CARE! SO GET OUT OF HERE! F*** YOU! I'll make videos all I want to.

We can see that CopperCab is trying to reciprocate IshatOnU's request to make more videos (note the irony implicit in his moniker, IOU). When he did make the video, IshatOnU, living up to his moniker, responded with an offensive video so vile that we will not mention it here. CopperCab then responded in a video titled "I DON'T CARE!!" saying, "I thought you were better than that, I thought you had respect for others. APPARENTLY, I WAS WRONG!" In the next video response from IshatOnU, we see an annotation bubble that states, "me and CopperCab have no beef, i like the kid, i was just trollin." This exchange differs from what we saw with peachofmeat in that CopperCab did not relent after being called out and "scammed" by a troll (in one final gesture, peachofmeat sold his YouTube channel on E-Bay for $2,300, as TheWillofDC reported in January 2011). Rather, CopperCab stubbornly kept posting videos discussing various topics, including revealing that his offline friends had abandoned him because he was "embarrassing" ("I'D NEVER DO THAT!!"), but most notably targeting his haters and relating the experience of being "a ginger," to which, again, countless comments, hateful parodies, and sympathetic response videos were generated. In the video "I'D NEVER DO THAT!!" CopperCab first apologizes for not making a video in a while, relates the story about his friends abandoning him, and then reveals that, because of his two-week hiatus from video making, rumors circulated that he had committed suicide (hence, the title of the video). This revelation then became its own Internet meme, as people continue to post that CopperCab has committed suicide on any number of his videos. In fact, just two days before this writing, someone posted a comment about CopperCab's apparent suicide on his "I DON'T CARE!!" video: a video that has now been on YouTube for over three years.

As we can see, the layers of interaction and the gaming going on with just this one example make it difficult to simply say that the vlogger (CopperCab) makes hermeneutic guesses about what his haters may mean when they post hateful comments. Such an action is futile and nearly impossible; rather, the hateful and other comments, video responses, and related videos all remain alongside one another in a community of singularities. The vlogger (speaker) and the video (medium) make up just a portion of what Brooke and Rickert refer to as "information density." They call dynamic, social sites a technology in the "third order of informatics" which rely on tags to "constitute, associate, aggregate, and network" (252). No doubt the practice of tagging has created CopperCab's YouTube cloud; he tags his videos with no less than thirty tags on nearly every video. While Brooke and Rickert are discussing the social bookmarking site Delicious, their arguments can be transferred to any social, dynamic online space, and particularly to You-Tube. Brooke and Rickert explain, "this density significantly enhances a user beyond the range of individual performance because its externalized form generates interactions that amount to the incorporation of the knowledge of many" (251–52). And in "the many," at least on YouTube, and especially in CopperCab's case, are haters and flamers, all existing alongside each other.

Among other things, the "community" that sprang up around Cop-perCab's videos created and organized "Ginger Pride 2010," a gathering of "gingers" and their supporters who seek to make their voices heard on and off YouTube. Moreover, as of this writing, CopperCab has become a spokesperson for antibullying campaigns in California (see "STOP THE BULLYING!! MY HAPPY VALENTINE'S DAY!!"). There is more to this story than I could ever cover in a book chapter devoted to the theoretical question on the discourse of mastery, but it suffices to say that CopperCab's videos and the thousands of pieces of associated material, form a living, complex network of not only communication exchanges, but human interaction it-self, and that, at least in part, exemplify the language games in the electrate apparatus and participatory culture.

From Severity and Demand to Postconflict "Touching"

We now approach the final discussion of this chapter: one having to do with three versions of pedagogy that I cannot help but connect to both the theory articulated here and the CopperCab example. When I first read Kevin Por-ter's article, "A Pedagogy of Charity," I was struck by the articulation of the "pedagogy of severity," which I connected directly to Lyotard's second prag-matic. Watching what happens when those who were once listeners and are now speakers (authorities) seemed, to me, the best illustration of the danger involved in not recognizing or moving toward Lyotard's third pragmatic. I now think that explicating the "pedagogy of severity" in reference to the hating and flaming pervasive throughout video and participatory cultures pulls the discussion back into the realm of rhetoric and composition and also, perhaps, gives it lasting power. Hating and flaming can be compared, in pedagogical terms, to what Porter has articulated as a "pedagogy of severity," which he discusses in the context of students responding to other students' writings. Porter's "pedagogy of severity," while tied specifically to a writing classroom, adds to what I have already put forward, since Porter claims that "severity" occurs when those formerly in the position of the listener are suddenly granted the position of the master. Porter begins by investigating how his students, if given the authority, would "grade" their peers' writing. Peer critiques teach students to look at papers from a teacher's perspective (reversing the roles as described in Lyotard's first pragmatic). In this case, Porter specifically asks his students "to grade *as if they were an instructor* a sample paper [Porter] had written under a pseudonym" (577). What ensued from this exercise is telling. As Porter reports, severity in students' responses was extremely prevalent. The pedagogy of severity (also following Lyotard's second pragmatic) insists on "student passivity" (580). Even more dangerous, "it often transforms students into the kind of harsh, antagonistic reader that they would otherwise resent" (577). Thus, Porter finds that his students mostly focus on faults and problems: creating responses that eerily echo domineering "masters" of the past. These severe assertions, especially put forth as punishment for not writing "correctly," stay in the body of the student-subjects long after they have occurred. Then, when they are suddenly placed in the privileged position, the severe assertions come to the forefront, despite "knowing" to do otherwise; the student-subjects respond with the same severity, and replicate the position (albeit constructed) of the master. Porter's experiment carries some interesting insights regarding the embedded responses of severity that surface when students are placed in the position of the master.

While Porter's experiment was blatant in terms of its "declaring" the students to be in the position of power, we may nevertheless connect this example to the case of CopperCab, with whom we see this "pedagogy of severity" happening when IshatOnU takes advantage of CopperCab's invitation for reciprocity. Instead of complying, IshatOnU portended to take the place of the master, since he had the upper hand at the moment (by accumulating more subscribers and views). However, as we saw, IOU, as I now like to call him, never gained authority; rather, he remained alongside CopperCab and all of the other Tubers. We can imagine (and have probably participated in) pedagogical spaces that resemble both of these instances; how many times have students been "declared" by their masters that they are unfit for writing? We might compare these instances of incorporeal transformation to the incorporeal transformations they have also experienced in an adjacent, cloud-driven community and see what we get. While I have not done this, I imagine that the results of such a comparison would be telling.

For the same reasons that I brought the pedagogy of severity into the mix, I turn to Alcorn and specifically his explication of an experiment conducted by psychologist Stanley Milgram. The Milgram experiments are such that, at least for me, upon hearing of them, they remain in the body as any chilling and taboo subject may remain. Alcorn uses the Milgram experiment as an exemplar to demonstrate what he calls a "pedagogy of demand." A pedagogy of demand is much more dire than Porter's pedagogy of severity and is concerned with how desire functions under the discourse of mastery. Milgram set out to see why people obey those in control only after being given simple demands: even if the instructions include rendering pain on another human. Alcorn finds this inquiry useful because Milgram calls the learner in the experiment the "victim"; this learner is instructed to remember proper responses to verbal cues given by the authority figure. The authority figure in the experiment (which Alcorn calls "teacher") and the victim (learner) are both actors. The experimental subjects (whom Alcorn calls "students") are instructed by the teacher to deliver electric shocks "at levels they themselves found fit" (*Changing the Subject* 43) whenever the victim makes a mistake in responding to verbal cues. Even though the victim moaned and pleaded to the student to stop giving shocks, Milgram found that "the vast majority of people [students] administered very low shocks" (43). Alcorn concludes: "The students are, in principle, free to act on their own different desire" (48); yet they don't. Alcorn contrasts the students' desires with those of the teachers, who are, in several of the case scenarios, different and continues by saying, "the effect of demand prompts students to feel that they in fact, desire what the experimenter desires" (48). However, several of the "students" asked questions, exhibited slight resistance, or were disobedient. These types of resistance were usually met by the following response from the teacher: "It's absolutely essential to the experiment that we continue" (46; qtd. in Milgram 48). Those who kept questioning stopped shocking; those who were silenced by that demand kept shocking.

Milgram suggests that people were able to administer electric shock to those who need to "learn" because they did not see themselves as responsible; rather, they attribute "all initiative to the experimenter, a legitimate authority" (7–8). Thus, because the master demanded it, the subject found these demands as necessary and relinquished any ethical misgivings. Also, the discourse of mastery is deeply embedded in the traditional discourse of "science"; thus, the experimenter represents scientific authority: authority that (as in pragmatic one) controls language and deflects questioning. Alcorn concludes that the kinds of "simple demands" used by the teacher "silence the person who asks the question" (47). A pedagogy of demand thus "creates a subject fully submissive to the meanings of the master" (51). However, what is most pertinent to this chapter is that the people who did not obey in the Milgram experiment never stopped questioning, the authoritative answers given by the teacher did not silence them; rather, they continued to resist by persistently asking questions, and never accepting a final answer.

Viewing the teacher as authority figure has been critiqued at length over the past several decades; however, Alcorn suggests that, despite knowing otherwise, the pedagogy of demand is still greatly in practice: even under various guises of "teacher as facilitator" or "teacher as nurturer" (see also D. Davis, *Breaking Up*). Perhaps this helps explain why Porter's students were readily able to access the pedagogy of severity in their responses. Alcorn's description coincides with Lyotard's first and second pragmatics, but emphasizes the inherent danger in such a pedagogy. Alcorn takes this a little further by making the following claim: "Demand . . . does not simply facilitate particular truth effects; it also structures a specific set of libidinal relations between subjects. These libidinal relations, and not the meaning of the signifiers that circulate in the relations, determine the role discourse plays in society" (49). Recall that Lange suggests that "the interplay between flames and flame claims" ("What is Your Claim to Flame?") is crucial when attempting to understand the larger, cultural role of flaming. We can think of CopperCab's persistence in posting videos from this perspective, as many commentators simply advise him to stop posting videos and everything will be "OK." But CopperCab does not stop. His desire takes him elsewhere, and even if it makes sense rationally to just stop posting and all the hating will cease, CopperCab does not see it that way. We can now see how this connects to Alcorn's assertions about libidinal relations. While hating occurs in an online environment, it still has the same effects as are brought to light by the Milgram experiments. That is, on YouTube, and especially on vlogging videos, the body is present, so studying the interactions that take place there from a hermeneutic or discourse perspective will only solve a piece of the ever-changing puzzle involved in human interaction online.

However, what I find puzzling when thinking about the Milgram experiments in the context of hating and flaming, is the fact that the "haters" administer metaphorical shocks with no perceived authority present. Could it be that the act of hating is symbiotic with the deoedipalized subject? We could argue that Kuhn's "alien bureaucracy" on YouTube constitutes an authority, but my research suggests otherwise, especially since Tubers often work to hack and break the rules of YouTube so they can be remade under different conditions. Because they have to navigate the "alien-ness" of the invisible bureaucracy, and, are presumably found guilty before proven innocent (see Kuhn), Tubers' only possible authority may be said to be other Tubers and subscribers. Thus, to gain popularity or win subscribers, Tubers make sure to leave traces of their participation all over the site. To be sure, users like peachofmeat have hacked the so-called authority of the Tubing community, taking away from the importance of "sub for sub," for example. Yet, as singularities, Tubers Tubing are also Touching in adjacent relationships and loose communities, thereby creating and re-creating the network by their levels of participation.

I conclude where I began. The second epitaph for this chapter comes from Haynes's article "Postconflict Pedagogy: Writing in the Stream of Hearing," a piece that unsettles me, *wounds* me, yet repeatedly reels me in. "Postconflict Pedagogy" works with Lyotard's *Just Gaming* in a similar manner as I have done in this chapter; however, its exemplars from video culture are no less than two of the most violent and repulsive instances of Internet video posted. Ever. One is the unthinkable beheading of journalist Daniel Pearl, who, in 2002, "was brutally beheaded in Pakistan by terrorists who filmed the slaughter and posted it on the Internet" (209), and the second is the on-camera, overdose suicide of Abraham Biggs in 2008, streamed live from his webcam on *justin.tv*, for hundreds of people to witness (227). These videos, the implications arising from Haynes's pointing to them as exemplars of the listening game, and her call for postconflict pedagogy resonate deeply with what I have already discussed in this chapter. While I have focused the listening game on hating that does not result in physical death, Haynes virtually throws death in our faces, where we must confront it. For me, Haynes's effort is one of bravery and resistance: something I simply struggle with handling in this short treatment of her thoughtful piece. Therefore, I will try my best to connect the violence already suggested by Alcorn by way of Milgram to Haynes's description of postconflict pedagogy.

Haynes tells us that, after watching the Daniel Pearl execution video in 2002, it has taken her nearly seven years and multiple writing projects to come up with a way not to

> write arguments on Danny's behalf ... but to bear witness to such cruelty by confronting the *mediation* of his murder—to confront its discourse and style—not by joining in the discourse of counterterrorism, but by situating language and image outside the logic of war, for that is where Danny lived. The challenge: how to find a postconflict means of argument in a post-9/11 world. (209)

What proceeds, then, is a series of riffs that form a network of possibilities for a postconflict pedagogy. Among other things, what strikes me the most is Haynes's discussion of Daniel's forced statement moments before his death: "My father is Jewish. My mother is Jewish. I am Jewish" (227). Daniel was forced to "declare" *himself* in front of his murderers, literally solidifying his own image before his death with no chance of an incorporeal transformation. However, this declaration resonates deeply with viewers who are thus incorporeally transformed themselves. By forcing Pearl to make this declarative statement under clearly staged circumstances, his murderers compound the process of the discourse of mastery by making him turn it back on himself in a double act of violence.

Biggs's video is equally disturbing, and as in the Pearl video, Haynes tells us, the "listening takes place as writing a fatal hearing" (227). Yet, Biggs's streaming webcam suicide was not a rehearsed, cinematic spectacle. Rather, it unfolded in real time with viewers unsure of what was happening. Haynes relates the following: "Viewers who watched the video for twelve hours while he died did not wish to contend in the conflict playing out before them. Abraham's conflict with himself and life was a public event. People posted as it happened, egging him on, taunting him and belittling him. In such instances writing a hearing becomes writing a drive-by shouting" (227). We can see that this "writing a hearing," this "drive-by shouting" is a "live" version of hating, and, like CopperCab, the hating ironically drives the invention of future material. However, unlike CopperCab, Biggs's future "material" became his falling into death itself, which stopped the flow and granted authority to the haters. Additionally, as Emily Friedman reports for ABC News, many viewers said they thought Biggs's suicide was a hoax, since he had apparently "threatened to kill himself before and faked it," so they posted typical hater-like comments, thinking they would spawn more material. This can be connected directly to CopperCab, who, as I mentioned, consistently receives comments announcing his own suicide. However, the difference is that Biggs's life has ended. The game is over. In the same regard, while discussing the ethics of language games on the Internet, Haynes turns to the concept of "netplay," which, she explains,

> suggests the Internet is more of an ambiguous outpost where the incompatibility between language games reveals the paradox in playing just. What is unthinkable is to stop the play. Lyotard is adamant that —absolute injustice would occur if the pragmatics of obligation, that is, the possibility of continuing to play the game of the just, were excluded. That is what is unjust
>
> (226; cf. Lyotard and Thebald, *Just Gaming* 66).

Here is where Biggs and the viewers watching him die went wrong. They stopped the play. And here is where IOU comes back into the discussion: because of the pragmatics of obligation swirling around the YouTube community of singularities, IOU, in his perpetual state of owing, kept the game going. This possibility of playing the game remains open. Thus, postconflict pedagogy is a new game, that "jam[s] and locate[s] the source of terrorism with postconflict thinking—with audacious audition" (214).

The pedagogy of severity, the pedagogy of demand, and especially the call for postconflict pedagogy, respond in complex ways to the question, "Who speaks when something is spoken?" and take the question into the realm of video culture. I contend we should follow Haynes in her persistence when working toward a postconflict pedagogy. I see this piece as an act of resistance. In "Resisting a Discourse of Mastery," Lyotard notes that the value of knowledge in the university has changed completely (from the *Aufklarung* (enlightenment) to the training to work in a specific field). As a result he conceives of writing as *active resistance* and describes it as follows: "To advance or want something that is not clear, and to discover a means of giving testimony of that which is precisely not yet included in the circulation of commodities; it is not yet known . . . this is active resistance . . . to resist the already done, the already written, the already thought." Despite the usual connotations, "active resistance" requires remaining open, listening, and generating responses as a listener, and we see active resistance percolating in online networks as, using Haynes's term, "audacious auditions." The possibility of "playing nice" in video culture may be absurd, but it entails actively resisting the discourse of mastery. Engaging in perpetual questioning might indeed engender negative resistance from those who would expect answers; however, in direct conjunction with electrate listening, and as we will see in chapter 5, teaching in an electrate manner does not require prescriptions but rather reading, writing, and listening with the other.

5. Participatory Pedagogy: Merging Postprocess and Postpedagogy

> From Plato to the present, one of the invidious tests for whether or not a notion or practice has any value is to determine whether it can be generalized (is generic) and whether it is transferable (codifiable, teachable). If not, usually the assumption is that there is no method but merely a knack, an irrationality that is left to the forces of chance.
> —Victor Vitanza (by way of Richard Young), "From Heuristic to Aleatory Procedures"

> We must enter in the space of amnesia, of phantom pain, and ask some cold titanium questions. Is it enough to resist seeing composition and the computer as tools of empowerment or to resist seeing technology as a threat to autonomy? Or is it time to risk the final amputation of a decaying pedagogy?
> —Cynthia Haynes, prosthetic_rhetoric@writing.loss.technology

> But perhaps the most controversial aspect of postprocess's introduction was its unapologetic resistance to simple pedagogical application.
> —Sidney Dobrin et al., "A New Postprocess Manifesto: A Plea for Writing"

As one of the field's enduring areas of contention, the rift between theory and practice in rhetoric and composition still elicits strong response and creates distressing separations between "irresponsible," "abstract" theory and "responsible," "real-life" practice. For electracy, as Ulmer has shown in most of his works (most notably *Teletheory* and *Heuretics*), theory is practice; that is, theories in electracy are discovered through the act of engaging in practice. However, it is not enough to simply say that theory and practice merge in electracy; rather, the long-lasting disciplinary debate needs unpacking for viability in the electrate apparatus. Thus, this chapter, based on Victor Vitanza's third counterthesis in "Three Countertheses: or, A Critical In(ter)vention into Composition Theories and Pedagogies," will attempt to show that splitting theory and practice is ultimately unproductive in participatory culture and the electrate apparatus for several reasons, most notably the contention that we are part of the living networks we create. In chapter 4 I forwarded the claim that "teaching" language games is extremely necessary in our networked world, where, as Collin Brooke and Thomas Rickert state, "we, too are transformed" (248), which indicates that movement never slows down enough for mastery; yet I would argue that learning and teaching in this manner produces more possibilities for writing and more productive knowledge. While I left this claim to resonate in chapter 4, I can now address it directly.

As we will see in the third counterthesis, Vitanza puts forward one of the first calls for moving toward postpedagogy, a pedagogy not based on any theory or predetermined form. Since then, other versions of postpedagogy have circulated, and have ranged from Vitanza's "just drifting" to valuing "element[s] of surprise" (Rickert, *Acts of Enjoyment* 172), and, for the most part, work to lift the notion of a "finished" curriculum from the pedagogical situation. Postpedagogy relies on making and forging connections among disparate, "fuzzy" fragments that, in print culture, appear irrational or simply coincidental. Critiques of postpedagogy typically point out the impracticality of not working with predetermined models or genres or being so "loose" that patterns in the learning process are not captured coherently (see Brooks and Anfinson). Thus, it is the aim of this chapter to both interrogate the perceived split between theory and practice, and then contribute to the discussions of postpedagogy by calling for a move toward participatory pedagogy.

How Do We Communicate What We Know?
Sizing Up the Postprocess Mindset

> Postprocess theory must continue to be insensitive to composition's most cherished disciplinary concerns. Among other things, this means that composition studies' traditional issues of ethical accountability, agency, and pedagogy, to name a few, cannot be the sole guarantors of a new postprocess theory of writing. Our endeavor requires an entirely new logic (or perhaps paralogic) to deny the danger of disciplinary affirmation.
> —Sidney I. Dobrin, J. A. Rice, and Michael Vastola, *Beyond Postprocess*

Vitanza's third counterthesis

states (from a postmodern, "third sophistic" perspective) that theory as the game of knowledge cannot help as a resource, because theory of this

sort resists finally being theorized, totalized. . . . This third counterthesis is
in reference to the third, but modified, proposition of Gorgias (if 'it' could
be known, it cannot and should not be communicated [that is, taught]).

("Three Countertheses" 159)

As we already know, the matter of relying on theories to improve classroom
practices is an age-old point of contention. Before getting into the third counterthesis more directly, I would like to both contextualize it and drift with it
by bringing the notion of "postprocess theory" into the mix. I do this for two
reasons. First, postprocess addresses the theory/practice split head on and
second, postprocess—especially the updated version—offers a competing
rhetoric for electracy that I have only briefly addressed. Postprocess theory
got its start in Thomas Kent's edited collection, *Post-Process Theory: Beyond
the Writing-Process Paradigm*, though many of its tenets had already been
articulated by prior publications. The initial collection continues intrigue me,
since it at once challenged the status quo of "writing-as-a-process" while, I
initially thought, simultaneously upheld the status quo of empowerment-oriented and critical pedagogies. However, more than a decade later, we have
a new version of "post-process theory" entitled *Beyond Postprocess*, edited
by Sidney I. Dobrin, J. A. Rice, and Michael Vastola, and this collection
challenges its predecessor in more ways than did my initial treatment of
the collection. I had the great advantage of viewing the collection prior to
publication, and doing so has given me much inspiration for this chapter.
Beyond Postprocess revisits the first collection and meditates on the so-called
postprocess movement spawned from it. In the first collection, Kent stresses
in his introduction that "most post-process theorists hold three assumptions
about the act of writing: (1) writing is public; (2) writing is interpretive; and
(3) writing is situated" (1). In *Beyond Postprocess*, Kent's preface updates this
a bit: he argues for "righting writing" not by way of postprocess theory (as it
never was a body of theoretical work or a "movement") but "the postprocess
mindset," which "rights writing by placing textual production, which is always interpretive, public, and situated, as the right object or our attention"
(16). One of the major debates surrounding postprocess then and now has to
do with whether or not this set of theoretical assumptions can or should be
imported into the classroom. We see Kent's hedging in this regard when he
calls postprocess not a theory but a mindset, but I think that it is now worth
examining a valuable exchange that took place a few years ago regarding
whether or not postprocess theory could be "turned" into a pedagogy.

Both Gary Olson and Thomas Kent responded to Lee-Ann M. Kastman
Breuch's essay, "Post-Process 'Pedagogy': A Philosophical Exercise." The

larger issue that emerges from this exchange questions the significance of making a necessary separation between theory and pedagogy. What ensues is a fitting and timely example of how discussions about theory and pedagogy in rhetoric and composition (despite occurring throughout the past several decades) still rely on outdated assumptions created for a different time, space, and apparatus. For instance, a specific question that emerges is whether or not *postprocess theory* is "mature" enough to be *turned into* a pedagogy or to even generate pedagogical insights, since it has emerged only in the past few years (see Breuch 140; cf. Dobrin, "Paralogic Hermeneutic Theories").

The idea that theories should mature before being applicable to practice is part of the apparatus of print and literacy. For electracy, as I will explain in the latter sections of this chapter, this notion changes from "turning" a theory into practice to *practicing the theory as it is emerging.* And it is important to note that practicing a theory as it is emerging will not reduce or compromise its legitimacy. Breuch claims that pedagogical implications are indeed found in postprocess theory even though they are not highlighted in a "productive" way (127). She thus proceeds to explicate how, exactly, *postprocess theory* is more aptly understood as *postprocess pedagogy*, since proponents of postprocess theory, such as Kent and Dobrin, "are not specific enough to outline any pedagogy that could be labeled 'post-process,' thus increasing the resistance to applying post-process theory to pedagogy" (124). Breuch's characterization of postprocess theory as "not specific enough" is predicated on the assumption (embedded in the apparatus of literacy) that, in order to be relevant and legitimate in the discipline of rhetoric and composition, new theories must have clear links to pedagogy: hence her deliberate name change from *theory* to *pedagogy.*

Alongside Breuch's explication of postprocess theories, and backing up several years, we can see that this very discussion also occurs in Vitanza's third counterthesis. The third counterthesis responds directly to the shift occurring at the time from *inner-directed* (expressive, cognitive, and foundational) to *outer-directed* (social-epistemic and antifoundational) theories and practices. The problem questions the possibility or impossibility of a "stable topology" that can be known, communicated throughout the discipline, and taught to students ("Three Countertheses" 160). Vitanza's response is still very valid, especially in light of the aforementioned attempt to necessarily "apply" postprocess theory. Interestingly, Vitanza and those who espouse the "postprocess mindset" (particularly Kent) appear to be advocating similar ideas and even, at times, use some of the same terms. However, there are distinct differences on which I will focus; illuminating

these differences will help with the task of inventing the apparatus of electracy and what I will advocate as participatory composition.

The issues brought forth by both Vitanza and Kent are well known by
now, but a brief review will shed some light on how they are implicated in
participatory composition. Kent devises another conceptual scheme for what
he calls "internalist" and "externalist" rhetorics (linked to Vitanza's inner-directed and outer-directed). Internalist rhetorics take "human subjectivity"
as "the starting place for every investigation of meaning and language use"
(*Paralogic Rhetoric* 98). Thus, Kent places all of the aforementioned rhetorics
(expressive, cognitive, social-epistemic, antifoundational) as well as schools
of literary criticism (Russian Formalism, Anglo-American New Criticism,
Czech structuralism, and poststructuralist "concerns") as that which relies
on internalist assumptions (182 n. 3; see also D. Davis, "Finitude's Clamor"
126). He thus argues for an "externalist" rhetoric that claims to:

> Shift from an internalist conception of communicative interaction—the
> notion that communication is a product of the internal workings of
> the mind or the workings of the discourse communities in which we
> live—to an externalist conception that . . . would challenge us to drop
> our current process-oriented vocabulary and to begin talking about our
> social and public uses of language. (169)

This description is linked to one of the central tenets of postprocess theory:
that "all writing is public" (Kent, *Post-Process Theory* 1). In the updated
version of this claim, Kent modifies this a bit by saying "the postprocess
mindset, then, rights writing by placing textual production, which is always
interpretive, public, and situated, as the rightful object of our attention
(Preface 16). He continues by maintaining that writing never constitutes a
"thing in-itself" and makes the following assertion: "To produce a text or
to read a text means that we must possess already an incredibly wide range
of communicative competence, and when we write effectively, we always
produce texts that call upon this unique competence and that cannot be
reproduced through the application of a process, system, or pedagogy" (18).
Through these claims, we can see that Kent maintains his critique that
theories are inherently "internalist," which mistakenly stand as a conceptualized body of knowledge to eventually be mastered and passed on to
students without acknowledging the unique communicative act of trian-
gulation always present in communicative interactions. Thus, Kent's externalist pedagogy also endorses the notion that "neither writing nor reading
can be reduced to a systemic process or to a codifiable set of conventions"
(*Paralogic Rhetoric* 161).

These two passages can serve as starting places that link to the third counterthesis. In light of what I have explicated about postprocess theory, I will now discuss the third counterthesis more directly: both postprocess and the third counterthesis rehash the prominence of the theory/practice split in rhetoric and composition by eventually advocating theories that have no apparent link to pedagogy. However, I hope that juxtaposing them will illuminate the central tenets of the third counterthesis: tenets that seem to be the least understood yet extremely crucial for what I have been advocating throughout this book. I will then turn to describing the concept of heuretics as an example of merging theory and practice to produce the third option embedded in participatory culture for electracy. The final section of this chapter will put forward attempts for practicing participatory composition. These examples do not necessarily come from classrooms, yet their practices can be thought of as exemplars for participatory pedagogy in both composition and the digital world at large. Following the trend my book has put forward so far, many of the examples come from video culture, wherein participatory pedagogy is most evident.

From Postpedagogy to Participatory Pedagogy: Inventing/Teaching/Paralogy

The basic assumption in many of the Socratic dialogues is that to know something, to call it knowledge, one has to be able to teach it, to reproduce the means by which it is transferred to and acquired by another human being.

—Victor Vitanza, "Three Countertheses"

As a caveat and a response to the inevitable reaction from "the discipline" in 1991, Vitanza realized that a "recently proud profession must reject [the third counterthesis] as ridiculous" ("Three Countertheses" 161). Now, two decades later, after surviving the trauma of the countertheses, the contentions raised by the third counterthesis are ready to be discussed at length, especially in the context of electracy and participatory composition. The third counterthesis can provide insight into what happens to pedagogy when the conditions, values, and purposes for writing change (which had only begun to be discussed in 1991). The third counterthesis, Vitanza argues, can be "restated (with greater precision) in two other ways, which have an overall immediate, direct relevance to rhetoric and composition and, most important, a direct relevance to pedagogy" (159–60). Vitanza's use of the word *relevance* in relation to pedagogy is crucial, since he will not tell us how to apply the third counterthesis to pedagogy; instead, the third counterthesis will *create the conditions* for thinking about pedagogy in a wholly different manner: "The first way to restate counterthesis 3 is to declare a moratorium on attempting to turn theory into praxis/pedagogy. The field of composition demonstrates a resistance *to* theory by rushing to apply theory to praxis without ever realizing the resistance *of* theory itself to be theorized and applied" (160). Declaring a moratorium, however, does not include mourning for that which is lost; the void created by not turning a theory into practice is indeed where practice occurs: the former whole, now a hole, remains a w/hole: constantly reassembled into new combinations by the practitioners involved. The slash between the "w" and the "h" indicates that this kind of writing uses several meanings of the words "whole" and "hole": traces left behind from choric inventions. The "wholeness" of theory and practice should simultaneously be thought of as a perpetual "hole": never to be filled, completed, or "whole" enough to be *turned into* a stable practice. Once a theory is appropriated by theorizing it or applying it, the theory itself resists, unravels, and forges new connections. During this unraveling, elements that had to be excluded in the name of clear communication and teaching eventually return to disrupt the analytical appropriation or application. Holes appear, and the rush to communicate how the theory works as a Theory, a master narrative, then, again fills in those holes, only to be unraveled once again. Gilles Deleuze and Felix Guattari, in *What Is Philosophy?* further explain theory's resistance to application. They suggest:

> Philosophical concepts are fragmentary wholes that are not aligned with one another so that they fit together, because their edges do not match up. . . . Every movement passes through the whole of the plane by immediately turning back on and folding itself and also by folding other movements or allowing itself to be folded by them, giving rise to retractions, connections, and proliferations in the fractalization of this infinitely folded up infinity. (33, 38)

"Giving rise" to connections does not entail consciously turning the concept into application; rather, these connections appear and reappear, never completely fitting together, but, by passing through the plane, creating the conditions for the possibility of becoming and learning, which are then disassembled and reassembled into new combinations. "Giving rise" to connections also explains how theory and practice work together simultaneously as production.

When Breuch claims that postprocess theory does indeed have direct links to pedagogy, she searches for explicit examples where it has been applied most appropriately; for example, Bruce McComiskey's "social-process rhetorical inquiry" and Raul Sánchez's one-to-one mentored relationship between teacher and student (Breuch 125). These applications—while both very different—are practical, "how to" accounts of actual classroom practices stemming from postprocess theory. While I would not disagree with Breuch that these different applications are indeed occurring and benefiting students, I would question her quest to demonstrate that, contrary to what its proponents say, postprocess theory must necessarily elicit overt pedagogical application. We can go back to the third counterthesis to work with this some more. In his second restatement of the third counterthesis, Vitanza says

> that during the moratorium, we will gain time (yes, I'm optimistic!) for enough of us to realize that (critical) theory paradoxically can, but cannot, be employed to critique and to found theoretical praxis. Theory has become, for the field of composition, the will to unified theory (see a nostalgic expression of this will in Bizzell, "On the Possibility"); it has become "theory hope."
>
> (Vitanza, "Three Countertheses," 160; also see Fish, "Consequences," and Fish, "Anti-Foundationalism")

The notions of theory hope and anti-foundationalism in rhetoric and composition have been centers of debate for the past several years; debates have generally been focused on three general areas. The first can be summarized as the attempt to turn the theory of antifoundationalism into a pedagogy for teaching writing (see Bizzell; Curry; and Rassmussen). Second, other scholars have argued that doing so results in only "theory hope" (see Gale; Jarratt; Smit; and Summerfield), which is summarily dismissed as a futile exercise, or, in Smit's terms, a "hall of mirrors." Finally, some have attempted to see the usefulness of theory in a field that has been historically aligned with practical application (see Daniell; Harkin; and Harris). Of course, this list is not exhaustive, but I have included it to demonstrate the extent to which these ideas have infiltrated and influenced scholarship in the discipline consistently over the last two decades.

It appears that Breuch follows the first group in that she argues that, with further theorization, these theories will elicit more direct links to pedagogy, and the actual scene of teaching might change (moving to more of a tutorial model, for example); Breuch takes literally the postprocess claim that writing cannot be taught and equates it with being potentially irresponsible by emphasizing that "post-process theory does not mean an avoidance of the teaching of writing; it does not mean becoming irresponsible teachers" ("Post-Process 'Pedagogy'" 146). And Kent concurs, echoing the ethical imperative that Breuch puts forth: "Giving up the search for a principled pedagogy will help us all become more responsible teachers" ("Principled Pedagogy" 433). We can now recall the epitaph I cited at the beginning of this chapter by the editors of *Beyond Postprocess*, where they insist that postprocess must be insensitive to composition's "most cherished" concerns: "among other things, this means that composition studies' traditional issues of ethical accountability, agency, and pedagogy, to name a few, cannot be the sole guarantors of a new postprocess theory of writing" (32). It was quite surprising for me to read this, as I have believed for quite some time that these ethical imperatives keep driving an even stronger wedge between theory and practice. Breuch claims that we are only "responsible" teachers if we search for principles in the theories and then apply them to teaching; Kent claims that we are only "responsible" teachers if we stop doing what Breuch suggests. However, both of these claims of "responsibility" still uphold the belief that presupposes the binary separation of "responsible" practice and "irresponsible" theory, and it is the mission of the writing teacher to be dedicated to responsibility.

The ethical imperative and accusations of responsibility or irresponsibility can now be explained in more detail by further elaboration from the third countertheses. Following Stanley Fish's description of "theory hope," Vitanza thus explains his similar notion of "pedagogy hope."[1] He writes, "Pedagogy hope has, as its supposed beneficent ends, the improvement of our teaching of composition. . . . We hope for improved modes of production (a set of *techne*) to create an improved product; we hope for *arête* (political virtue) that will sustain the capitalist/socialist polis at the expense of the social in the individual" ("Three Countertheses" 61). Moving away from pedagogy hope would be to move from pedagogy to *postpedagogy*: what Vitanza calls "a *pedagogy other(wise)*, what we want is a pedagogy without criteria . . . what we desire is a counterpedagogy, which expresses the 'desire to escape to pedagogical imperative: a desire . . . to do away with pedagogy altogether'" (161; qtd. in Felman 23; cf. Crowley, "Perilous"; Berthoff, "Teaching"). "Doing away with" pedagogy, however, does not mean that students will stop coming to class and we will no longer teach, thus making us irresponsible. To take this literally, as Breuch has, we would assume that we would no longer be teaching students in universities (or online, for that matter) as we do now, that the *act* of teaching is no longer necessary under the conditions being described.

In his reply to Breuch's essay, Olson first states: "it saddens me to hear all the resistance to and mischaracterization (unintentional, I am sure) of post-process theory" ("Why Distrust" 423), and he adamantly stresses, "nothing pedagogically has changed. What changes is your own understanding of what you are doing in the classroom" (427). In other words, our practices are inherently implicated in the theories that resonate for us. We are neither "doing away with" pedagogy by not teaching anymore, nor are we trying to make critical pedagogy work better under these new conditions (i.e., one-to-one tutorial situations). Rather, we are doing away with the notion that what we teach and how we teach it are predicated on the codified assumptions of a theory (legitimized by the discipline) that is first interpreted and then acted upon. Thus, as Vitanza says, a postpedagogy:

> Realizes legitimization by paralogy . . . as a (para) process, paralogy is contrary to such commonly accepted virtues as control and efficiency . . . For paralogy, the goal is not renovation but innovation; not a stochastic series based on rules that allow us to guess effectively and efficiently but a paradoxical series that invites us to break with the former rules altogether.
>
> ("Three Countertheses" 165–66)

Paralogy, then, as a space for innovation, affirms inventions that do not conform to preestablished conditions or ideologies. D. Diane Davis has written extensively about how both Kent (by way of Davidson) and Vitanza (by way of Lyotard) turn to paralogy to help redescribe pedagogy. However, and as she has pointed out, "Kent puts [paralogy] into the service of hermeneutics" and "Lyotard's paralogy, however, aligns itself with a *post* hermeneutic impulse [that] strives to 'impart a stronger sense of the unpresentable'" ("Finitude's Clamor" 128–29; cf. Lyotard, *Postmodern* 81). Kent links paralogy to guesswork, which has as its end successful interpretation about the meaning of others' utterances (see Kent, *Paralogic Rhetoric* 5). Kent deems this "guesswork" paralogical because "no logical framework, process, or system can predict in advance the efficacy of our guesses" (5). Davis goes on to point out that the difference, then, is that while Kent would have understanding as his "aim," understanding "in an entirely different and rigorous sense [is] Lyotard's [and Vitanza's] target" (129). We can sense the unpresentable but cannot articulate it. Its sense comes across—"gives rise"—in our actions, and this is precisely how we can get out of the theory/practice split.

Thus, in terms of the third counterthesis, the goal of paralogic postpedagogy would not be *understanding* predicated on "Socratic pedagogy" (Vitanza, "Three Countertheses" 166) wherein there is a predetermined conclusion to every inquiry. Vitanza describes this traditional practice as a "philosophical trick and a language game all too damaging to human beings" (166). Dobrin et al. address this when they question whether or not postprocess has "ushered in postpedagogy," which they define as "a point within composition studies where new ways of thinking about writing fundamentally refuse any codifiable notion of the relationship between the writing subject and the texts it produces, as well as the 'practical' scholarship expected to proceed from that relationship" (*Beyond Postprocess* 27). I hope to move this discussion into the participatory realm by showing how, in video culture, and as I explained at length in chapter 4, the "rules" for the game constantly change depending on any number of factors. In fact, it is not difficult to connect "paralogic postpedagogy" back to each chapter in this book where I turn to video culture, particularly chapter 2, where I describe Internet memes as phenomena that require remixing and reinvention with each "writing" act. Both Vitanza's and Dobrin et al.'s explanations are telling; they tell us to question the very values and purposes that have been constants in pedagogy, despite various surface level changes that have taken place (such as collaborative learning, student-centered classrooms, and rearranging the classroom itself, for example). It will thus be the purpose of the rest of this chapter to discuss how the notion of postpedagogy can morph with participatory pedagogy for electracy.[2]

Given that this chapter began with a timely call for rethinking theory and practice for an electrate apparatus, I hope to show that we can engage the theory/practice split by practicing theories as they emerge: by both working with established forms as well as inventing new ones as they become timely and necessary. This act requires letting go of the idea that when we teach writing in all of its manifestations, we are transmitting a body of knowledge based on a solid theoretical foundation. For instance, Ulmer describes the classroom as "a place for invention rather than of reproduction" (*Applied Grammatology* 163–64). However, as I mentioned in chapter 1, he is not saying that we should simply place a stronger focus on the canon of invention in writing courses, as was the case throughout the 1980s and early 1990s in rhetoric and composition (see, for example, Sharon Crowley's *Methodical Memory*). Rather, any pedagogical situation should be considered as a scene for inventions to come into appearance by creating the conditions for participation. We relinquish the discourse of mastery. We place value on the aspect of chance and emerging networks. We access a choric space for writing and teaching.

Theory/Practice: A Heuretical Emergence

Inventions may be written—generated—without having to be thought first.

—Gregory Ulmer, *Heuretics*

The students are helping to invent the future of writing. This attitude and relationship to learning has to be made explicit and encouraged, since students are unaccustomed to working in an experimental way.

—Gregory Ulmer, *Internet Invention*

I place the above citation from Ulmer's *Internet Invention* on nearly all of my course syllabi in order to let students know that they are involved in creating the coming rhetoric for electracy. I share this anecdote not to set off the association that the rest of this chapter will be the "syllabus" for my book, but rather to indicate that the practices and examples I share for participatory pedagogy will also require participation from those who will join my effort and the many others who have been working for electracy. I thus address a final concept for participatory composition in electracy, namely, heuretics, and then move toward the examples and metaphors for enacting its practices. Along with chorography (chapter 3), heuretics, as a method of invention, helps theories come to the forefront as they are simultaneously practiced. Ulmer emphasizes that method "becomes invention when it relies on analogy and chance" (*Heuretics* 8); therefore, the method emerges as it is being invented.[3] This concept is crucial. If inventions can be generated or written without having been thought first, then the notion that we turn theories into practices is not possible. Ulmer claims that many problems exist in a "tangle" but are lost when reduced to parts ("Toward Electracy"). Recall that in the space of chora, inscription is erased immediately, thereby leaving traces, which can then become part of an evolving network.

Heuretics (deriving from the combination of hermeneutics + ethics + heretics + heuristics, diuretics, etc.) is predicated on inventing using chorography.[4] The concept of heuretics is implicit in everything I have been advocating in each chapter of this book. I address it directly in this chapter, however, because its central aims, like chorography, are inventive; yet, with heuretics, we see direct folding of theory and practice and proairetic examples for a participatory pedagogy. Heuretics can be better understood as a counterpart to traditional interpretation, or hermeneutics. Ulmer explains that heuretics encounters inventors before they have discovered anything; heuretics focuses on production, and on not always being strictly tied to the notion that, in order to teach or learn something, we first have to master it. Loosely defined, heuretics allows us to understand something while also participating in its invention. Heuretics serves as the methodology for participatory composition.

To locate the relevance of heuretics, Ulmer returns to Peter Ramus, who "oversaw the change in the apparatus (from manuscript to print) that involved institutional practices as much as it did technology . . . the methodological innovation initiated by Ramus culminates in the 5-paragraph theme" (*Heuretics* 34, 35). Ulmer also attributes to Ramus the immense simplification of the experience of learning: "Once the move was made from manuscript to print, at least two foundational principles of medieval schooling were abandoned: mnemonic training and scholastic logic" (*Internet Invention* 4). This is relevant because, according to Ulmer, we are amid the same shift today; translating the literate categories that organize knowledge into digital culture shows that the necessary disciplinary separations and specializations (English, history, sociology, physics, architecture, engineering) are relative to the apparatus of literacy and "have no absolute necessity" in the electrate apparatus (4). The logic of electracy is associative and imagistic; what is important is "the creating of a MOOD or atmosphere . . . Mood is a holistic, emergent kind of order" ("Toward Electracy"); the space from which the mood emerges can be thought of by means of chora. Recall from chapter 3 that choric inventions make up of a network of associations, and, in video culture, mood is paramount in all aspects of participation. Vitanza suggests that what is central to heuristics is the concept of *connectionism*, which serves as "a new concept of memory . . . Opposed to the classical concept of memory as not storing information in some specific locale from which it may be retrieved, connectionism designs memory as not stored at any specific locus . . . but in the myriad relationships among various loci, topoi-cum-chora" ("From Heuristics to Aleatory Procedures" 197).[5] Connectionism emerges through writing by way of choragraphy and happens when writers/readers construct patterns from disassociated parts. In fact, in *Lingua Fracta*, Collin Brooke renames the canon of arrangement, *pattern*, precisely for this purpose, since constructing associational patterns is central in electracy. Similarly, choragraphy reasons with a different concept of memory, which we can align with Brooke's *persistence*. Ulmer calls this kind of "reasoning" memory a "psychological gesture." The psychological gesture "remembers an emotion: the body remembers" (213). Memory comes to the forefront in the electrate apparatus, since the apparatus itself is emerging in response to the technological ability to capture the sound and motion of the human body, which, as we have seen in chapters 2, 3, and 4, manifests at lightning speed in video culture. Ulmer uses the concept of "felt" to describe how memory acts as a conduit for making networks of associational connections. Different from a woven textile, a "text" invented by way of choragraphy is not a text but a "felt": felt, in this case, carries multiple meanings. One corresponds to the emotional qualities arising from punctums of recognition "felt" and remembered by the body. The second is "felt" as material. Ulmer writes: "we have forgotten that 'text'—the common name for written compositions—derives from 'textile' [woven fabric]." He thus links to "felt," which "replaces 'textile' as a fabric craft to be developed as a vehicle for the tenor of imaged compositions" (*Internet Invention* 35). Felt is rolled, mashed, and difficult to break into pieces or sections. To further this discussion, Deleuze and Guattari describe felt (as different from woven fabric) as follows:

> Felt is a supple solid product that proceeds altogether differently, as an anti-fabric. It implies no separation of threads, no intertwining, only an entanglement of fibers obtained by fulling (for example, by rolling the block of fibers back and forth). What become entangled are the microscales of the fibers. An aggregate of intrication of this kind is in no way homogeneous: it is nevertheless smooth, and contrasts point by point with the space of fabric.
>
> (36; qtd. in Deleuze and Guattari, Thousand Plateaus 475)

From this description of felt, Ulmer moves to an explanation of how to make felt, which then serves as the metaphor for choric writing. These linkages—moving from a discussion of writing to the process of making felt—do not make sense logically, yet they still generate and invent a new method based on multiple meanings of the words in question. These linkages also cannot be summarily codified and transmitted; the paralogy involved here does not make communication easier. Instead, it opens up even more possibilities and linkages. That is, we would not apply hermeneutics to a theory and then wait for it to mature before realizing application possibilities. Rather, practices would emerge and become invented as the theory unfolds and refolds. Recall that for heuretics, information is evoked rather than found; hence, these evocations, connectionism, and distributed memories, "function by means of pattern making, pattern recognition, pattern generation" (Ulmer, *Heuretics* 36). Patterns and networks become crucial for using theory to invent new practices, since it is the recognition of a pattern as it is occurring that drives the new invention.

Circling back to the distinction between Vitanza's and Kent's conceptualizations of paralogy, we can now see how heuretics functions as a postpedagogy. Ulmer further describes heuretics as follows: "As a pedagogy, heuretics encounters inventors before they have discovered anything. Hermeneutic teaching does a good job of covering all the solutions to problems found so far. Heuretic teaching complements hermeneutic pedagogy by approaching invention from the side of not knowing" ("I Untied the Camera of Tastes" 578). Instead of creating "masters" of heuretics, heuretic pedagogy would create consultants working alongside one another to forge connections. The connections the consultants experience bring the materials of a problem into "sudden, unexpected relationship with other areas of a thinker's experience" (*Heuretics* 142). The experience of a "felt" results in connecting memories and moods to make and thus write new discoveries. This is thinking through the body, taking into consideration the feelings a particular environment evokes and linking them accordingly.

Heuretics offers an alternative to pedagogy hope and the pedagogical imperative in composition. Davis suggests: "the pedagogical imperative has been responsible for perpetuating a subtle reign of terror in universities and schoolhouses" (*Breaking Up* 213): a reign of terror based on exclusion and deflection of "felt" knowledge not "appropriate" for academic knowledge. Participatory pedagogy, realized through choragraphy and heuretics, allows for felt knowledge to be realized and linked, which is another way to describe how theory and practice work in the electrate apparatus.

Sites for Participatory Pedagogy

In this final section, I discuss sites for participatory pedagogy that may inspire future reinventions for teaching. As I explained at length in the preceding sections, the notion that theories mature before being set into practice is not an accurate reflection of the apparatus of electracy. Rather, and by way of heuretics, theories and practices emerge simultaneously. We can see countless instances of this on YouTube, and following Ulmer's assertion that entertainment in electracy is to schooling in literacy, we will look at how YouTube itself has been reinvented for participatory purposes. This repurposing aims to elicit even more participation and ramp up the possibilities for action in video culture.

I stumbled on this event when first researching the concept of "tubing," which Geof Carter and I develop in our article "Tubing the Future: Participatory Pedagogy and YouTube U in 2020." We both thought it showed participatory pedagogy in action and aimed to explore it further. Created by designers Jeff Crouse and Aaron Meyers, "The World Series of Tubing" is a competition in which participants, in real time, compete on a stage with a preselected "hand" of several YouTube videos. Players select their "hands" of videos for various reasons, and each player's "hand" is displayed on a screen. Two players display their videos simultaneously on a screen and then audience members vote for the best hand via laser stylus pens. We found this practice can serve as a metaphor for the participatory pedagogy of the future for several reasons. First, participants must preselect their favorite videos on YouTube before heading onstage to compete. Once onstage, participants are given augmented reality cards on which their videos are loaded, and they begin to manipulate the cards to display the video images on the screen. Once the audience begins seeing this virtual "deck of cards," they can begin voting. This technologically complex yet culturally simple method illustrates participatory practices because the outcome is, of course, not known in advance. Participants "play" because they want to see how their selections fare out with audiences in a real-time situation.

Second, and more connected to this chapter, participants' videos resemble an assemblage of material not unlike Ulmer's "popcycle" (discussed in chapter 1): a range of conductively associated images, texts, etc., that make up a collage of our subjectivities and communities and are usually defined by the institutions of our lives, such as family, entertainment, community, and education (rom *Internet Invention* 6). Interlinking these four sites brings about a pattern, which serves as the method for constructing a MyStory. The pattern forms "not at the level of meaning or theme . . . Rather, the pattern forms at the level of repeated signifiers—words and graphics" (6): a sampling as such. Ulmer explains: "to compose a mystory is to map one's location in a discourse network. A discourse network is not determined in advance, and there are infinite networks" (14). Let this not be confused with the 1980s talk of "discourse communities"; discourse networks are not communities; they are radical singularities: paralogic linkages that arise from experiencing ourselves as images from, as Ulmer puts it, our "pictographic archives."[6] This image archive resides in the body but must be evoked through the network; recall from chapter one that the popcycle assists in accessing the unpresentable, looking for paralogic linkages by way of the accidents that have occurred in several areas of people's lives. When I suggested that we add a more overtly participatory element to the MyStory in chapter one, I can now show that the World Series of Tubing does just that.

To be sure, the World Series of Tubing may seem to have no connection at all to the popcycle; however, I see the act of rapidly selecting a "deck" of videos, placing them in some order to appear, one by one, on the screen, and changing the order as the audience responds as a version of the popcycle that emerges in even more of a lateral and associative fashion. Since participants' popcycles receive immediate audience feedback, they make adjustments as they go, and, when it is all said and done, they can look back at their sequences of videos and the ratings they received on each one. These decks do not come to life until they enter into the participatory ring, and they very likely represent all areas of the popcycle, with which players have some sort of connection. If we looked at the videos selected in retrospect, we could conductively associate them with the categories of the popcycle. I see the World Series of Tubing as a metaphor for what might occur in a pedagogical situation, and while we cannot literally recreate the game, we can simulate it and learn from it.

Third, each "tubing" session indeed sets off other unexpected juxtapositions for audience members and future participants. With two sets of videos flashing before their eyes, audience members call up associations to help them decide which video resonates for them more. This direct participation could likely lead to the generation of new material and the evolution of new ideas. Again, while The World Series of Tubing may not necessarily be replicated in the classroom, the ways in which ideas are generated and subjects as singularities throw themselves "out there," can give us a sense of how participatory pedagogical practices may emerge.

Interestingly, Crouse and Meyers are also working on the projects "You3b" and "YouCube" (Crouse, Meyers), which aim to put the participatory elements from the World Series of Tubing into actual motion online. You3b and YouCube are both dynamic sites online and take the participatory elements of both You-Tube in general and The World Series of Tubing in particular to new levels. You3b invites participants to create "sets" of videos, juxtaposed in three windows, which play simultaneously. Participants rate and comment on the sets of three videos in the same fashion as they do on YouTube. The goal of You3b is to intensify the practice of juxtaposition, which in turn sets off more associations in viewers. When watching these "sets," participants engage directly with unexpected juxtapositions and then create their own sets. It goes without saying that watching these sets on You3b takes a certain mindset, since three videos play at the same time; that said, however, creating these juxtapositions has lasting effects. Similarly, Meyers's YouCube asks participants to enter the URLs of four videos, which are then repurposed on a rotating, 3-D cube. The purpose of the cube is the same as the strip of juxtaposed videos on You3b: users upload content in order for it to be remixed and repurposed. Yet, the "cube" is in constant motion, which, unlike You3b, only allows traces of the videos to be seen at any one given viewing. The video cube that emerges, then, has the potential for setting off literally countless associations. In fact, if we recall my brief description of my own popcycle in chapter 1, I envision each of the scenarios depicted there on the YouCube, which will allow for several associated linkages to arise in viewers. Plus, as the cube rotates, viewers would only see snippets of each video clip at a time, thereby increasing the capability of remix. You3b and YouCube extend traditional remixing to include multiple videos; that is, the remixes are of the videos themselves as well as the juxtapositions and connections they may elicit. This complex notion of participation is exactly what I envision when for participatory composition. If we take, for example, the three major videos I discussed in chapters 2, 3, and 4 (posted by ToshBabyBoo, the liztomania meme, and CopperCab, respectively) and placed them in juxtaposition on You3b, what would we see? What associations would we make? Taking this a step further, what if we made YouCubes from these videos' video responses? Or remixes in response to them? It is not difficult to see that the possibilities are endless.

I would like to end by turning to Paul Kameen, who, in, *Writing/Teaching: Essays toward a Rhetoric of Pedagogy,* sees *writing* and *teaching* as always symbiotic in their relationship and suggests that what and how we teach comes from certain "texts" that repeat for us. Kameen's insight might be thought of, loosely, as our "theories" and closely resembles Ulmer's popcycle. I do this to bring the chapter back around to its initial inquiry about the theory/practice split in our field. While my discussion above may seem a far cry from the writing classrooms we inhabit, the practices introduced there illuminate how we might teach in electracy. Kameen's reference to writing can be stretched out to "writing" at large, as I have been working with it in this book. Kameen suggests that "texts," these loosely defined "theories," carry "felts" for us; we respond to them because we feel a connection with them (a la the popcycle) beyond trying to "turn" them into lessons for the classroom. Rather, "after enough re-readings, you start to carry those voices into the classroom with you—not so much as in conscious thinking but more in the mode of productive, inaudible bickering over what exactly to do, and why, and how, and when" (144). Kameen explains, however, that just because he has these "texts" that help make him the teacher he is, he definitely does not emulate or even vaguely resemble any of them. Instead, these "texts" come out as "samples," "remixes" for particular students at particular times and are necessarily remixed each time a new group of students arrives. This requires writing teachers, as intensities, to tap into their own as well as their students' "texts" (as felts). These felts work as part of a singular collage that fosters what happens in the classroom throughout the course of the semester or quarter. Then the collage loosens and is reassembled into different combinations for the next pedagogical scene.

Kameen's attitude toward teaching can also be explained through Barthes, who calls writing a "tissue of quotations" (see *Roland Barthes by Roland Barthes*); this "tissue," as it relates to teaching comes from embedded bodily responses: responses that guide what we do when we write and teach. It is important to keep in mind, then, that one can intervene in inventing the electrate apparatus without using the texts and theorists I've cited in this book. Intervening requires putting together a remix of our own and our students' texts and assignments, which very well may include some of the texts I've explicated. Hopefully, and as Ulmer has tirelessly argued before me, in the emerging electrate apparatus, we will stop thinking of theory and practice as necessarily separate and instead see them as working side by side to evoke those inventions that have yet to be thought. Doing so will keep the buzz alive and will encourage practices not yet invented to emerge.

6. Afterword: Productive Knowledge, Participatory Composition

> Thus, as students learn the things we ostensibly teach, we might also ask what students are not learning. What other forms of writing and thinking are being shut down or distorted—forms of writing that have their own, different powers and inventive allure?
> —Thomas Rickert, *Acts of Enjoyment*

Participatory composition, inspired by Ulmer's early articulation of "videocy" (see chapter 1) and suitable for the emerging apparatus of electracy, offers a way to link writing, participation, and video culture from multiple perspectives. I hope this effort both contributes to and offers a different take on the growing numbers of rhetorics for electracy and presents readers with an alternative for both participating and teaching in the digital world. Along with the text of this book, I also offer our own Long Beach version of the "Phoenix Lisztomania Brat Pack Mash Up" video meme, and the videos "The Dancing Floor" and "Choric Slam Tilt: Unpinning the Table," all of which are posted on YouTube, to forward *Participatory Composition's* ideas (links can be found in the introduction). We hope these videos will accompany chapter 2 and 3's arguments and serve as exemplars for participatory composition. The series of videos "Being Placed (Not!): 1970s Pop Music and the Cadence of Small Town Life" are also posted on YouTube and show my popcycle, discussed in chapter 1, in action.

Along with the examples I've cited throughout this book and my own work that serve as exemplars, I conclude *Participatory Composition* with two more examples of electrate writing, all produced by students after they had studied electracy, participatory culture, and the theories and practices associated with both. Including student examples may seem like a tired, clichéd practice in our discipline, particularly since the process by which the examples evolved can never be captured in a book. That said, however, I hope these examples serve as simply a starting place for others' engagement with participatory composition. These particular pieces are not exactly the most outstanding projects, yet they show a sort of raw articulation of how students both take in and repurpose participatory material. Recall that one of the main contentions of chorography, or choric invention, is that each practitioner makes discoveries by working with established forms (a la platforms online) and invents new trajectories from them; these trajectories serve as conceptual starting places for others to contribute to rhetorics for electracy. The two examples I include here stand out to me, simply because both of them respond to the call of heuretics: of learning, inventing, and knowing while doing.

Ever since I have been advocating for the buzz created by participatory pedagogy, electracy and composition, the most common question people ask is, "How can you teach this way?" In fact, Kevin Brooks raises this very question when he cites my previous work, which identified with postpedagogy (and by extension electracy), in his article (with Aaron Anfinson) "Exploring Post-Critical Composition: MEmorials for Afghanistan and the Lost Boys." Taking my claim that, in postpedagogy, chorography, and electracy, each practitioner must repurpose the theories and practices that resonate for them quite literally, Brooks and Anfinson write, "Rather than assume that students will seek the path of reproduction and repetition, it seems just as likely to assume that they will re-invent a genre and rework a model if given an opportunity" (78). While I greatly appreciate Brooks and Anfinson's concerns, I point out that postpedagogy does not simply mean "anything goes" in a sort of wild, anarchistic fashion. Rather, students study electracy and heuretics, learn about associative connections and paralogic linking and then immediately engage in production, almost always within a structure of an established platform online (YouTube, for example) or by using the popcycle or other formats for organizing the uncanny associations they make. In fact, Brooks's own wiki space on Ulmer has been extremely useful for both me and my students.

Since my initial engagement with electracy over a decade ago, I have changed my thinking in what to call the teaching that arises from the electrate apparatus. First, and following Vitanza from the third counterthesis (chapter 5), I turned to postpedagogy. I then adopted Ulmer's and others' notion of post-criticism to argue for a "post-critical" composition. I did this in order to set electrate work off from the (then and still now, to an extent) popular practice of "critical pedagogy." Through various research projects and through teaching in the manner I was always trying to describe (through postpedagogy and post-critical composition), I came to realize that the concepts I was using were not adequate, and that Brooks was right:

students should invent and reinvent established genres like the MyStory and MEmorial. Brooks's work with Ulmer's genre of the MEmorial is impressive; the sites his students produce highlight electrate composition, and I suggest that readers visit his "Exploring MEmorials 2" site, which is rich with both exposition and performance of the Memorial.

The notion of participatory composition—suggested to me by my colleague Geof Carter, to whom I am deeply indebted—resonated greatly and, I hope, by way of video culture, better articulates the network of possibilities for writing in electracy. Participatory composition inherently includes working with the technologies that help bring the composition to life, and part of the task for students is always finding and locating the best format or platform within which to work. That is, while each class I teach has a social media platform, students do not necessarily use the platform itself to create and compose their assignments. The practice of both creating content and learning the structure of a particular platform, to me, really places the participatory pedagogical notion at the forefront, since students have to invent not only the content for their projects but also the site in which the projects will be hosted. Until this practice evolved, the participatory element of my pedagogy was not yet visible. I remember asking students to buy zip disks and CDs to turn in "hard" copies of their multimedia work. By turning in a video, for example, as a hard copy, it has no life beyond the professor's computer, and thus, aside from the actual production of the video, does not actualize in a dynamic space. However, when the technology to upload, download, share, link, and embed video became available, suddenly the participatory element thrived. In that regard, Collin Brooke and Thomas Rickert's assertion that "language and technology are constitutive and transformative" (250) deeply resonates. Searching, traveling, and locating an appropriate site is as integral as the space itself, and the dynamics involved in the space are part of the composition. Figuring out the technical issues of any one of the free platforms students use is also part of the composition, and, by the end of any given semester, students have gained technical skills by simply participating in their fellow students' compositions.

The following examples are from students enrolled in my graduate seminar on digital rhetoric. Both students had no prior exposure to electracy before taking the course. The social media site I use for the course can be located at http://electracy.ning.com. I chose these particular examples to show a juxtaposition of possibilities not confined to the MyStory, though, ironically, one example evolved into a MyStory. While this may seem contradictory, I do this because this MyStory interestingly began as a video entitled "Sunshine and Noir," and after we watched the video in class and listened to how its contents came about, we could not help but encourage the student to pursue a MyStory. The students in the class responded to the initial video, and their responses helped invent what would become a MyStory. Plus, the impetus for making the video "Sunshine and Noir" was participatory in nature, as we will see when the author explains how people from his old neighborhood came together on Facebook. Prior to this encounter, the author wanted to explore the connections he felt to his old neighborhood via a memoir, but the project stalled several times. After many discussions with people he hadn't seen in years, he finally began to take pictures of his old neighborhood, post them on Facebook, and participate in discussions about them. Alongside his initial postings, his friends on Facebook posted their own images and videos, and, interestingly, one of the videos his friend unearthed and posted became a central facet of the ensuing MyStory. This act then drove him to create the video "Sunshine and Noir" out of these participatory experiences. While this part of the project is not visible to readers, it is extremely important to the eventual invention of the MyStory, as are the comments and responses this student received during class and online. Thus, the MyStory "Transformational Grammars" was invented, and to me, the blending of the private and public in it is so intricate that it works as both critique and performance. Since it began on Facebook through several interactions among friends and then morphed into the video "Sunshine and Noir," the MyStory is not exactly like other MyStories out there; it is a participatory MyStory.

The second example, "Mi Papa Es Su Papa: MEMEorializing Ernest Hemingway," shows one of the first attempts at producing what Geof Carter and I call a "MEMEorial" (see "Tubing the Future"), which is a spin-off of Ulmer's aforementioned MEmorial. While the project is deeply personal for the student, since it connects Hemingway's suicide to her own father's, it is also inherently participatory. Hemingway is alive and well in meme culture through memes such as "Hipster Hemingway," "Bored Hemingway," and "Awesome Hemingway," and this project connects the humor associated with Hemingway memes with the seriousness of alcoholism and suicide. It began with an online survey, which included questions about Hemingway, meme culture, and suicide in general and then morphed into a depiction of suicide that resonates both personally for the student and publically for anyone who has a connection to suicide. The project shows an alternative way to raise awareness about and cope with the effects that suicide can have on family members.

Both of these works show, first, how students brand new to the concepts of electracy and participatory culture interacted with the goal of aiming for inventive and productive knowledge; second, how students grapple with the differences between electrate and literate learning and work to combine both electrate and literate practices; and third, how the process of discovery and heeding to unrelated connections aids in building new knowledge. I will share excerpts from each student's written explanation of the projects and provide links to the online versions. The first student's written portion reflects on writing with electracy, experimenting first with video, working intensely with comments and responses, and finally composing the MyStory. The electronic version entails the performance. This example also highlights videocy, and represents, I contend, what Ulmer was aiming for when articulating the concept in *Teletheory*. By beginning with a video and then moving toward MyStory (which, incidentally, includes many videos), we see the interconnectedness of videocy and electracy. The second student's written portion explains the process of moving from a MEmorial to constructing the MEMEorial, reflects on the delicate balance among the personal and public, and explains the uncanny connections that led to the production of the MEMEorial video.

EXAMPLE 1. Transformational Grammars: Virtual Exiles and MyStory
By Mark R. Olague
Located at http://www.wix.com/markolague/transformationalgrammar

In the first excerpt below, Mark summarizes the inception of the project and his relationship to the work of Roland Barthes. We see that Mark's initial connection to Barthes's mourning in Camera Lucida *led to the subsequent connections that led to both his video and MyStory*

> [*Excerpt 1*]: In its first incarnation my project sprang from Roland Barthes's theory of the *punctum* expressed in *Camera Lucida* coupled with Gregory Ulmer's notion of *biographemes*, those intellectual totems embodied in certain images and concepts in Barthes's work gathered together to produce a "body of knowledge" or critical monument to the late French theorist. Like Barthes, I started from the death of my own mother, submitting myself to the elusive, fragmentary logic of grief. In its first "mediation" I constructed a video essay, which I entitled "Sunshine and Noir" in reference to the opening chapters of Mike Davis's Foucauldian study of the

class antagonisms in his urban history of Los Angeles, *City of Quartz*. Guided by the punctums I experienced while watching the films of Quentin Tarantino I saw an analogy between the "hidden" neighborhoods in Los Angeles used as backdrops for the director's early films with the one I grew up in Bell, California. For the purpose of the Mystory I re-mediated some of the components and made further connections by organizing my material under the four institutional discourses initially delineated by Ulmer in his "Popcycle."

The following, more lengthy excerpt explains each section of Mark's MyStory and the choric experiences of assembling the connections. I maintained most of the original text, so readers could get a glimpse at the process with which Mark engaged in turning his initial video into a MyStory based on interactions he had on Facebook with old friends from the neighborhood as well as discussions in class with his peers. This is what makes Mark's MyStory participatory.

[*Excerpt 2*]: Like intuition, serendipity plays a key role in the analogical reasoning of the Mystory process. It was only by luck that while reading *Camera Lucida* this semester . . . [that I discovered] the *New Yorker* excerpted the critic's *Mourning Diary*, a collection of handwritten entries Barthes intermittently scribbled on quarter strips of paper soon after [his mother's] death. I have hyperlinked images of these entries on my site with the article in the *New Yorker*, including a photo of the theorist being held by his mother Henriette as a child. . . . In some ways, the newly published diary represents a *remediation* of Barthes' grief, a fact resonating deeply with me because of my own mother's death from cancer two years ago. Like Barthes, I too was grief-stricken, struggled with the desire to express my grief that honored its formless, chora-like nature. Print technology, in particular genres like the literary memoir, seemed cognitively "pre-mapped" by sentimentality, hermeneutics, and self-absorption—too seductive it was to describe and define grief, to attempt to make it "meaningful" to its subject, than to trace or be directed by its elliptical and fragmentary nature. The trick was to find a form that made it more productive to me, to watch patterns emerge rather than to impose any upon it—to become, in effect, a *choragrapher*.

. . . And so like the photo of black and white of Barthes and the one with his mother, I added pictures of my mother, formatted to appear as if someone was flipping through them. Some of the pictures were of my mother before she was married to my father, including one of my favorites: an employee ID when she worked at Norris Industries in Maywood, CA, a defense contractor and major employer during the post-WWII industrial boom in Southern California. This allowed me to think about the decline of defense manufacturing throughout Southern California, including major employers like Norris Industries in the 1990s, and its effect on communities like the one I grew up in, a fact which I connect later in more detail in the "Noir City" section of my Mystory. But while reading and discussing Barthes's theory of the emotional impact of photographic stills, I begin to speculate how Barthes's theory of the *punctum* would have applied to cinematic images had he lived.

. . . Barthes's discussion of cinematic spectatorship (in "Upon Leaving the Movie Theater") brings me to the next two parts of my Mystory in which I hope to link Barthes's *jouissance* or the "erotic" bliss of watching a film with the "seductions" of ideology. I've designed the page to include an image of an empty movie theater from a spectator's point of view in which I place at the blank screen a *YouTube* clip showing a scene (which I explain below) from Quentin Tarantino's *Pulp Fiction*. I link the image of the local movie house of my childhood, the Liberty 3 (formally the Alcazar Theater), with Tarantino's film aesthetics—"grindhouse" and the commensurate concept "film noir." Guided by the logic of the *punctum,* I riffed on the ideological subtexts of cinematic genres like "noir" and "grindhouse."

For a while, I have been trying to theorize the films of Quentin Tarantino beyond the typical lens of

hermeneutics-centered film criticism. Few of the critical
exegesises of Tarantino's films I have come across locate
specifically what I happen to find appealing about them. It is
not *only* the endless citationality or intertextuality of Tarantino's vaunted pastiche technique that explains their power.
Like Barthes's analysis of Eisenstein's films, there appears a
"third" or "obtuse meaning" also. As Barthes explained, the
obtuse meaning has "something to do with disguise," a past-
ing over of the Real, which he believed, irrupted in fragmentary form in the film still image. What is sensed by the viewer
of such images is an "emotion which simply designates
what one loves, what one wants to defend," explains Barthes
("Third Meaning" 59).

Tarantino himself has admitted and implicated Barthe-
an-like cinephilia as the motive behind his 2007 co-directed
Grindhouse project with fellow director Robert Rodriguez.
Grindhouse is an homage to the low-budget, exploitation
cinema of the 1970s, whose excessive sex and violence belied
its much less penchant for tackling social issues, sometimes—
as in the case of the war in Vietnam—before mainstream
movies did so. But more importantly, as its moniker connotes,
it was the financially low-end movie houses and the working
class audiences they appealed to (an element most Tarantino
film criticism ignores) that influenced the aesthetics of these
films than just their reputed low budget auteurism. The term
"grindhouse" could also refer to the "grinding" or "churn-
ing" release frequency (the "mass industrialization" of film
content mirroring the nation's manufacturing economy of the
period) of such films, whose stock content, usually exagger-
ated in garish film posters, elicited the desires of filmgoers,
the working class cinephillic. Director Richard Rodriguez,
accounting for his half of the *Grindhouse* project, the qua-
si-sci-fi horror film *Planet Terror*, stated his intention was
to "make good" on what many cinematic posters of the era
promised audiences but ultimately failed to deliver: sex, gore,
and violence. This promise to deliver *jouissance* to today's film

audience with an outmoded style of moviemaking seems, on
the surface, anachronistic: how could today's film audience
appreciate a film aesthetic so specific to a particular era? I felt
the answer was in both my and Tarantino's past—the local
movie theater in my neighborhood in Bell, CA, The Liberty 3
and Tarantino's early breakthrough films, *Reservoir Dogs* and
Pulp Fiction.

In Pulp Fiction, *the punctum* for me occurs nearly half-way
through the film when the scheming Boxer Butch (played by
Bruce Willis) returns to his apartment to retrieve the watch
his father, a P.O.W. killed in Vietnam, has given to him,
while gangsters he has betrayed look for him throughout the
city. Like the scene with Mr. Blonde, the *punctum* occurs
when background suddenly melds into foreground: Butch
makes his way cautiously through the back entrances of his
apartment, alongside secret passage ways, cutting through
a chain-link fence, pushing aside towels draped over a fence
drying. Like the previous scene, it is devoid of dialogue, silent
except for low sounds of a distant television drifting from
nearby apartments, punctuated by the cry of a child and the
musical horn of a passing lunch truck. Again, as in the scene
with Mr. Blonde, it situates me in a landscape that I not only
know but one I formally inhabited: a working class suburb
in Los Angeles largely absent or effaced from the usual filmic
images of the city. Thus the much-discussed "noir" aspects of
Tarantino's films are linked to their virtually much-ignored
class dimensions. While I am not claiming Tarantino's films
are intentionally political, they do contain, in my reading of
my responses to them, a political dimension: a working-class
self-recognition. Yet this presence of my past evoked onscreen
covers up a loss in the present: my working class neighborhood, like the manufacturing industries and public invest-
ment that abandoned it nearly thirty years ago, no longer
exists. If Barthes compared the darkness of the cinema to
the maternal womb, then the image of my mother, too, is
invoked. Certain images are "uncanny" in the Freudian sense,

Barthes acknowledged, because they invoke a sense of home that is no longer home. Thus "noir" seems a perfect metaphor for what is "hidden" and "repressed" in the city.

The theoretical recognition of my working class origins occurred when I read Mike Davis's *City of Quartz* when it was published in the 1990s. It is no coincidence that Davis's Foucauldian analysis of Los Angeles, whose introductory chapter fashions a critical dialectic connecting the literary and cinematic "noir" aspects of the city with its history of class antagonisms, emerges around the same time as Tarantino's first films. Davis's book demarcates the historical "power" and "class" lines in the city, as well as charts the decay of the city's "utopian" promise of self-creation and abundance to its "sinister equivalent" in the metaphor of film *noir*—the city whose "dark underbelly" of corruption and greed is revealed at night, only in its shadows, its dark corners. While noir is the guiding trope of Davis's book, this idea of the "repressed" ideological history of my neighborhood also connects with the film noir's investigations more explicit subject matter: the "seedier" side of human nature, the repressed secrets of personal trauma.

In the "Intimate Chora" part of my Mystory, I have laid out photos and images from my neighborhood when I lived there from 1976–1985 in an effort to evoke, as a *chorographer*, the closeness of the community. In my first video I talked about how social networking sites like *Facebook* allowed me to reconnect with former residents of my neighborhood— known simply as "Chanslor" after the quarter-mile street we lived on—to share memories. In fact, one of the emphases in my video, "Sunshine and Noir," was for emphasizing the community "reforming" capabilities of social networking sites like Facebook as a way for "imagined" communities to reconstitute themselves and enact cultural memories. What I found after talking to some of the people who lived in the neighborhood during that time is that many shared the same narrative threads about the rise and fall of the neighborhood.

For instance, many of us agreed that the death of my older brother Roland and a childhood friend of mine, Jose Carlos Rubio, both in their early 20s, were turning points for the neighborhood.

I have included a picture of my brother on this page taken the same year he died, 1985, of a drug overdose. Because [of] my own family's reticence to talk about it, many rumors and innuendo surrounded his death, which I was able to dispel, including the rumor that he was "murdered" because he had started the street gang in the neighborhood, which, unfortunately, still exists today. I also included the pictures of two classmates who were killed (one by the other) in gang violence. In fact the death of Jose Carlos Rubio, a close friend of mine since kindergarten until the day I moved, who was shot while attending a birthday party of a friend in a house full of witnesses, compelled many families to leave the neighborhood because of the increasing violence. My mother herself often cited our move out of the neighborhood as a strategic move to save me from falling into the same influences that were consuming my friends—a fact that further connects my project to her. In the video clip I've put on my page, visitors can see a home video posted by a friend of mine of us kids (including myself at 14) playing football at the park in our neighborhood (fleeting images of Rubio come in and out of frame at 3:01 in the video) the same year my brother died. In many respects these personal aspects are, in my opinion, as important to mapping *chora* as the impersonal social history of my neighborhood. Since, besides these deaths, Chanslor's decline was emblematic of the urban problems besetting many similar urban neighborhoods in Los Angles reeling from divestment of public expenditures Davis attributes to the passing of Proposition 13, the capping of annual property taxes during the late 1970s, in *City of Quartz*. The deindustrialization of the economy and decline of manufacturing too had a devastating effect on working-class industrial suburbs like Bell. By the 1990s Bell was considered a "dangerous" neighborhood plagued by gangs and drug violence, one of the many urban "infernos" besieged by the national crack epidemic. For many of us who escaped this, including myself, there was a sense of loss and alienation that only later, here, while undergoing the Mystory process was I able to connect with the "discipline" or "career" portion concluding my project: my research interests in the themes and tropes of exile and nostalgia, and all the various textual approaches to express these conditions.

If there were any explicit "Eureka!" moments to the Mystory process I experienced they were reserved for the final aspect of my project. In some respects, these insights inadvertently responded to the drawbacks or reservations critics like O'Gorman complained about with the Mystory. His disdain for "nostalgia" specifically echoed my own undergraduate and graduate research interests in literary exile as it pertained to writers from the former Soviet Union and Eastern Europe who lived in the west. Serendipitously, Ulmer's conception of chora and monumentality, including his construction of the MEmorial, connected with the cultural critic, Svetlana Boym's theory of "reflective nostalgia" and "virtual exile" in her text, *The Future of Nostalgia*. In her book, Boym theorizes about a nuanced "reflective nostalgia" that acknowledges the imperfect images of the past, acknowledges the ambivalences and the ironies against the drive for pure and impossible restoration. Reflective nostalgia is an "intermediary between collective and individual memory," writes Boym, and it is often expressed in cultural forms like art and literature which meditate on the "common landmarks of everyday life" now lost to exiles and emigrants from certain vanished communities (53–54).

. . . To reflect this I have included a "gallery of exiles" on my page, mostly the pictures of well-known literary exiles such as Vladimir Nabokov, Joseph Brodsky, the late Serbian writer, Danilo Kis, Albanian writer Ismail Kadare, and Croatian writer Dubravka Ugresic among others (if there is a central "exile's" image it is that of James Joyce, whose portrait

I include in the gallery). I have also included an image of the Russian artist installation, *Toilets, 1992* including a link to Boym's discussion of Kabakov's art in ArtForum online. *Toilets* depicts a communal toilet during the Soviet era and thus expresses the "banal" grandeur of vanished social spaces that, punctum-like, bring to the surface the many mixed emotions of those who lived during the era—their disillusion with the failed Soviet promise of utopia against Soviet day-to-day reality as well as the "ironic" solidarity such loss provokes. This is why I have included the equally banal image of the "catwalk" or passageway I photographed when I recently visited my old neighborhood. As I posted the images, I received tons of comments by those who wanted to share the memories and feelings the image evoked, an image not likely to resonate to those who did not live in the area. From this, I meditated on the "virtual" aspects of exile, how feelings of estrangement and alienation so common to political exiles in Eastern Europe were similar if not equivalent to my own "reflective nostalgic" feelings for my old neighborhood. In a sense, this connection provided me an insight into why I identified with the work of certain writers and why certain themes, *biographemes*, seem to unconsciously repeat in me.

EXAMPLE 2. Mi Papa Es Eu Papa: MEMEorializing Ernest Hemingway

By Lisa J. Brown (vimeo profile name: lisa b)

Video located at http://vimeo.com/42531459

In the following excerpt, Lisa contextualizes her MEMEorial. She cites the article "Tubing the Future: YouTube U in 2020" written by Geof Carter and me to describe the MEMEorial, which is a version of Ulmer's genre the MEmorial. Our explanation of the MEMEorial moves the genre into the participatory realm.

[*Excerpt 1*]: Gregory Ulmer defines the MEmorial as "a new kind of monument" that embodies the electrate sensibility through its reconfiguration and juxtaposition of personal

stories of sacrifice and loss alongside an existing monument,
as exemplified by the AIDS Memorial Quilt. Through the
lens of videocy, Ulmer prompts us to "treat the internet as
an inhabitable monument in which tourist-theorists in a
collective middle voice learn how to make national identify
formation self-conscious through the creation of ephemorials
(ME-morials)" (Ulmer, *Electronic Monuments* 302). Because
video does not translate mimetically into existing forms of
academic discourse, the current method of segregation with
respect to various forms of discourse has been revealed to
be counterproductive (Ulmer, *Teletheory* 12, 34). As such, we
must adopt a new hybridity of critical and creative strategy in
order to respond within the medium.

That Ulmer should denote the MEmorial as an ephemeral
memorial is not surprising, given that the nature of video
culture is both transitory and lasting—a series of disjointed
fragments collaged and joined together fluidly, occupying
an elusive yet unending present through the phenomenon
of Derridean trace. The question, then, is how to best transition from MEmorial to MEMEorial, which Geoffrey Carter
and Sarah Arroyo describe as necessary "to enact participatory tubing" ("Tubing the Future" 295) in that MEMEorials—"open at both ends and capable of all sorts of recombi-
nant interfaces"—enable us to move beyond personal history
to a fully participatory space or digital commons. In "Participatory Publics: From MEmorials to MEMEmorials," Carter
and Cortney Smethurst trace the "Bed Intruder" meme from
its original broadcast to the Gregory Brothers autotuned
remix and beyond, giving us at least an initial glimpse at the
productive possibilities of collective creativity with respect to
the project of memorializing a given moment in time. . . . But
how to make the leap from commemorating somewhat ob-
scure moments in popular culture to a memorial that might
conceivably be deemed "relevant" or "meaningful" in a larger
cultural—and scholarly—context?

In the following excerpt, Lisa explains the process of following con-
nections to assemble her MEMEorial. In Lisa's explanation, we see
how she takes the joy/sadness axis for electracy, plays with it, and
evokes simultaneous grief and laughter. Lisa's decision not to discuss
her own grief specifically exemplifies the project of the MEMEorial,
since its goal is spreadability and not personal mourning.

[Excerpt 2]: What I think of when I think about Hemingway . . .
I decided to begin my MEMEorial with a process similar to
that adopted by Ulmer for his MyStory, "Derrida at the Little
Bighorn," collapsing the public and private sphere through a
personal connection to an historical event. I knew I wanted
to focus on a significant literary figure, which made Ernest
Hemingway the most logical choice. A lifelong bookworm, the
quickest and easiest way for me to relate to other people has
always been to find a book or an author that we share in common, as this creates a common ground and provides me with
a safe space from which to speak. That being said, I was only
ever able to bond with my dad over a single book: Hemingway's *The Old Man and the Sea*, which he described as the only
book he ever read for school and enjoyed. Much like Hemingway, my dad also had an unhealthy relationship with the bot-
tle. They both owned guns. They both loved to fish. They both
suffered from depression. And they both took their own lives:
Ernest Hemingway on 2 July 1961, my dad on 17 Jan. 2009.

Confident in my starting point, I then followed a variety of connections in order to assemble the bulk of my raw
material. I'm unable to disentangle the fact of Hemingway's
own shotgun-assisted suicide from that of Gonzo journalist
Hunter S. Thompson, who appeared on Late Night with David Letterman where he discussed his proclivity for killing.
This anecdotal evidence was discovered through what might
reasonably be described as free-form YouTube research:
entering in search terms, browsing through clips, following
threads I might otherwise not ever have stumbled upon by
clicking through various suggested/related videos, and so

forth. The list of writers whose work I love and who also committed suicide trails off from there: Charlotte Perkins Gilman, John O'Brien, Sylvia Plath, John Kennedy Toole, Virginia Woolf, and, of course, David Foster Wallace—who hanged himself, as did my father, which brought me full-circle back to Hemingway.

. . . Two of my desert island top 5 quotes from literature are straight from the pages of Hemingway as well. The first: "Isn't it pretty to think so?" And the second: "Man was not made for defeat. A man can be destroyed, but not defeated." While the first comes from my favorite piece of Hemingway's work, *The Sun Also Rises*, the second quote has always hit closer to home, since it comes from the book that encapsulates a special bond I felt with my father. As such, several months after he died, I decided to get the words "destroyed, but not defeated" tattooed across an anatomical heart—which is arguably when the physical germination of this MEMEorial actually began. Although prior to the tattoo—in fact, nearly immediately after my dad killed himself—I began to experience the Baader-Meinhof phenomenon, or frequency illusion, a form of cognitive bias in which something that has recently been brought to your attention is "suddenly everywhere" with alarming frequency and regularity. I couldn't pick up a book, open a magazine, turn on the television, go to the movies, listen to the radio, or browse the internet without some reference to suicide psychically bitch-slapping me. . . . Just like when you buy a new car and are instantly surrounded by the exact make and model wherever you turn, it appeared that suicide was with me to stay.

. . . Or, What We Think of When We Think about Hemingway

This conclusion seemed to be supported by some additional research I conducted through YouTube, which ultimately led me to the TED website. While telling his own story of attempted suicide for the first time in a public forum through TEDYou at TEDActive 2011, Stanford Graduate School of

Business Professor J. D. Schramm notes, "Research shows that 19 out of 20 people who attempt suicide will fail. But the people who fail are 37 times more likely to succeed the second time." Due to cultural taboos regarding suicide, Schramm asserts, friends and family members of suicide survivors often find themselves unsure of how to respond—and so they opt to say nothing at all. The result, then, is an increasingly at-risk population with very few resources in a culture that discourages them from participating in social and critical discourse. To that end, Schramm encourages survivors of suicide—both those who attempted to take their own lives as well as though who lost a loved one to suicide—to speak out and share their stories, as this is "a conversation worth having, an idea worth spreading."

One need only look at the criminalization of suicide to realize just how marginalized this at-risk population is in our culture. It's no coincidence that we say one commits suicide, after all. In a society that condemns people who opt to end their own suffering, how can we expect those experiencing such an extreme degree of pain (whether psychic, physical, or both) that they can't bear the thought of remaining alive to suffer any longer to come forward and seek help? After all, we're constantly bombarded by rein-forcement through media, pedagogy, and religious institu-tions that suicide is not only a crime, it is also a sin—and an unforgivable one at that. This is not a discourse conducive to healing and recovery; it is rampant vilification that will do nothing other than to ensure that people who might have otherwise sought help will continue to suffer silently rather than be publicly condemned until they simply can't take it anymore. By MEMEorializing Hemingway in a way that confronts and attempts to understand his death while also celebrating his work and his life, I hope to participate in a conversation that works toward a new discourse that no longer criminalizes suicide and the attendant mental health issues that surround it.

[Excerpt 3]: The issue at stake appears to be the subversion
of a hegemonic print-based culture that privileges mimetic
representation over creative invention in favor of new, more
fluid forms of discourse that reject marginalization in order
to occupy a choral space, thus paving the way for more egal-
itarian modes of knowledge production and acquisition. As
Thomas Rickert explains:

> What the chōra allows Ulmer to do is theorize and practice
> how this seeming inconsistency or paradox [between the
> impossibility of the chora and its nevertheless pervasive
> existence] is actually productive. It is part of what enables
> or gives rise to rhetoric (as the receptacle), but it also
> withdraws, which in turn necessitates nothing more than
> another beginning, or another inventio.
>
> ("Towards the Chora" 270)

Because chora is inherently and inextricably tied to a sense of
movement (hence both "choreography" and "chorography"),
it cannot be fixed physically or temporally. Nevertheless, as
invention crosses boundaries and doubles back upon itself, it
continuously emerges through the very space within which
it defies definition (270). As such, it is through the essential
paradox of its very existence that the chora asserts its own
necessity. Each new invention (or beginning) immediately
insists upon a past that can then be remembered from the
new(ly) invented present; yet this simultaneously assumes
that a subsequent invention (and hence a new beginning) will
dislodge the previous invention from its location within the
present moment—thus destabilizing its position while ultimately insisting upon it. By MEMEorializing Hemingway, we
dislocate his work, relegating it to the field of memory so that
new (or, at least, newer) inventions may act upon it respectively. And yet, given that both occupy the present, both can
be understood as existing within the same choral network or
space. I can think of no better way to construct the project of
cultural memory than through a liberating series of lateral
connections we need only navigate through experience.

The Future of Participatory Composition

I hope these and the many examples cited throughout this book help enact a participatory composition now and in a future where new technological capabilities and cultural practices will soon arrive. As Ulmer has relentlessly argued, electracy is still in its infancy, so the practices with which we engage will continue to change and morph. We are just beginning to grapple with the cultural effects of video culture, and, as I stated in the opening lines of this book, the space for investigation and participation is wide open. I suspect that the "underbelly" aspects, which I've started to explore here, will engage scholars and students in the coming years, since, presently, we see so many instances of people becoming irrevocably changed, for better and for worse, because of their participation in video culture. We also have to no doubt consider how the study of video culture impacts policies in place for our own scholarly work, especially for peer-review, since, as we have already seen, we are exposed *in* our scholarship when it is video-based, as aptly explored in Alex Reid's "Exposing Assemblages." All of that said, however, I am certain that the study of video culture within the framework of electracy has a bright future. It is best, then, to end the way *Participatory Composition* began: embed. like. share. comment. check in. upload . . . participate.

NOTES

WORKS CITED

INDEX

NOTES

1. Introduction: Electracy, Videocy, and Participatory Composition

1. Richard Fulkerson's essay "Composition at the Turn of the Twenty-First Century" offers a follow-up taxonomy to his 1980 effort "Four Philosophies of Composition." Interestingly, in updating his taxonomy for rhetoric and composition, Fulkerson points out in a note that he intentionally omitted practices he did not consider major "approaches" to composition: one of these practices was "computers and composition" (682 n 5). His move surprisingly aligns with what I aim to accomplish by placing participatory composition alongside prominent "approaches"; participatory composition aims to add cultural and technological complexity to "computers and composition," thereby not making it into a new approach, but rather inviting further exploration and participation in its emergence.

2. This skepticism can be dispelled by looking at the project of the EmerAgency, a virtual consultancy, which Ulmer has worked to create for over a decade. The Emer-Agency aims to intervene in public policy problems using electrate reasoning. I will not discuss the EmerAgency at length in this book, but it has been a very helpful concept for study when teaching about electracy and civic issues. Additionally, as seen in the invention of my popcycle, the concept of the EmerAgency is a driving force behind my own engagement with the electrate apparatus.

3. Thanks to Dobrin, I was able to work with the second Postprocess collection before its official publication, so I am forever grateful to him for sharing it with me.

2. Recasting Subjectivity for Electracy: From Singularities to Tubers

1. Rickert also explains that "many Composition scholars have taken up the challenge to transform or at least critically engage student subjectivities, as well as the contested notion of what subjectivity is and how is it constructed discursively and ideologically" (*Acts of Enjoyment* 12–13). Rickert refers to James Berlin, Patricia Harkin and John Schilb, Lester Faigley, and Sharon Crowley and suggests that much of the postmodern scholarship in rhetoric and composition from the early to mid-1990s focused on subjectivity, which responded to antifoundationalist, postmodern theory (13).

2. Lynn Worsham has provided a powerful explanation of the violence inherent in this misconception in "Going Postal: Pedagogic Violence and the Schooling of Emotion." It is in this article that Worsham defines the "oedipalized subject" upon which

Rickert expands. She defines it like this: "Oedipalization—or the internalization and identification with an authority figure to which one is attached emotionally—is the specific way the patriarchal and bourgeois family produces individuals whose affective orientation to authority best supports the early period of capitalist development."

Worsham continues with a description of the deoedipalized subject, which is crucial to my forthcoming use of Giorgio Agamben's "whatever" being. Worsham writes, "More specifically, postmodernism produces a subject who is variously described as de-oedipalized, narcissistic, feminized, lost, fragmented, and schizophrenic. The de-oedipalized subject is deeply ambivalent because it is locked in a perpetual crisis of abjection in which it oscillates between self-exaltation and dejection, between euphoria and hostility or rage."

3. To add to what I have said about the "whatever" singularity as positive, I turn specifically to Vitanza. Vitanza equates "oedipalization" with negation. To be oedipalized is to be defined under the sign of negation. Following Deleuze and Guattari (and I add Agamben), Vitanza argues, "the unconscious has no 'No' there. (Hence, again, one postmodernist activity is to denegate this negative that modernists, such as Freud, have planted there in perpetual acts of colonization.) But what did Freud do? He simply negated consciousness; hence, the *un*conscious. . . . Freud, however, proceeded nonetheless to territorialize the *un*conscious. He specifically said, when he sailed to that country (where Id was there Ego shall be), that he found Oedipus there. Found Castration there. Found lack there. The Oedipus story is a story of prohibition/of the negative. Of repression. Therefore, in the negative (the *un*conscious), Freud tells us, we have the negative (prohibition, lack). Which leads to negation in infinite regress" (*Negation, Subjectivity, and the History of Rhetoric* 318). This passage is crucial. The conceptualization of a subject/singularity that is a deoedipalized "whatever" being would not view the unconscious as that which is under negation; instead, it would become a place of affirmative desiring production. This production does not "lack"; its holes are kept perpetually open.

3. The Question of Definition: Choric Invention and Participatory Composition

1. The status of rhetoric and composition, as well as its assorted conceptions at various universities, makes defining its object of study a central concern, since defining "what we do" is something that occupies not only institutional conversations but also frequents our journals and conferences more so than other disciplines. In other words, for such a young discipline, rhetoric and composition has spent a considerable amount of time on defining its object of study. In fact, Helen Foster's *Networked Process: Dissolving Boundaries of Process and Post-Process* argues at length for a name change from rhetoric and composition to rhetoric and writing studies, and her book represents a study interrogating the very notion of what the discipline does.

2. Jacques Derrida, out of whom Ulmer primarily works, addresses this at length in several works, most notably, *Specters of Marx*. However, I will be using Ulmer's work as primary texts since he has remotivated Derrida (and Barthes) in his own line of flight. Avital Ronell has also written about this at length, especially in *Dictations: On Haunted Writing*. Refusing and unable to define precisely those out of whom she works, Ronell's writings are always "haunted" by the specters of events/other people she does not name.

3. The article we are referring to appeared in 1997. While Anderson has modified her views since then (see "Property Rights: Exclusion as Moral Action in 'The Battle of Texas'"), we still believe that the earlier article is relevant, because it demonstrates how many successful critical pedagogues use elements from the Classical tradition to support their practices.

4. Anderson specifically critiques Dale Bauer's class, which advocates radical pedagogy, because her students are *so* resistant to the idea of a radical pedagogy.

4. Who Speaks When Something Is Spoken?
Playing Nice in Video Culture

1. Others in rhetoric and composition, including Linda Adler-Kassner, Vicki Tolar Collins, Nancy DeJoy, Anne Ruggles Gere, Rebecca Moore-Howard, Andrea Lunsford, and Krista Ratcliffe, have also challenged the issue of authorship but by way of the question of textual ownership. These challenges rely on feminist theories to disrupt "restrictive theory and practice." Joy Ritchie and Kathleen Boardman see feminisms as "our best hope for inclusion and proliferation of difference, multiplicity, and uncontrollable excess" ("Feminism and Composition" 603). While I affirm what Ritchie and Boardman "hope for," I also question that this "hope" may be the very thing that stifles their dream for a liberating rhetoric.

Lee-Ann M. Kastman Breuch also contributes to this conversation by suggesting that one of the most useful concepts from what has been put forth as post-process theory is the "rejection of mastery," since "many post-process scholars associate the process movement with mastery" ("Post-Process 'Pedagogy'" 127). Breuch goes on to say that the reason for this rejection is that process theory suggests that writing is a "thing" or an object to be mastered. I return to Breuch's article at length in chapter five.

2. Alcorn explains that desire is tangled up in interactions involving discourse and thus works extensively to introduce desire into discourse. In doing so he links Kinneavy's "persuasive" discourse with Lacan's "master discourse" because "it fixes desire in relation to knowledge" (*Changing the Subject* 68). Next, Alcorn links Kinneavy's informative discourse with Lacan's "university discourse" because it is concerned purely with the transmission of knowledge" (68). Alcorn suggests that university discourse works when "subjects desire to put aside their real desires, to serve as keepers or transmitters for signification. Persuasion, on the other hand, works when subjects desire to put aside their divided nature to promote a potentially disputable truth" (68).

3. Yarbrough also discusses Stanley Fish, whom I will not delve into in this chapter. He discusses Fish's notion of "knowledge communities" and "theory hope" and concludes that, by way of Fish, "it does not really matter how we teach composition" (*After Rhetoric* 219). He objects to Fish's use of interpretive communities by arguing that discourse creates communities instead of the other way around. This helps him support his claim that the required composition course should be abolished and replaced with a course on discourse studies. Yarbrough claims: "to teach at all we must teach objects. There can be no teaching of 'language' or 'culture' or 'life' or 'the world' any more than, as Fish says, we can teach 'the situation' or even particular situations. What we can teach are the objects affecting situations, including responses to those marks and noises people make within situations. Attempts to 'improve student writing' in general are useless—we can only help students' abilities to effect changes

through discourse regarding this object or that" (237). Yarbrough thus remains with the notion that we can and should turn students into "masters" of objects, which will "empower our students as speakers and writers" (234). While I have discussed the rhetoric of empowerment at length in chapter 2, I want to stress that the notion of "empowering" someone is predicated on eventually becoming a master, which necessarily excludes those who are not yet empowered, and grants the new master the position of the speaker (as in Lyotard's first pragmatic).

4. Giorgio Agamben explains immanence as such: "Starting with Husserl, immanence becomes immanent to a transcendental subjectivity, and the cipher of transcendence thus reappears at its center" (*Potentialities* 230). Thus, the open space created by the *compearance* of singular beings, moves away from immanence as transcendent as a whole toward remaining a hole. I have decided to quote Nancy at length here, instead of in the text, since his explanation is quite long; but what he says is very important for the notion of community this chapter advocates. Nancy suggests that attempting to articulate community (as the sharing of our exposure, our finitude) is somewhat difficult, especially in terms of the "hole" in immanence. Nancy writes:

> By itself, articulation is only a juncture, or more exactly, the play of the juncture: what takes place where different pieces touch each other without fusing together, where they slide, pivot, or tumble over one another, one at the limit of the other—exactly at its limit—where these singular and distinct pieces fold or stiffen, flex or tense themselves together and through one another, unto one another. (*Inoperative* 76)

Nancy then suggests that this whole, which reaches for totality, "does not close in around the singularities to elevate them into [totality's] power: this whole is essentially the opening of singularities in their articulations, the tracing and the pulse of their limits" (76). It is not difficult to see this "tracing" in the examples from video culture I cite in this chapter.

5. Participatory Pedagogy: Merging Postprocess and Postpedagogy

1. Lynn Worsham calls pedagogy hope the "will to pedagogy" ("Writing against Writing" 96) and explains that the pedagogical imperative is "at the heart of a discipline requiring every theory of writing to translate into a pedagogical practice or at least some specific advice for teachers" (96).

2. Vitanza cites several people who (in 1991) also provide examples of attempts at postpedagogies (see "Three Countertheses" 170 n. 12). Ulmer is one of those people; however, Vitanza does not yet explicate Ulmer's work. Vitanza cites Ulmer's "post(e)pedagogy" as explicated in *Applied Grammatology: Post(e)-Pedagogy from Jacques Derrida to Joseph Beuys* and "Textshop for Post(e)pedagogy" as an example of avoiding pedagogy hope, but he does not go further. Since the publication of "Three Countertheses," however, Vitanza has fully accepted Ulmer's grammatological writing and postpedagogy. This acceptance is exemplified by his numerous references to it in his later work and especially by publishing Ulmer's textbook, *Internet Invention*, in his series. Bump Halbritter and Todd Taylor published a "scholarly film" in the journal *JAC* in 2006; they confess that they were "trying to imagine what a scholarly film might look like with no apparent models" ("Remembering Composition" 395). This is an act of paralogy, of writing and producing in an electrate manner.

3. Ulmer links "method" with the practice of method acting, which is another metaphor for interface ("to gain access to the unfamiliar by means of the familiar" (*Heuretics* 115). He explains method acting as follows: "The value of Method as analogy for choragraphy concerns the way it requires the actors to merge their personal culture with that of the play, whose themes and scenes are translated in rehearsal, using the technique of Affective memory, into the actor's own experiences, cultural backgrounds, and memories. During rehearsal a series of improvisational exercises, often far removed from the words of the script, remake the play in terms of the actors' autobiographies, finding equivalents and analogies in their life stories for the Idea, Objectives, and Actions that emerged from the table work" (116). These "improvisational exercises" are not part of the final "product" of the play, but are key in making it work. Ulmer would be more interested in the content of those exercises than in the product itself. Ulmer stresses that the key to method acting is the psychological gesture: "the actors found the gestural trigger of the emotion (anger, love, envy, hate) by reconstructing the physical setting of a memory" (117–118). The details of the physical setting, the punctums present in the image, provide linkages to the script, which help get the actor "in character."

Additionally, relating this concept to the emerging apparatus of electracy, Ulmer stresses: "we are inventing electracy. Electracy does not already exist as such, but names an apparatus that is emerging 'as we speak,' rising in many different spheres and areas, and converging in some unforeseeable yet malleable way" (*Internet Invention* 7). Echoing this statement, Ulmer, in his CCCC talk I cited in chapter 1, emphatically stated: "Electracy is happening." Because electracy is already happening, the possibility of ignoring it is becoming more and more impossible, so the exigency to come up with theories and methods designed for electracy resonates strongly.

4. Michael Jarrett provides some historical information on the word *heuretics* at http://www.yk.psu.edu/~jmj3/defheu.htm. He explains:

> While readers might associate *heuretics* with a varied set of connotators—eureka, heuristics, heretics, and, yes, diuretics—the word originated as a theological term, as the flip-side or repressed Other of hermeneutics. One could interpret scripture (read through a hermeneutic), or one could employ scripture as a means of invention (read it heuretically). Hermeneutics asks, What can be *made of* the Bible? Heuretics asks, What can be *made from* the Bible? Hermeneutics was secularized early on. It provided methodologies of reading, legitimated the study of texts and, in effect, created the Renaissance humanist. Heuretics enjoyed neither prestige nor currency, and though I suspect the word popped up now and again during witch trials (in the mouths of prosecutors), its systematic use has been largely confined to the fine arts.

Jarratt also suggests that Ulmer's *Teletheory* is the first to use heuretics in critical discourse, and, as I have also suggested, Ulmer develops it in *Heuretics*.

5. Vitanza's article "From Heuristic to Aleatory Procedures" is a very succinct exposition of heuretics and especially Ulmer's CATTt heuristic, which he describes as "the stand-in" for the impossibility of the chora (196). I will not address the CATTt heuristic here, since I do not think it corresponds with what I have been advocating

as a electrate composition. As Vitanza has suggested, the CATTt (Contrast, Analogy, Theory, Target, tale) serves as a stand-in to describe chora, which resists and evades description. I have found that choragraphy does indeed explain how a electrate composition works without having to resort to the specifics of the CATTt, which might be confused as a "heuristic" designed for the literate apparatus.

6. Thomas Rickert provides an explanation of this type of network in his response essay "Enjoying Theory." He equates it with "theory" and writes: "It is important to note that 'theory' is not an object so much as a contentious discursive network, always seeking, adapting, questioning, postulation, and creating. This means that it is wildly recursive.... Whatever our relation to theory, it is not something we can simply escape or abandon through praxis. Nor is it, finally, something to be controlled or corralled, precisely because its recursiveness will exceed all bo(u)nds" (636 n. 5). This explanation links to how theory is conceptualized in an electrate manner; in other words, theory is not an object to be "used," but is instead a force and intensity in itself, coming to life as it is invented and practiced.

WORKS CITED AND CONSULTED

Adler-Kassner, Linda. "Ownership Revisited: An Exploration in Progressive Era and Expressivist Composition Scholarship." *College Composition and Communication* 49.2 (1998): 208–33. Print.

Agamben, Giorgio. *The Coming Community.* Trans. Michael Hardt. Minneapolis: U of Minnesota P, 1993. Print.

——. *The Man without Content.* Trans. Georgia Albert. Stanford: Stanford UP, 1994. Print.

——. *Means without Ends: Notes on Politics.* Trans. Vincenzo Bintti and Cesare Casarino. Minneapolis: U of Minnesota P, 2000. Print.

——. *Potentialities: Collected Essays in Philosophy.* Stanford: Stanford UP, 1999. Print.

Alcorn, Marshall W. *Changing the Subject in English Class: Discourse and the Constructions of Desire.* Carbondale: Southern Illinois UP, 2002. Print.

——. "Changing the Subject of Postmodernist Theory: Discourse, Ideology, and Therapy in the Classroom." *Rhetoric Review* 13 (1995): 331–49. Print.

Amerika, Mark. "Expanding the Concept of Writing: Notes on Net Art, Digital Narrative, and Viral Ethics." *Leonardo* 37.1 (2004): 9–13. Print.

Anderson, Chris. "Film School: Why Online Video Is More Powerful than You Think." *Wired* 19.1 (2011): 112–17.

——. "How YouTube Is Driving Innovation." YouTube 15 May 2010. Web. 2 Sept. 2010.

Anderson, Virginia. "Confrontational Teaching and Rhetorical Practice." *College Composition and Communication* 48.2 (1997): 197–214. Print.

——. "Property Rights: Exclusion as Moral Action in 'The Battle of Texas.'" *College English* 62.4 (2000): 445–72. Print.

AnthroVlog. "Participatory Cultures." YouTube, 11 Nov. 2007. Web. 9 Feb. 2011.

——. "Returning the Favor." YouTube, 25 Aug. 2010. Web. 16 Feb. 2011.

——. "What Defines a Community?" YouTube, 3 Oct. 2007. Web. 15 Feb. 2011.

Aristotle. *On Rhetoric: A Theory of Civil Discourse.* Trans. George A. Kennedy. New York: Oxford, 1991. Print.

Arroyo, Sarah J., and Geoffrey V. Carter. "Tubing the Future: Participatory Pedagogy and YouTube U in 2020." *Computers and Composition* 28.1 (2011): 292–302. Print.

Ballif, Michelle, D. Diane Davis, and Roxanne Mountford. "Negotiating the Differend: A Feminist Trilogue." *JAC* 20.3 (2000): 582–625. Print.

Ball, Cheryl, and James Kalmbach, eds. *RAW: (Reading and Writing) New Media.* Cresskill: Hampton, 2010. Print.

Barthes, Roland. *Camera Lucida: Reflections on Photography*. Trans. Richard Howard. New York: Hill and Wang, 1981. Print.

———. "From Work to Text." *Image, Music, Text*. Trans. Stephen Heath. New York: Hill and Wang, 1977. 155–64. Print.

———. "Inaugural Lecture: College de France." *A Barthes Reader*. Trans. Richard Howard. Ed. Susan Sontag. New York: Hill and Wang, 1982. Print.

———. *Mourning Diary*. New York: Hill and Wang, 2010. Print.

———. *Roland Barthes by Roland Barthes*. Trans. Richard Howard. Los Angeles: U of California P, 1977. Print.

———. "The Third Meaning." *Image, Music, Text*. Trans. Stephen Heath. New York: Hill and Wang, 1977. Print.

———. "Upon Leaving the Movie Theater." *The Rustle of Language*. New York: Farrar, Straus, and Giroux, 1986. Print.

Bastick, Tony. *Intuition: How We Think and Act*. New York: John Wiley, 1982. Print.

Bauer, Dale M. "The Other 'F' Word: The Feminist in the Classroom." *College English* 52 (1990): 385–96. Print.

Benkler, Yochai. *The Wealth of Networks*. New Haven: Yale UP, 2007. Print.

Berlin, James. "Composition and Cultural Studies." *Composition and Resistance*. Ed. C. Mark Hurlbert and Michael Blitz. Portsmouth: Boynton, 1991. 47–55. Print.

———. "Poststructuralism, Cultural Studies, and the Composition Classroom." *Rhetoric Review* 11 (Fall 1992): 16–33. Rpt. in *Professing the New Rhetoric*. Ed. Theresa Enos and Stuart C. Brown. Englewood Cliffs: Prentice Hall, 1994. 461–80. Print.

———. "Rhetoric and Ideology in the Writing Class." *College English* 50 (1988): 477–94. Print.

———. *Rhetoric and Reality*. Urbana: NCTE, 1996. Print.

———. *Rhetorics, Poetics, and Cultures: Refiguring College English Studies*. Urbana: NCTE, 1996. Print.

———. *Writing Instruction in 19th Century American Schools*. Urbana: NCTE, 1983. Print.

Berthoff, Anne. "Is Teaching Still Possible? Writing, Meaning, and Higher Order Reasoning." *College English* 48.6 (1984): 743–55. Print.

Bingham, Art. "Review of Walter J. Ong's *Orality and Literacy*. Northern Illinois University Writing across the Curriculum website. 6 May 2011.

Bizzell, Patricia. "A Response to 'Fish Tales: A Conversation with the Contemporary Sophist.'" *Philosophy, Rhetoric, Literary Criticism: (Inter)views*. Ed. Gary Olson. Carbondale: Southern Illinois UP, 1994. 68–71. Print.

Blakesley, David. Rev. of *Remediation: Understanding New Media*, by J. David Bolter and Richard Grusin. *Kairos* 6.1 (Spring 2001): n. pag. Web.

Bolter, Jay David. *Writing Space: Computers, Hypertext, and the Remediation of Print*. Cambridge: MIT Press, 1991.

Boyle, Casey. Rev. of *Lingua Fracta: Toward a Rhetoric of New Media*, by Collin Gifford Brooke. *Kairos* 15.1. (Fall 2010): n. pag. Web.

Boym, Svetlana. *The Future of Nostalgia*. New York: Basic Books, 2001.

Brandt, Deborah, et al. "The Politics of the Personal: Storying Our Lives against the Grain." *College English* 64.1 (Sept. 2001): 41–62. Print.

Breuch, Lee-Ann M. Kastman. "Post-Process 'Pedagogy': A Philosophical Exercise." *JAC* 22.1 (2002): 119–50. Print.

Brooke, Collin Gifford. "Forgetting to Be (Post) Human: Media and Memory in a Kairotic Age." *JAC* 20.4 (Summer 2000): 773–95. Print.

———. *Lingua Fracta: Toward a Rhetoric of New Media.* Catskill: Hampton, 2009. Print.

Brooke, Collin, and Thomas Rickert. "Being Delicious: Materialities of Research in a Web 2.0 Application." Dobrin, Rice, and Vastola 163–82.

Brooks, Kevin. "Exploring MEmorials 2." Web. 17 Feb. 2011.

———. "Lecture 1: Ulmer in Context." *Career-Compass Wikispace.* Web. 27 June 2011.

Brooks, Kevin, and Aaron Anfinson. "Exploring Post-Critical Composition: MEmorials for Afghanistan and the Lost Boys." *Computers and Composition* 26.2 (June 2009): 78–91. Print.

Brown, Jim. "Clinamen Home." 18 May 2009. Weblog. 2 Feb. 2011.

Brown, Lisa J. "Mi Papa Es Su Papa: MEMEorializing Ernest Hemingway." Vimeo, 19 May 2012. Web. 14 June. 2011.

Burgess, Jean, and Joshua Green. *YouTube: Online Video and Participatory Culture.* Malden: Polity, 2009. Print.

Burke, Kenneth. *Rhetoric, Poetics, and Philosophy.* Ed. Don M. Burks. West Lafayette: Purdue UP, 1978. Print.

Carter, Geoffrey V. "inter.Virtual.Vitalism.views." *Currents in Electronic Literacy* (2011). Web. 15 Feb. 2011.

Carter, Geoffrey V., and Sarah J. Arroyo. "Video and Participatory Cultures: Writing, Rhetoric, Performance, and the Tube." *Enculturation* 8 (2010). Web. 14 Oct. 2010.

Carter, Geoffrey V., and Cortney Smethurst. "Participatory Publics: From MEmorials to MEMEorials." YouTube, 15 May 2011. Web. 14 May 2012.

Carter, Michael. *Where Writing Begins: A Postmodern Reconstruction.* Carbondale: Southern Illinois UP, 2003. Print.

Chmielewski, Dawn. "Google in preliminary talks to buy online site Hulu." *Los Angeles Times,* 1 July 2011. Web. 13 July 2011.

Cisco Visual Networking Index (VNI) Forecast, 2009-2014. Cisco, 2 June 2010. Web. 2 June 2010.

Clark, J. Elizabeth. "The Digital Imperative: Making the Case for a 21st Century Pedagogy." *Computers and Composition* 27.1 (2010): 27–35. Print.

Clifford, John. "The Subject of Discourse." Harkin and Schilb 38–51.

Clifford, John, and Elizabeth Ervin. "The Ethics of Process." Kent 179–97.

Clifford, John, and John Schilb, eds. *Writing Theory and Critical Theory.* New York: MLA, 1994. Print.

Collins, Vicki Tolar. "The Speaker Respoken: Material Rhetoric as Feminist Methodology." *College English* 61.5 (May 1999): 545–73. Print.

Conley, Thomas M. *Rhetoric in the European Tradition.* New York: Longman, 1990. Print.

Connerton, Paul. *How Societies Remember.* New York: Cambridge UP, 1989. Print.

CopperCab. "ATTENTION HATERS!!" YouTube, 19 Jan. 2010. Web. 14 Feb. 2011.

———. "I'D NEVER DO THAT!!" YouTube, 3 Mar. 2010. Web. 17 Feb. 2011.

———. "I DON'T CARE!!" YouTube, 26 Jan. 2010. Web. 17 Feb. 2011.

———. "STOP THE BULLYING!! MY HAPPY VALENTINE'S DAY!! YouTube, 14 Feb. 2011. Web. 17 Feb.2011.

Crary, Jonathan. "Eclipse of the Spectacle." *Art after Modernism.* Ed. Brian Wallis. Boston: Godine, 1984. Print.

Crouse, Jeff. Personal email to Geof Carter and Sarah Arroyo. 22 Aug. 2010.

———. *You3b*. 21 February 2011. Web.

Crowley, Sharon. *Composition in the University: Crisis and Change*. Pittsburgh: U of Pittsburgh P, 1998. Print.

———. *The Methodical Memory: Invention in Current Traditional Rhetoric*. Carbondale: Southern Illinois UP, 1990. Print.

———. "The Perilous Life and Times of Freshman English." *Freshman English News* 14.3 (1986): 11–16. Print.

———. "Reimagining the Writing Scene: Curmudgeonly Remarks about *Contending with Words*." Harkin and Schilb 189–97.

Crowley, Sharon, and Debra Hawhee. *Ancient Rhetorics for Contemporary Students*. New York: Macmillan 1996. Print.

Curry, Judson B. "A Return to 'Converting the Natives'; or, Antifoundationalist Faith in the Composition Class." *Rhetoric Review* 12.1 (1993): 160–67. Print.

Dalton, David W., and Michael J. Hannafin. "The Effects of Word Processing on Written Composition." *Journal of Educational Research* 80.6 (1987): 338–42. Print.

Danielewicz, Jane. "Personal Genres, Public Voices." *College Composition and Communication* 59.3 (2008): 420–50. Print.

Daniell, Beth. "Theory, Theory Talk, and Composition." Clifford and Schilb 127–40.

Davidson, Donald. "A Nice Derangement of Epitaphs." *Truth and Interpretation: Perspectives on the Philosophy of Donald Davidson*. Ed. Ernest Le Pore. New York: Blackwell, 1986. 433–46. Print.

Davis, D. Diane. *Breaking Up [at] Totality: A Rhetoric of Laughter*. Carbondale: Southern Illinois UP, 2000. Print.

———. "Finitude's Clamor: or, Notes toward a Communitarian Literacy." *College Composition and Communication* 53.1 (2001): 119–45. Print.

Davis, Mike. *City of Quartz: Excavating the Future in Los Angeles*. London: Verso Books, 2006.

De Certeau, Michel. *The Practice of Everyday Life*. Trans. Steven F. Rendell. Berkeley: U of California P, 1984. Print.

Deleuze, Gilles. *Empiricism and Subjectivity: An Essay on Hume's Theory of Human Nature*. Trans. Constantin V. Boundas. New York: Columbia UP, 1989. Print.

———. *The Fold: Leibniz and the Baroque*. Trans. Tom Conley. Minneapolis: U of Minnesota P, 1993. Print.

———. *Pure Immanence: Essays on a Life*. Trans. Anne Boyman. New York: Zone Books, 2001. Print.

Deleuze, Gilles, and Félix Guattari. *Anti-Oedipus: Capitalism and Schizophrenia*. Trans. Robert Hurley, Mark Seem, and Helen R. Lane. Minneapolis: U of Minnesota P, 1983. Print.

———. *A Thousand Plateaus: Capitalism and Schizophrenia*. Trans. Brian Massumi. Minneapolis: U of Minnesota P, 1987. Print.

———. *What Is Philosophy?* Trans. Hugh Tomlinson and Graham Burchell. New York: Columbia UP, 1994. Print.

Deleuze, Gilles, and Claire Parnet. *Dialogues*. Trans. Hugh Tomlinson and Barbara Habberjam. New York: Columbia UP, 1987. Print.

The Deleuze Dictionary. Ed. Adrian Parr. Rev. ed. Edinburgh: Edinburgh UP, 2010. Print.

Derrida, Jacques. "*Geschlecht*: Sexual Difference, Ontological Difference." Trans. Ruben Berezdivin. *Research and Phenomenology* 13 (1983): 65–83. Print.

———. *Of Grammatology*. trans. Gayatri Spivak. Baltimore: Johns Hopkins UP, 1976.

———. *Of Spirit: Heidegger and the Question*. Trans. Geoffrey Bennington and Rachel Bowlby. Chicago: U of Chicago P, 1987. Print.

———. *Specters of Marx: The State of the Debt, the Work of Mourning, and the New International*. Trans. Peggy Kamuf. New York: Routledge, 1994. Print.

Dickson, Alan Chidsey, et al. "Interchanges: Responses to Richard Fulkerson, *Composition at the Turn of the Twenty-First Century*." *College Composition and Communication* 57.4 (2006): 730–62. Print.

Dobrin, Sidney I. "Paralogic Hermeneutic Theories, Power, and the Possibility for Liberating Pedagogies." Kent 132–48.

———. *Postcomposition*. Carbondale: Southern Illinois UP, 2011.

Dobrin, Sidney I., J. A. Rice, and Michael Vastola, eds. *Beyond Postprocess*. Logan: Utah State UP, 2011. Print.

Donahue, Patricia. Rev. of *Writing/Teaching: Essays toward a Rhetoric of Pedagogy*, by Paul Kameen. *JAC* 21.1 (2001): 231–35. Print.

Downs, Douglas, and Elizabeth Wardle. "Teaching about Writing, Righting Misconceptions: (Re) Envisioning 'First Year Composition' as 'Introduction to Writing Studies.'" *College Composition and Communication* 58.4 (2007): 552–84. Print.

Dubisar, Abby M., and Jason Palmeri. "Palin/Pathos/Peter Griffin: Political Video Remix and Composition Pedagogy. *Computers and Composition* 27.2 (2010): 77–93. Print.

Durst, Russell. "Interchanges: Commenting on William Thelin's 'Understanding Problems in Critical Classrooms'; Can We Be Critical of Critical Pedagogy?" *College Composition and Communication* 58.1 (2006): 110–14. Print.

"Ecology." *Oxford English Dictionary*. Nov. 2010. Oxford UP. Web.

Edutopia. "Big Thinkers: Henry Jenkins on New Media and Implications for Learning." YouTube, 19 Feb. 2010. Web. 8 June 2010.

Egsvideo. "Victor Vitanza. Lyotard: Hesitating Thought 2010 11/19." YouTube, 12 Nov. 2010. Web. 15 Feb. 2011.

Elbow, Peter. *Embracing Contraries: Explorations in Learning and Teaching*. New York: Oxford UP, 1986. Print.

Emerson, Ralph Waldo. "On Education." *A World of Ideas: Essential Readings for College Students*. Ed. Lee A. Jacobus. Boston: Bedford/St. Martins, 2006. 247–59. Print.

Faigley, Lester. "Competing Theories of Process: A Critique and a Proposal." *College English* 48.6 (1986): 527–42. Print.

———. *Fragments of Rationality: Postmodernity and the Subject of Composition*. Pittsburgh: U of Pittsburgh P, 1992. Print.

Felman, Shoshana. "Psychoanalysis and Education: Teaching Terminable and Interminable." *Yale French Studies* 63 (1982): 21–44. Print.

Fiore, Kyle, and Nan Elasser. "'Strangers No More': A Liberatory Literacy Program." *College English* 44 (1982): 115–28. Print. Rpt. in *Perspectives on Literacy*. Ed. Eugene Kintgen, Barry Kroll, and Mike Rose. Carbondale: Southern Illinois UP, 1988. 286–99. Print.

Fish, Stanley. "Anti-Foundationalism, Theory Hope, and the Teaching of Composition" and "Interview with Stanley Fish." *Current in Criticism*. Ed. Clayton Koelb and Vergil Lokke. West Lafayette: Purdue UP, 1987. 65–98. Print.

———. "Consequences." *Against Theory*. Ed. W. J. T. Mitchell. Chicago: U of Chicago P, 1985. 106–31. Print.

Fleckenstein, Kristie. "CFP: The Believing Game." WPA-L Listserv. 15 Sept. 2008. Web.

Flower, Linda. "Literate Action." *Composition in the Twenty-First Century: Crisis and Change.* Ed. Lynn Bloom, Donald Daiker, and Edward White. Carbondale: Southern Illinois UP, 1996. 249–60. Print.

Flynn, Elizabeth. "Writing as Resistance." *JAC* 16.1 (1996): 171–76. Print.

Foster, David. "The Challenge of Contingency: Process and the Turn to the Social in Composition." Kent 149–62.

Foster, Helen. *Networked Process: Dissolving Boundaries of Process and Post-Process.* Lafayette: Parlor, 2007. Print.

Foucault, Michel. Preface. *Anti-Oedipus: Capitalism and Schizophrenia,* by Gilles Deleuze and Felix Guattari. Minneapolis: University of Minnesota Press, 1983. xi–xiv. Print.

Freeman, John Craig. "Imaging Place: The Choragraphic Method." *Rhizomes* 18 (2009). Web.

Freire, Paulo. *Pedagogy of the Oppressed.* Trans. Myra Bergman Ramos. New York: Continuum, 1990. Print.

Friedman, Emily. "Florida Teen Live-Streams His Suicide Online." *ABC News.* 21 Nov. 2008. Web. 18 Feb. 2011.

Fulkerson, Richard. "Composition at the Turn of the Twenty-First Century." *College Composition and Communication* 56.4 (2005): 654–87. Print.

———. "Four Philosophies of Composition." *College Composition and Communication* 30 (Dec. 1979): 343–48. Print.

Gale, Fredric. "Don't Know Much about Automobiles: Fish's Anti-Theory Theory." *JAC* 13.1 (1993): 7–8. Print.

Gere, Anne Ruggles. "Revealing Silence: Rethinking Personal Writing." *College Composition and Communication* 53.2 (2001): 203–23. Print.

Giroux, Henry. "Private Satisfactions and Public Disorders: *Fight Club,* Patriarchy, and the Politics of Masculine Violence." *JAC* 21.1 (2001): 1–31. Print.

———. "What Is Critical Pedagogy?" *Rage and Hope.* 22 Nov. 1999. Web.

Gopnik, Adam. "The Information: How the Internet Gets inside Us." *New Yorker* 11 Feb. 2011. Web.

Greenbaum, Andrea, ed. *Insurrections: Approaches to Resistance in Composition Studies.* New York: State U of New York P, 2000. Print.

Gruber, Howard E. "Darwin's 'Tree of Nature' and Other Images of Wide Scope." *On Aesthetics in Science.* Ed Judith Wechsler. Cambridge: MIT P, 1978. 121–40.

Guattari, Félix. *Chaosmosis: An Ethico-Political Paradigm.* Trans. by Paul Bains and Julian Pefanis. Indianapolis: Indiana UP, 1995. Print.

Gye, Lisa. "Halflives, a Mystory: Writing Hypertext to Learn." *Fibreculture Journal* 2 (2003). Web.

Gye, Lisa, and Darren Tofts. eds. "Illogic of Sense: The Gregory L. Ulmer Remix." Alt-X Press. 2007. Web.

Hairston, Maxine. "Diversity, Ideology, and Teaching Writing." *College Composition and Communication* 43 (1992): 179–93. Print.

Halbritter, Bump, and Todd Taylor. "Remembering Composition (the Book): A DVD Production." *JAC* 26.3–4 (2006): 389–96. Print.

Hancock, John D., dir. *Bang the Drum Slowly.* 1973. Film.

Haraway, Donna. "Writing, Literacy, and Technology: Toward a Cyborg Writing." Interview with Gary A. Olson. *Women Writing Culture.* Ed. Gary A. Olson and Elizabeth Hirsh. Albany: State U of New York P, 1999. 45–77. Print.

Hardin, Joe Marshall. "Putting Process into Circulation: Textual Cosmopolitanism." Dobrin, Rice, and Vastola 61–74.

Harkin, Patricia. "The Postdisciplinary Politics of Lore." Harkin and Schilb 124–38.

Harkin, Patricia, and John Schilb, eds. *Contending with Words: Composition and Rhetoric in a Postmodern Age.* New York: MLA, 1991. Print.

Haroian-Guerin, Gil, ed. *The Personal Narrative: Writing Ourselves as Teachers and Scholars.* Portland: Calendar Islands, 1999. Print.

Harris, Joseph. "The Rhetoric of Theory." Clifford and Schilb 141–47.

Havelock, Eric. *The Muse Learns to Write: Reflections of Orality and Literacy from Antiquity to the Present.* New Haven: Yale UP, 1986. Print.

Hawisher, Gail. "Studies in Word Processing." *Computers and Composition* 4 (1986): 6–31. Print.

Hawisher, Gail, and Cynthia Selfe, eds. *Passions, Pedagogies, and 21st Century Technologies.* Logan: Utah State UP, 1999. Print.

Hawk, Byron. "Bystory: 'An Unrelated Story That's Time Consuming.'" George Mason University, 2003. Web. 25 Jan. 2011.

———. *A Counter-History of Composition: Toward Methodologies of Complexity.* Pittsburgh: U of Pittsburgh P, 2007. Print.

———. "Hyperrhetoric and the Inventive Spectator: Remotivating *The Fifth Element.*" *The Terministic Screen: Rhetorical Perspectives on Film.* Ed. David Blakesley. Carbondale: Southern Illinois UP, 2003. 70–91. Print.

———. "Reassembling Postprocess: Toward a Posthuman Theory of Public Rhetoric." Dobrin, Rice, and Vastola 75–93. Print.

Hawk, Byron, David M. Reider, and Ollie Oviedo, eds. *Small Tech: The Culture of Digital Tools.* Minneapolis: U of Minnesota P, 2008. Print.

Hawkins, Joan. "When Bad Girls Do French Theory: Deconstructing National Trauma in the Shadow of 9/11." *CTHEORY: Theory, Technology, and Culture* 24.3 (2001). Web.

Haynes, Cynthia. "Postconflict Pedagogy: Writing in the Stream of Hearing." Dobrin, Rice, and Vastola 145–62.

———. "prosthetic_rhetoric@writing.loss.technology." *Literacy Theory in the Age of the Internet.* Ed. Todd Taylor and Irene Ward. New York: Columbia UP, 1998. 79–92. Print.

Haynes, Cynthia, and Jan Rune Holmevik. *High Wired: On the Design, Use, and Theory of Educational MOOs.* Ann Arbor: U of Michigan P, 2001. Print.

Heidegger, Martin. "Language." *The Norton Anthology of Theory and Criticism.* Ed. Vincent B. Leitch et al. New York: Norton, 2001. 1118–34. Print.

Heilker, Paul. "Twenty Years In: An Essay in Two Parts." *College Composition and Communication* 58.2 (2006): 182–212. Print.

Hesford, Wendy S. *Framing Identities: Autobiography and the Politics of Pedagogy.* Minneapolis: U of Minnesota P, 1999. Print.

Hillis Miller, J., and Manuel Asensi. *Black Holes: J. Hillis Miller; or, Boustrophedonic Reading.* Stanford: Stanford UP, 1999. Print.

Hotz, Robert Lee. "Read My Lips: I'm Learning Language." *Dallas Morning News* 9 Sept. 2002: C2. Print.

IshatOnU. "CopperCab (I Don't Care) Response." YouTube, 26 Jan. 2010. Web. 17 Feb. 2011.

Isseling, Samuel. *Rhetoric and Philosophy in Conflict: An Historical Survey*. The Hague: Martinus Nijhoff, 1976. Print.

Jacobs, Dale. "Marveling at the Man Called Nova: Comics as Sponsors of Multimodal Literacy." *College Composition and Communication* 59.2 (2007): 180–205. Print.

"Jacques Derrida." *Internet Encyclopedia of Philosophy*. 21 June 2011. Web.

jaimedelaguilayrei. "phoenix lisztomania brat pack mashup." YouTube, 26 July 2009. Web.

Jameson, Fredric. "Marxism and Dualism in Deleuze." *South Atlantic Quarterly* 96.3 (Summer 1997): 393–416. Print.

Jarrett, Michael. "Defining Heuretics." Michael Jarrett's Webpage. 25 Jan. 2003.

———. *Drifting on a Read: Jazz as a Model for Writing*. Albany: State U of New York P, 1999.

———. "On Hip Hop: A Rhapsody." *Illogic of Sense: The Gregory L. Ulmer Remix*. Ed. Darren Tofts and Lisa Gye. 7 May 2007. Electronic Book Review. Web. 2 May 2009.

———. "Toward Electracy: Heuretics in the Classroom." Michael Jarrett's Webpages. 25 Jan. 2011.

Jarratt, Susan. "Feminism and Composition: The Case for Conflict." Harkin and Schilb 105–23.

Jaschilk, Scott. "Academically Adrift." *Inside Higher Education*. 18 Jan. 2011. Web.

Jenkins, Henry. *Convergence Culture: Where Old and New Media Collide*. Cambridge: MIT Press, 2006. Print.

———. "If It Doesn't Spread, It's Dead (part one): Media Viruses and Memes." *Confessions of an Aca/Fan*. 11 Feb. 2009. Web.

———. "If It Doesn't Spread, It's Dead (part two): Sticky and Spreadable—Two Paradigms." *Confessions of an Aca/Fan*. 13 Feb. 2009. Web.

———. "Learning from YouTube: An Interview with Alex Juhasz, Part One." *Confessions of an Aca-Fan*. 20 Feb. 2008. Web.

———. "Learning from YouTube: An Interview with Alex Juhasz, Part Two." *Confessions of an Aca-Fan*. 22 Feb. 2008. Web.

Jenkins, Henry. With Katie Clinton, Ravi Purushotma, Alice J. Robison, and Margaret Weigel. *Confronting the Challenges of Participatory Culture: Media Education for the 21st Century*. Cambridge: MIT Press, 2009. Print.

jimmy. "Ching Chong! Asians in the Library Song (Response to UCLA's Alexandra Wallace)." YouTube 15 Mar. 2011. Web. 20 Apr. 2011.

John Craig Freeman. "Ulmer Tapes 4.04." YouTube 10 Sept. 2010. Web. 25 Oct. 2010.

Johnson, T. R. "School Sucks." *College Composition and Communication* 52.4 (June 2001): 620–50. Print.

Johnson-Eilola, Johndan. *Datacloud: Toward a New Theory of Online Work*. Cresskill: Hampton, 2005.

Jones, Donald C. "Beyond the Postmodern Impasse of Agency: The Resounding Relevance of John Dewey's Tacit Tradition." *JAC* 16 (1996): 81–102. Print.

JTOTokay. "RE: The Truth about the Community—LOL." YouTube, 11 Mar. 2010. Web. 16 Feb. 2011.

Juhasz, Alex. *Learning from YouTube*. Cambridge: MIT P, 2011. Web.

———. "MediaPraxis." Weblog.

———. "Why Not (to) Teach on YouTube." *Video Vortex Reader: Responses to You-Tube.* Ed. Geert Lovink and Sabine Niederer. Amsterdam: Institute of Network Cultures, 2008. 133–40. Web.

KalebNation. "RE: The Truth about the Community [AKA YouFraud]." YouTube, 10 Mar. 2010. Web. 11 Feb. 2011.

Kameen, Paul. "Rewording the Rhetoric of Composition." *Pre/Text* 1 (1980): 73–93. Print.

———. *Writing/Teaching: Essays toward a Rhetoric of Pedagogy.* Pittsburgh: U of Pittsburgh P, 2000. Print.

Kelly, Kevin. "Becoming Screen Literate." *New York Times Magazine* 21 Nov. 2008. Web. 12 Dec. 2010.

Kent, Thomas. *Paralogic Rhetoric: A Theory of Communicative Interaction.* London: Bucknell UP, 1993. Print.

———, ed. *Post-Process Theory: Beyond the Writing-Process Paradigm.* Carbondale: Southern Illinois UP, 1999. Print.

———. Preface: "Righting Writing." Dobrin, Rice, and Vastola xi–xxii.

———. "Principled Pedagogy: A Reply to Lee-Ann M. Kastman Breuch." *JAC* 22.2 (2002): 428–33. Print.

Khanacademy. "A Short Overview of the Khan Academy." YouTube, 14 Dec. 2009. Web. 10 June 2011.

Kill, Melanie. "Acknowledging the Rough Edges of Resistance: Negotiation of Identities for First-Year Composition." *College Composition and Communication* 58.2 (2006): 213–325. Print.

Kinneavy, James L. *A Theory of Discourse.* 1971. New York: Norton, 1980. Print.

Kipnis, Laura. *Ecstasy Unlimited: On Sex, Capital, Gender, and Aesthetics.* Minneapolis: U of Minnesota P, 1993. Print.

Kopelson, Karen. "Tripping over Tropes: Of 'Passing' and Postmodern Subjectivity—What's in a Metaphor?" *JAC* 25.3 (2005): 435–67. Print.

Kuhn, Virginia. "The YouTube Gaze: Permission to Create?" *Enculturation* 7 (2010). Web.

Kundera, Milan. *The Book of Laughter and Forgetting.* Trans. Aaron Asher. New York: Harper Perennial, 1996. Print.

———. *Immortality.* Trans. Peter Kussi. New York: Harper Collins, 1990. Print.

kyburz, bonnie lenore. "Status Update." *Enculturation* 8 (2010). Web.

Landow, George. *Hypertext 2.0: The Convergence of Contemporary Critical Theory and Technology.* Baltimore: Johns Hopkins UP, 1997.

———. *Hyper/Text/Theory.* Baltimore: Johns Hopkins UP, 1994.

Lange, Patricia. "Achieving Creative Integrity: Reciprocities and Tensions." *Enculturation* 8 (2010). Web.

———. "(Mis) Conceptions about YouTube." *Video Vortex Reader: Responses to You-Tube.* Ed. Geert Lovink and Sabine Niederer. Amsterdam: Institute of Network Cultures, 2008. 87–99. Web.

———. "Publicly Private and Privately Public: Social Networking on YouTube." *Journal of Computer-Mediated Communication* 13 (2008): 361–80. Print.

———. "Videos of Affinity on YouTube." *The YouTube Reader.* Ed. Pelle Snickars and Patrick Vonderau. Stockholm: National Library of Sweden, 2009. Print.

———. "The Vulnerable Video Blogger: Promoting Social Change through Intimacy." *Scholar and Feminist Online* 5.2 (2007): 1–5. *Barnard Center for Research on Women.* Web. 15 Feb. 2011.

————. "What Is Your Claim to Flame?" *First Monday* 11.5 (2006). Web. 17 Feb. 2011.

Lau, Anna. "(Why) Do Asian Americans Have a Target on Their Back?" *Psychology Today*. 16 Mar. 2011. Web.

Lauer, Janice. *Invention in Rhetoric and Composition*. Lafayette: Parlor, 2004. Print.

LeFevre, Karen Burke. *Invention as a Social Act*. Carbondale: Southern Illinois UP, 1987. Print.

Lessig, Lawrence. "Re-examining the Remix." YouTube. 1 June 2012. Web. 13 July 2011.

Lisztomania (phenomenon). (n.d.). *Wikipedia*. 17 June 2011. Web.

Lovett, Ian. "UCLA Student's Video Rant against Asians Fuels Firestorm." *New York Times* 15 Mar. 2011. Web.

Lunsford, Andrea. "Rhetoric, Feminism, and Textual Ownership." *College English* 61.5 (1999): 529–44. Print.

Lyotard, Jean-François. *The Differend: Phrases in Dispute (Theory and History of Literature)*. Trans. Georges Van Den Abbeele. Minneapolis: U Of Minnesota P, 1989. Print.

————. *The Inhuman: Reflections on Time*. Trans. Geoffrey Bennington and Rachel Bowlby. Stanford: Stanford UP, 1988. Print.

————. *Just Gaming*. Trans. Wald Godzich. Minneapolis: U of Minnesota P, 1979. Print.

————. *The Postmodern Condition: A Report on Knowledge*. Trans. Geoff Bennington and Brian Massumi. Minneapolis: U of Minnesota P, 1979. Print.

————. "Resisting a Discourse of Mastery: A Conversation with Jean-Francois Lyotard." Interview with Gary Olson. *JAC* 15 (1995): 391–410. Print.

Lyotard, Jean-François, and Jean-Lupe Thebald. *Just Gaming*. Trans. Wald Godzich. Minneapolis: U of Minnesota P, 1985. Print.

Manning, Erin. *Relationscapes: Movement, Art, and Philosophy*. Cambridge and London: MIT P, 2009. Print.

Marks, John. *Gilles Deleuze: Vitalism and Multiplicity*. London: Pluto, 1998. Print.

Mauer, Barry. "Lost Data, 2." *Rhizomes* 18 (2009). Web.

McComiskey, Bruce. "The Post-Process Movement in Composition Studies." *Reforming College Composition: Writing the Wrongs*. Ed. Ray Wallace, Alan Jackson, and Susan Lewis Wallace. London: Greenwood, 2000. 37–53. Print.

————. Rev. of *Literacy Matters: Writing and Reading and the Social Self*, by Robert P. Yagelski. *College Composition and Communication* 53.4 (June 2002): 751–54. Print.

McLuhan, Marshall. *Understanding Media: The Extensions of Man*. Cambridge: MIT P, 1994. Print.

Memmott, Talan. "Beyond Taxonomy: Digital Poetics and the Problem of Reading." *New Media Poetics: Contexts, Technotexts, and Theories*. Ed. Adalaide Morris and Thomas Swift. Cambridge: MIT P, 2006.

Meyers, Aaron. *YouCube*. Web. 1 Oct. 2010.

Milgram, Stanley. *Obedience to Authority: An Experimental View*. New York: Harper, 1975. Print.

Miles, Libby, Michael Pennell, Kim Hensley Owens, Jeremiah Dyehouse, Helen O'Grady, Nedra Reynolds, Robert Schwegler, and Linda Shamoon. "Interchanges: Commenting on Douglas Downs and Elizabeth Wardle's 'Teaching about Writing, Righting Misconceptions.'" *College Composition and Communication* 59.3 (2008): 503–11. Print.

Miller, Susan. "The Feminization of Composition." *The Politics of Writing Instruction: Postsecondary.* Ed. Richard Bullock and John Trimbur. Portsmouth: Boynton/Cook, 1991. 39–54. Print.

MissSarah537. "Haterz be hatin' on dis." YouTube, 25 Mar. 2010. Web. 9 Feb. 2011.

Moor, Peter J. "Flaming on YouTube." MS Thesis. U of Twente, Enschede, The Netherlands, 2008. Web.

Moore-Howard, Rebecca. "Sexuality, Textuality: The Cultural Work of Plagiarism." *College English* 62.4 (2000): 473–91. Print.

Moulthrop, Stuart. "Rhizome and Resistance: Hypertext and the Dream of a New Culture." *Hyper/Text/Theory.* Ed. George P. Landow. Baltimore: Johns Hopkins UP, 1994. 299–319. Print.

———. "You Say You Want a Revolution? Hypertext and the Laws of Media." *Postmodern Culture* 1.3 (1991). Web. 15 Feb. 2013.

Murray, Donald. "The Listening Eye: Reflections on the Writing Conference." *College English* 41.1 (1979): 13–18. Print.

Nancy, Jean-Luc. *The Inoperative Community.* Ed. Peter Connor. Trans. Peter Connor, Lisa Garbus, Michael Holland, and Simona Sawhney. Minneapolis: U of Minnesota P, 1991.

Neel, Jasper. *Aristotle's Voice: Rhetoric, Theory, and Writing in America.* Carbondale: Southern Illinois UP, 1994. Print.

O'Gorman, Marcel. "From Mystorian to Curmudgeon: Stalking toward Finitude." *Illogic of Sense: The Gregory Ulmer Remix.* Ed. Darren Tofts and Lisa Gye. Boulder: Alt X, 2007. Web.

Olague, Mark R. "Transformational Grammars: Virtual Exiles and MyStory." Web. 5 Dec. 2010.

———. Personal website. 11 Nov 2012.

Olson, Gary. "The Death of Composition as an Intellectual Discipline." *Composition Studies* 28.2 (Fall 2000): 33–41. Print.

———. "Fish Tales: A Conversation with 'The Contemporary Sophist.'" *JAC* 12.2 (1992). Web.

———. "Toward a Post-Process Composition: Abandoning the Rhetoric of Assertion." *Dialogue on Writing: Rethinking ESL, Basic Writing, and First-Year Composition.* Mahwah: Erlbaum, 2002. Print.

———. "Why Distrust the Very Goals with Which You Began?" *JAC* 22.2 (Spring 2002): 423–28. Print.

Omizo, Ryan. "Vulnerable Video: A New Vernacular." *Enculturation* 8 (2010). Web.

Ong, Walter. *Orality and Literacy: The Technologizing of the Word.* New York: Routledge, 1982. Print.

Polyani, Michael. *Personal Knowledge: Toward a Post-Critical Philosophy.* New York: Harper & Row, 1964. Print.

Porter, James. "Recovering Delivery for Digital Rhetoric." *Computers and Composition* 26.4 (2009): 207–24. Print.

Porter, Kevin J. "Literature Reviews Re-Viewed: Toward a Consequentialist Account of Surveys, Surveyors, and the Surveyed." *JAC* 23.2 (2003): 351–77. Print.

———. "A Pedagogy of Charity: Donald Davidson and the Student-Negotiated Composition Classroom." *College Composition and Communication* 52.4 (June 2001): 574–611. Print.

Prelinger, Rick. "The Appearance of Archives." *The YouTube Reader*. Ed. Pelle Snickars and Patrick Vonderau. Stockholm: National Library of Sweden, 2009. 268–74. Print.

Pullman, George. "Stepping Yet Again into the Same Current." Kent 16–29.

Rajchman, John. *The Deleuze Connections*. Cambridge: MIT P, 2000. Print.

Rassmussen, Terry. "Antifoundationalism: Can Believers Teach?" *Rhetoric Review* 13.1 (1994): 150–63. Print.

Reid, Alexander. "Exposing Assemblages: Unlikely Communities of Digital Scholarship, Video, and Social Networks." *Enculturation* 8 (2010). Web.

———. *The Two Virtuals: New Media and Composition*. Lafayette: Parlor, 2007. Print.

Rice, Jeff. "1963: Collage as Writing Practice." *Composition Forum* 12.1 (2001): 19–39. Print.

———. "The 1963 Hip-Hop Machine: Hip-Hop Pedagogy as Composition." *College Composition and Communication* 54.3 (2003): 453–71. Print.

———. Rev. of *Race in Cyberspace*. By Beth Kolko, Lisa Nakamura, and Gilbert Rodman. *Kairos* 6.1 (Spring 2001). Web.

———. *The Rhetoric of Cool: Composition Studies and New Media*. Carbondale: Southern Illinois UP, 2007. Print.

Rice, Jeff, and Marcel O'Gorman, eds. *New Media/New Methods: The Academic Turn from Literacy to Electracy*. West Lafayette: Parlor, 2008. Print.

Rickert, Thomas. *Acts of Enjoyment: Rhetoric, Zizek, and the Return of the Subject*. Pittsburgh: U of Pittsburgh P, 2007. Print.

———. "Enjoying Theory: Zizek, Critique, Accountability." *JAC* 22.3 (Summer 2002): 627–40. Print.

———. "'Hands Up, You're Free': Composition in a Post-Oedipal World." *JAC* 21.2 (Spring 2001): 287–320. Print.

———. "Toward the Chora: Kristeva, Derrida, and Ulmer on Emplaced Invention." *Philosophy and Rhetoric* 40.3 (2007): 251–73. Print.

Ritchie, Joy, and Kathleen Boardman. "Feminism in Composition: Inclusion, Metonymy, and Disruption." *College Composition and Communication* 50.4 (1999): 585–606. Print.

Ronell, Avital. *Stupidity*. Urbana: U of Illinois P, 2002. Print.

Rosen, Jeffrey. "The Web Means the End of Forgetting." *New York Times Magazine* 21 July 2010. Web.

Roudinesco, Elisabeth. *Jaques Lacan & Co.: A History of Psychoanalysis in France, 1925–1985*. Trans. Jeffrey Mehlman. Chicago: U of Chicago P, 1990. Print.

Sahay, Amrohini. "Cybermaterialism and the Invention of the Cybercultural Everyday." *New Literary History* 28.3 (1997): 543–67. Print.

———. ". . . is the riddle of history." *New Literary History* 28.3 (1997): 595–99. Print.

Sanchez, Julian. "The Evolution of Remix Culture." YouTube, 5 Feb. 2010. Web.

Saper, Craig. *Artificial Mythologies: A Guide to Cultural Invention*. Minneapolis: U of Minnesota P, 1997. Print.

———. "The Felt Memory of *YouTube*." *Enculturation* 8 (Sept. 2010). Web.

Schilb, John. "Pedagogy of the Oppressors?" *Gendered Subjects: The Dynamics of Feminist Teaching*. Ed. Margo Cully and Catherine Portuges. Boston: Routledge, 1985. Print.

———. "Reprocessing the Essay." Kent 198–214.

Schramm, J. D. "Break the Silence for Suicide Survivors." TEDActive 2011. TED Conferences, LLC. Web. 1 May 2012.

Seitz, David. "Review: Hard Lessons Learned since the First Generation of Critical Pedagogy." Review of *Teaching Composition as a Social Process*, by Bruce McComiskey; *Mutuality in the Rhetoric and Composition Classroom*, by David Wallace and Helen Rothschild Ewald; *Collision Course: Conflict, Negotiation, and Learning in College Composition*, by Russel K. Durst. *College English* 64.4 (2002): 503–12. Print.

Shirky, Clay. *Cognitive Surplus: Creativity and Generosity in a Connected Age*. New York: Penguin Press, 2010.

Shor, Ira. *Critical Teaching and Everyday Life*. Boston: South End, 1980. Print.

Sidler, Michelle. "Rhetorical Economy and Public Participation: The Challenges of Webbed Technologies in Composition." *Composition Forum* 12.1 (2001): 1–18. Print.

Sidler, Michelle, and Richard Morris. "Writing in a Post-Berlinian Landscape: Cultural Composition in the Classroom." *JAC* 18.2 (1998): 275–91. Print.

Sirc, Geoffery. "The Difficult Politics of the Popular." *JAC* 21.2 (2001): 421–33. Print.

———. *English Composition as a Happening*. Logan: U of Utah P, 2002. Print.

———. "Review: The Schoolmaster in the Bookshelf." Review of *Kitchen Cooks, Plate Twirlers & Troubadours: Writing Program Administrators Tell Their Stories*, ed. Diana George; *The Personal Narrative: Writing Ourselves as Teachers and Scholars*, ed. Gil Haroian-Guerin; *Framing Identities: Autobiography and the Politics of Pedagogy*, by Wendy S. Hesford; *Living Rhetoric and Composition: Stories of the Discipline*, ed. Duane H. Roen, Stuart C. Brown, and Theresa Enos; and *Coming to Class: Pedagogy and the Social Class of Teachers*, ed. Alan Shepard, John McMillan, and Gary Tate. *College English* 63.4 (2001): 517–29. Print.

Skinnell, Ryan. "Circuitry in Motion: Rhetoric(al) Moves in YouTube's Archive." *Enculturation* 8 (2010). Web.

Sloterdijk, Peter. *Critique of Cynical Reason*. Trans. Michael Eldred. Minneapolis: U of Minnesota P, 1987. Print.

Smit, David W. "Hall of Mirrors: Antifoundationalist Theory and the Teaching of Writing." *JAC* 15.1 (1995): 35–52. Print.

Snickars, Pelle. "The Archival Cloud." *The YouTube Reader*. Ed. Snickars and Patrick Vonderau. Stockholm: National Library of Sweden, 2009. 292–313. Print.

Soja, Edward. *Postmodern Geographies: The Reassertion of Space in Critical Social Theory*. New York: Verso, 1989. Print.

Sosnoski, James. "Postmodern Teachers in Their Postmodern Classrooms: Socrates Begone!" Harkin and Schilb 198–219.

Spellmeyer, Kurt. "Culture and Agency." *College Composition and Communication* 48.2 (1997): 292–96. Print.

"Statistics." YouTube, n.d. Web. 10 Feb. 2013.

Stivale, Charles J., ed. "Gilles Deleuze's ABC Primer, with Claire Parnet." Directed by Pierre Andre Boutang, 1996. Web.

"Storytelling." Center for Storytelling. Vimeo, 2010. Parts 2 and 4. Web.

Strenski, Ellen. "Fa[c]ulty Wiring? Energy, Power, Work, and Resistance." *Insurrections: Approaches to Resistance in Composition Studies*. Ed. Andrea Greenbaum. Albany: State U of New York P, 2001. 89–117. Print.

Strangelove, Michael. *Watching YouTube: Extraordinary Videos by Ordinary People.* Toronto: U of Toronto P, 2010.

Stubblefield, Thomas. "Dissembling the Cinema: The Poster, the Film, and In-Between." *Thresholds* 34. Web. 5 November 2010.

"Student Quits at UCLA over Rant." *New York Times* 19 Mar. 2011. Web.

Sumerfield, Judith. "Is There a Life in This Text? Reimagining Narrative." Clifford and Schilb 179–94.

Thelin, William. "Interchanges: Commenting on William Thelin's 'Understanding Problems in Critical Classrooms' A Response." *College Composition and Communication* 58.1 (2006): 114–18. Print.

———. "Understanding Problems in Critical Classrooms." *College Composition and Communication* 57 (2005): 114–41. Print.

thepinkbismuth. "phoenix—lisztomania *brooklyn brat pack mashup*." YouTube, 31 May 2009. Web.

TheWillofDC. "The Death of the YouTube Community." YouTube. 9 Mar. 2010. Web. 16 Feb. 2011.

———. "YouTube News: Selling Your Channel?" YouTube. 17 Jan. 2011. Web. 15 Feb. 2011.

TheWorldmonitortv. "Alexandra Wallace UCLA Student Racist Rant on Asians in the Library for Phoning Tsunami Victims." YouTube 15 Mar. 2011. Web. 28 June 2011.

Thomas, Harin Karum. "The Pedagogy of Whatever." *Computers and Composition* 20.1 (2003): 23–50. Print.

Thompson, Clive. "Clive Thompson on How Twitter Creates a Social Sixth Sense." *Wired* 15.07 (2007). Web. 15 July 2007.

Tobin, Lad, and Thomas Newkirk, eds. *Taking Stock: The Writing Process Movement in the '90s.* Portsmouth: Boynton/Cook, 1994. Print.

Tofts, Darren, and Lisa Gye. Introduction. *Illogic of Sense: The Gregory Ulmer Remix.* Ed. Tofts and Gye. Boulder: Alt X, 2007. Web.

ToshBabyBoo. "TO: All of My Friend on My Friends List on Stickcam. (Ms. New Booty) Ms Magoo." YouTube 26 Mar. 2009. Web. 18 Feb. 2011.

Trimbur, John. "Composition Studies: Postmodern or Popular." *Into the Field: Sites of Composition Studies.* Ed. Anne Ruggles Gere. New York: MLA, 1993. 115–32. Print.

———. "Cultural Studies and Teaching Writing." *Focuses* 1.2 (1988): 5–18. Print.

———. "The Politics of Radical Pedagogy: A Plea for 'A Dose of Vulgar Marxism.'" *College English* 56 (1994): 194–206. Print.

"UCLA Chancellor Appalled by Student Video." YouTube 14 Mar. 2011. Web. 20 Mar. 2011.

Ulmer, Gregory. *Applied Grammatology.* Baltimore: Johns Hopkins UP, 1985. Print.

———. "Barthes's Body of Knowledge." *Studies in 20th Century Literature* 5.2 (1981): 219–35. Print.

———. "The Chora Collaborations." *Rhizomes* 18 (Winter 2008). Web.

———. "Electracy: Writing to Avatar." *Computer Writing and Research Lab.* Austin: U of Texas Dept. of Rhetoric and Writing, Oct. 2008. Web.

———. "Electracy and Pedagogy." Companion website to *Internet Invention.* Pearson Higher Education. October 2003. Web. 5 April 2004.

———. *Electronic Monuments (Electronic Mediations)*. Minneapolis: U of Minnesota P, 2005. Print.

———. "Foreword/Forward (into Electracy)." *Literacy Theory in the Age of the Internet.* Ed. Todd Taylor and Irene Ward. New York: Columbia UP, 1998. iv–xii. Print.

———. "Heuretics: Inventing Electracy." WordPress.com. Web. 9 June 2009.

———. *Heuretics: The Logic of Invention.* Baltimore: Johns Hopkins UP, 1994. Print.

———. *Internet Invention: From Literacy to Electracy.* New York: Longman, 2003. Print.

———. Introduction. "Electracy." *Networked: A (Networked_Book) about (Networked Art)* by Authors and Collaborators of the Networked Book Project. 1 July 2009. Web. 5 May 2009.

———. "I Untied the Camera of Tastes (Who Am I?): The Riddle of Chool (A Reply and Alternative to A. Sahay)." *New Literary History* 28.3 (1997): 569–94. Print.

———. "Metaphoric Rocks: A Psychogeography of Tourism and Monumentality." *The Florida Landscape: Revisited*, 1992. Web. 25 June 2009.

———. "The Mr. Mentality Show." YouTube 3 Sept. 2009. Web. YouTube 28 June 2011.

———. "A Night at the Text: Roland Barthes's Marx Brothers." *Yale French Studies* 73 (1987): 38–57. Print.

———. "The Object of Post-Criticism." *The Anti-Aesthetic: Essays on Postmodern Culture.* Ed. Hal Foster. Post Townsend: Bay, 1983. 83–108. Print.

———. "RE: Question about Videocy in *Teletheory*." *Facebook* message correspondence with Sarah Johnson Arroyo. 7 June 2011. Web.

———. "A Response to *Twelve Blue*, by Michael Joyce." *Postmodern Culture* 8.1 (1997). Web.

———. "The Spirit Hand: On the Index of Pedagogy and Propaganda." *Theory/Pedagogy/Politics: Texts for Change.* Ed. Donald Morton and Mas'ud Zavarzadeh. Urbana: U of Illinois P, 1991. 136–51. Print.

———. *Teletheory: Grammatology in the Age of Video.* New York: Routledge, 1989. Print.

———. "Textshop for an Experimental Humanities." *Reorientations: Critical Theories and Pedagogies.* Ed. Bruce Henricksen and Thais E. Morgan. Urbana: U of Illinois P, 1990. 113–32. Print.

———. "Toward Electracy: A Conversation with Gregory Ulmer." *Beehive* 3.4 (2000). Web.

———. "What Is Electracy?" from Gregory Ulmer's website on the University of Florida Server [no longer available]. Web. Last accessed March 2005.

———. "The X Tables: Dialogues with the Prosthetic Unconscious." *Electronic Art in Universities.* 12 Aug. 1994. Web. 2 Feb. 2003.

Ulmer, Gregory, and Joseph Tabbi. "A Project for a New Consultancy." *Electronic Book Review*, 1996. Web.

vinimzoTube. "phoenix—Lisztomania Curitiba Brat Pack Mashup."YouTube, 16 Nov. 2010. Web.

Vitanza, Victor. "Abandoned to Writing: Notes toward Several Provocations." *Enculturation* 5.1 (2003): n. pag. Web.

———. "From Heuristics to Aleatory Procedures; or, Toward 'Writing the Accident.'" *Inventing a Discipline.* Ed. Maureen Daly Goggin. Urbana: NCTE, 2000. 185–206. Print.

———. "The Hermeneutics of Abandonment." *Parallax* 4.4 (1998): 123–39. Print.

———. *Negation, Subjectivity, and the History of Rhetoric*. Albany: State U of New York P, 1997. Print.

———. "An Open Letter to my 'Colligs': On Paraethics, Pararhetorics, and the Hysterical Turn." *PRE/TEXT* 11.3–4 (1990): 238–87. Print.

———. "The Shaping Force of Electronic Texts and Journals on Our Professional Work." *Writing Instructor* Beta 1.0. (June 2001). Web.

———. "Taking A-Count of a (Future-Anterior) History of Rhetoric as 'Libidinalized Marxism' (A PM Pastiche)." *Writing Histories of Rhetoric*. Ed. Victor Vitanza. Carbondale: Southern Illinois UP, 1994. 180–216. Print.

———. "Three Countertheses: or, A Critical In(ter)vention into Composition Theories and Pedagogies." Harkin and Schilb 139–72.

Walter, E. V. *Placeways: A Theory of the Human Environment*. Chapel Hill: U of North Carolina P, 1988. Print.

Ward, Irene. Rev. of *Paralogic Rhetoric: A Theory of Communicative Interaction*, by Thomas Kent. *JAC* 15.1 (1995). Web.

Weinberger, Dave. "The Virtual Revolution: How 20 Years of the Web Has Shaped Our Lives." *BBC*. Nov. 2009. Web. 15 Dec. 2010.

Westbrook, Steve. "Visual Rhetoric in a Culture of Fear: Impediments to Multimedia Production." *College English* 68.5 (2006): 457–81. Print.

White, Eric. *Kaironomia: On the Will-to-Invent*. Ithaca: Cornell UP, 1986. Print.

Wiseman, Mary Bittner. *The Ecstacies of Roland Barthes*. New York: Routledge, 1989. Print.

Worsham, Lynn. "Going Postal: Pedagogic Violence and the Schooling of Emotion." *JAC* 18 (1998): 213–45. Print.

———. "On the Rhetoric of Theory in the Discipline of Writing: A Comment and a Proposal." *JAC* 19 (1999): 389–409. Print.

———. "Writing against Writing: The Predicament of Ecriture Feminine in Composition Studies." Harkin and Schilb 82–104.

Wysocki, Anne Frances, Johndan Johnson-Eilola, Cynthia L. Selfe, and Geoffrey Sirc. *Writing New Media: Theory and Applications for Expanding the Teaching of Composition*. Logan: Utah State UP, 2004.

Yagelski, Robert P. *Literacy Matters: Writing and Reading the Social Self*. New York: Teacher's College Press, 2000. Print.

———. "Who's Afraid of Subjectivity? The Composing Process and Postmodernism, or a Student of Donald Murray Enters the Age of Postmodernism." Tobin and Newkirk 203–17. Print.

Yarbrough, Stephen. *After Rhetoric: The Study of Discourse beyond Language and Culture*. Carbondale: Southern Illinois UP, 1999. Print.

"YouTube Fact Sheet." YouTube, 2010. Web.

Zavarzadeh, Mas'ud. "Theory as Resistance." *Rethinking Marxism* 2.1 (1989): 50–70. Print.

Zhao, Ruijie. "Teaching Invention through YouTube." *Computers and Composition Online*. Web.

Zittrain, Jonathan. *The Future of the Internet and How to Stop It*. New Haven: Yale UP, 2008. Print.

Zizek, Slavoj. *The Sublime Object of Ideology*. New York: Verso, 1989. Print.

———. *Tarrying with the Negative: Kant, Hegel, and the Critique of Ideology*. Durham: Duke UP, 1993. Print.

INDEX

Adler-Kassner, Linda, 143
Agamben, Giorgio, 30, 34, 36, 37, 41, 63, 87, 142, 144
Alaei, Bahareh, ix, 13, 17, 24, 26
Alcazar Theater. *See* Liberty 3
Alcorn, Marshall W., 26, 32, 34, 80–81, 96–98, 143
aleatory procedures, 14–15
Amerika, Mark, 3
Anderson, Chris, 1, 65, 75
Anderson, Virginia, 53, 143
AnthroVlog, 9, 88
Aristotle, 35, 41, 52, 63–64, 72
Arroyo, Sarah J., and Geoffrey V. Carter, 27, 71–72, 115, 122, 131–32
assemblages, 32–33, 41, 63, 67–68, 73, 87
authorship, 2, 5, 49, 143

Ball, Cheryl, and James Kalmbach, 3
Ballif, Michelle, D. Diane Davis, and Roxanne Mountford, 68
Bang the Drum Slowly, 83, 85
Barthes, Roland, 52, 63, 118, 142; on the punctum of recognition, 14, 26, 49–50, 54–57; reread by Gregory Ulmer, 54–55, 57–58; in "Transformational Grammars: Virtual Exiles and MyStory," 123–28
Bauer, Dale M., 143
bed intruder, 132
"Being Placed (Not!)," 17, 119

Bell, California, 124, 127, 129
Benkler, Yochai, 80
Berlin, James, 51, 69, 141
Beyond Postprocess, 27, 102–3, 109, 111
Biggs, Abraham, 98–100
Bingham, Art, 6
Bizzell, Patricia, 108
Bolter, Jay David, 3, 63
Boyle, Casey, 59
Boym, Svetlana, 130–131
brat-pack, meme, 74–75; in Long Beach, California, 26, 119
Breuch, Lee-Ann M. Kastman, 27, 103–4, 107–9, 143
Brooke, Collin Gifford, 5; in "Being Delicious" (*see* Brooke, Collin gifford, and Thomas Rickert); in "Forgetting to Be (Post) Human," 67; on *pattern* and *persistence*, 113; on *proairesis*, 26, 50, 54, 58–59, 79
Brooke, Collin Gifford, and Thomas Rickert, 22, 81, 86, 88–89, 94, 102, 121
Brooks, Kevin, 15, 17, 102, 120–21; in "Exploring Post-Critical Composition" (see Kevin Brooks and Aaron Anfinson)
Brooks, Kevin, and Aaron Anfinson, 102, 120
Brown, Lisa J. (pseud. lisa b), 131–36
Burgess, Jean, and Joshua Green, 20–23, 44, 46, 58, 71, 73, 77, 80

Carter, Geoffrey V., ix, 121; in "Tubing the Future" (*see* Arroyo, Sarah J., and Geoffrey V. Carter)
Carter, Geoffrey V., and Cortney Smethurst, 132
Carter, Michael, 23, 25, 53, 86
CATTt, 145–46
chora, 8, 26, 112–13, 124, 129–30, 136, 145–46; as an inventional practice, 49–50, 53, 59–62, 65–68, 71–73
choragraphy. *See* choric invention
"Choric Arcade," 17, 24
choric invention, 26, 28, 49–50, 61, 63, 70–71, 74, 107, 113, 120, 142
"Choric Slam Tilt: Unpinning the Table," 24, 119
chronos, 67
Clark, J. Elizabeth, 3
Collins, Vicki Tolar, 143
complex ecology, 25, 60
conduction, 50, 59
conductive logic, 14
Conference on College Composition and Communication (CCCC), 6
Conley, Thomas M., 52
Contending with Words, 141
CopperCab, 92–95, 97, 99, 117
critical pedagogy, 24, 29, 31, 33, 37, 40, 44, 53, 68, 110, 120
Crouse, Jeff, 115, 117
Crowley, Sharon, 10, 53, 109, 111, 141
Crowley, Sharon, and Debra Hawhee, 53
cultural studies, 24, 31, 39–40
Curry, Judson B, 108

Dalton, David W., and Michael J. Hannafin, 3
Daniell, Beth, 108
Davidson, Donald, 26, 80, 83–85, 110
Davis, D. Diane, in *Breaking Up,* 2–3, 33, 35, 65, 68, 97, 115; in "Finitude's Clamor," 34–37, 46–47, 85–87, 105, 110; in "Negotiating the Differend," 68

Davis, Mike, 123, 128–29
Deleuze, Gilles, 33; and Claire Parnet, 67; and Félix Guattari (*see* Deleuze, Gilles, and Félix Guattari)
Deleuze, Gilles, and Félix Guattari: in *Anti-Oedipus,* 32; in *A Thousand Plateaus,* 36, 64, 67, 70, 73, 90, 114; in *What Is Philosophy?,* 107
deoedipalization, 36, 47
deoedipalized subject, 26, 79–80, 97, 142
dancing floor, 61–62; as "The Dancing Floor," 26, 119
Derrida, Jacques, 6, 36, 49, 60–61, 133, 142, 144; in "Derrida at Little Big Horn," 15, 17
desire, 12, 14, 46, 68, 81, 96–97, 109, 126, 143; felt by Roland Barthes, 54–55; and the social, 32–33, 41, 48
desire, 14, 46, 54–55, 68, 81, 96–97, 143; for a pedagogy other(wise), 109; and the social, 32–33, 41, 48
desiring production, 23, 37, 41, 63, 142
digital culture, 37–39, 44, 51, 58, 113
discourse of mastery, 26, 79, 86, 94, 96, 99, 100, 111
Dobrin, Sidney I., 5, 101, 104, 141
Dobrin, Sidney I., J. A. Rice, and Michael Vastola, 27, 102–3, 110–11
dreaming, the, 66–67
Dubisar, Abby M., and Jason Palmeri, 3
Durst, Russell, 29

ecology, 20, 25, 60–71–72, 88
electracy, ix, 57, 58, 65, 68, 79, 82, 106, 119–23, 133, 137, 141, 145; defined and envisioned through the lens of online video, 1–2, 4–8, 10–14, 16–19, 21–25, 29–27; and participatory pedagogy, 112–13, 115, 118; and postprocess, 101, 103–4; and subjectivity, 29–32, 35–41, 45–46; and videocy, 21, 45, 123

electrate reasoning, 18, 59–60, 69–71, 74, 141
electricity, 6–7, 59
emblem. *See* image of wide scope
entertainment, 7–8, 12, 14, 16, 19, 42, 45–46, 69, 115–16
European Graduate School (EGS), 83
exposure, 46–48, 68, 87, 89, 121, 144

Facebook, 11, 13, 21, 48, 77–79, 122, 124, 128
Faigley, Lester, 31, 141
Felman, Shoshana, 109
felt, 11, 24, 40, 64, 66, 68, 122, 127, 134; as emotional qualities and material, 113–14; as felt knowledge, 14, 115
finitude, 87, 89, 144
Fish, Stanley, 108–9, 143
flame, 90–91, 94, 97
flaming. *See* hating
Foster, Helen, 142
Freeman, John Craig, 3
Friedman, Emily, 99
Fulkerson, Richard, 31, 141

Gale, Fredric, 108
Gere, Anne Ruggles, 143
Glassnote Entertainment Group, 75
Gregory Brothers, 132
Gruber, Howard E, 15
Guattari, Félix. *See* Deleuze, Gilles, and Félix Guattari; *Thousand Plateaus, A*
Gye, Lisa, 4

haecceity, 67–68
Halbritter, Bump, and Todd Taylor, 144
Hancock, John D. See *Bang the Drum Slowly*
Hardin, Joe Marshall, 29
Harkin, Patricia, 108
Harkin, Patricia, and John Schilb. See *Contending with Words*

Harris, Joseph, 108
hater, 90–94, 97, 99
"Haterz be hatin' on dis," 91
hating, 27, 79, 88, 90–92, 94–95, 97–99
Havelock, Eric, 6
Hawisher, Gail, 3
Hawisher, Gail, and Cynthia Selfe, 3
Hawk, Byron, ix, 5, 24–25, 62, 65, 84; on Ulmerian genres, 15–17
Haynes, Cynthia, 3, 101; on post-conflict pedagogy, 26–27, 77, 80, 98–100
Haynes, Cynthia, and Jan Rune Hol-mevik, 3
Heidegger, Martin, 36, 68
Hemingway, Earnest, 122, 131, 133–36
Heuretics (book), 11, 14, 17, 49–50, 59, 61, 63, 65–66, 73, 88, 101, 111–12, 114, 145
heuretics (concept), 27, 106, 112–15, 120, 145
hole, 33, 51, 63, 67–68, 107, 144
holey space, 60, 62–64, 69
Hulu, 19

idiocy, 13–14; of videocy, 13
ideologies, 65, 110
ideology, 11, 12, 29, 33–34, 65, 125
image of wide scope, 15–17
immanence, 34, 36, 39, 87, 144
incorporeal transformations, 90, 95
invention, 7, 25–26, 37, 51–53, 99, 111–12, 114, 122, 136, 141, 145; and chora, 49–50, 60–67, 69–72, 74, 80, 120, 142; as *proairesis*, 54, 57–60; and video, 10, 12–15, 17. *See also* choric invention
IshatOnU, 92–93, 95

Jarratt, Susan, 108
Jarrett, Michael, 145
Jaschilk, Scott, 9
Jenkins, Henry, 9, 30, 33, 42, 44, 72–73, 88
Johnson-Eilola, Johndan, 3

Jones, Donald C., 31
Juhasz, Alexandra, 19, 21–22, 29,
    41–45, 69, 73, 77
Just Gaming, 77, 81–82, 98–99
juxtaposition, 68, 117, 121, 131

kairos, 67
Kameen, Paul, 118
Kimoto, Cortney, ix, 25–26, 49, 132
Kent, Thomas, 26–27, 35, 80–81, 83–88,
    91, 103–5, 108–10, 114; on herme-
    neutic guesses and hermeneutic
    guesswork, 81, 84, 93; on passing
    theories, 26, 84, 87
Khan Academy, 7–8
Kinneavy, James L., 81, 143
Kopelson, Karen, 31
Kuhn, Virginia, 80, 86, 97–98
Kundera, Milan, 89–92
kyburz, bonnie lenore, 48

Landow, George, 3
Lange, Patricia, 9, 21–22, 30, 47, 77,
    90–91, 97
Lau, Anna, 13
Lauer, Janice, 15, 53
Liberty 3 (formally the Alcazar The-
    ater), 125, 127
Lingua Fracta, 7, 58–59, 79, 113
listening game, 27–28, 82–83, 86–87,
    89, 91, 98
Liszt, Franz, 74
lisztomania, 26, 73–75, 119
Lunsford, Andrea, 143
Lyotard, Jean-François, 77, 87, 94–95,
    97–99, 144; his alternative to the
    Lacanian "discourse of the mas-
    ter," 26, 80, 100; his listening game
    (*see* listening game); and Victor
    Vitanza, 71, 81–85, 110

Manning, Erin, 59–60
Mauer, Barry, 4–5
McComiskey, Bruce, 107
McLuhan, Marshall, 6

MEMEorial, 122–23, 131–36
Memmott, Talan, 4
MEmorial, 17, 120–23, 130–32
memory, 16, 66, 88, 113, 130, 136, 145
Meyers, Aaron, 115, 117
"Mi Papa Es Eu Papa: MEMEorializ-
    ing Ernest Hemingway," 131–36
Milgram, Stanley, 96–98
mood, 24, 64, 66, 113–14
Moor, Peter J., 90
Moore-Howard, Rebecca, 143
Moulthrop, Stuart, 63
Mr. Mentality, 11
MyStory, 4, 14, 17–18, 66, 116, 121–25,
    128, 130, 133; as participatory
    mystory, 122

Nancy, Jean-Luc, 87, 91, 144
networks, 8–9, 19, 21–23, 38, 58–59,
    100, 102, 111, 113–14, 116

oedipalization, 142
oedipalized subject, 39, 141
O'Gorman, Marcel, 4, 17, 58, 130
Olague, Mark R., ix, 123–31
Olson, Gary, 103, 109
Omizo, Ryan, 47
Ong, Walter, 5–6

paralogy, 71,106, 110, 114, 144
participatory composition, 10, 18, 22–
    23, 27, 28, 36, 38, 41, 49, 105–6, 117,
    120–21, 137, 141–42; and electracy,
    1–2, 4, 24, 119; and heuretics, 112
participatory culture, 2, 5, 27, 33, 70,
    94, 102, 106; and electracy, 8–11, 18,
    119, 122; in relation to Roland Bar-
    thes's reading of photographs in
    Camera Lucida, 54; and YouTube,
    19–20, 22, 42, 44, 46, 58
participatory pedagogy, 25, 27–28,
    101–2, 106, 111–12, 115, 120, 144
"Participatory Publics: From MEmo-
    rials to MEMEmorials," 132
participatory subjects, 23

pattern, 4, 6, 57, 62, 86, 102, 114, 116, 125; in *Lingua Fracta*, 113
peachofmeat, 77–79, 93, 98
Pearl, Daniel, 98–99
pedagogical imperative, 27–28, 109, 115, 144
pedagogy, 4–5, 10, 27, 31, 34, 37, 42, 49, 51, 94, 103–11, 114–15, 121, 135, 143–44; of demand, 26, 80, 91, 96–97, 100; as empowerment-oriented, 31–32; of severity, 26, 80, 91, 94–97, 100. *See also* critical pedagogy; participatory pedagogy; postconflict pedagogy
pedagogy hope, 109, 115, 144
persistence, 113
Pew Center for Internet and American Life, 9
Phoenix (band), 73, 75
popcycle, 14–18, 116–20, 124, 141
Porter, James, 3, 22–23
Porter, Kevin J., 26, 80, 95–97
postconflict pedagogy, 26–27, 80, 91, 98–100, as "Postconflict Pedagogy," 77, 98
posthuman, 5, 36, 67
postmodernism, 25, 69, 142
postpedagogy, 27, 101–2, 106, 109–11, 120, 144
postprocess, 81, 84, 103–10, 141, 144
post-critical composition, 50, 59, 120
praxis, 63, 107–8, 146
Prelinger, Rick, 72
punceptual linkages, 66
punctum, 14, 49, 54, 56–57, 60, 62, 89, 123, 125, 131; and Pulp Fiction, 127; Ulmer's reappropriation of, 50, 57

question of definition, 25, 49–51, 54, 57–58, 60–62, 71, 74, 142

Rajchman, John, 64, 70–71
Rassmussen, Terry, 108
reciprocity, 30, 77–78, 95
Reid, Alexander, 5, 23–24, 58, 63, 72, 137

remix, 3, 28, 60, 89, 117–18, 132; and reappropriation, 26, 50, 59, 65; as stage one remix, 74; as stage two or social remix, 74–75
resistance, 32, 34, 39–40, 96, 98, 100–101, 104, 107, 109; as active resistance, 100
rhetorics, 18, 24, 39, 67, 119–120; as empowerment-oriented, 41, 46, 53; as "internalist" and "externalist," 105
rhizome, 68
Rice, Jeff, 4–5, 27, 61, 102–3
Rickert, Thomas, ix; in *Acts of Enjoyment*, 5, 24, 31–32, 40, 51, 69, 102, 119, 141–42; in "Being Delicious," 22, 81, 86, 88–89, 94, 102, 121; in "Enjoying Theory," 146; "'Hands Up, You're Free,'" 33, 34; and Lynn Worsham, 37, 79; in "Toward the Chora," 60–62, 66, 70, 72, 136
Ritchie, Joy, and Kathleen Boardman, 143
Ronell, Avital, 34, 142
Roussin, Sarah (pseud. MissSarah537), ix, 91

Sanchez, Julian, 74–75
Saper, Craig, 4–5, 11, 61
Schilb, John, 141
Schramm, J. D., 135
Selfe, Cyntihia L., 3
singularities, 29, 31, 39, 67, 116, 141, 144; community of, 30, 38, 47–48, 87, 91, 94, 100; subjects as, 32–33, 117; as Tubers, 37, 98, as whatever, 37, 46, 87
Sirc, Geoffery, 3, 40–41
Skinnell, Ryan, 72–73
Sloterdijk, Peter, 34
Smethurst, Cortney. *See* Cortney Kimoto
Smit, David W., 108
smooth space, 63–64, 70
Snickars, Pelle, 72

social-epistemic rhetoric, 51
social remix, 74–75
solon (raja shah zen solon), 16
Solon (the ancient Greek tourist), 16, 88
speaking as a listener, 26, 79–80, 82, 87–88
spirit hand, 35–36, 41
spreadable media, 26, 50, 75
stage one remix, 74
stage two remix. *See* social remix
Stivale, Charles J., 32
STOP BUSH, 39–41
STOP US, 40–41, 47
STOP U, 41, 47
"Storytelling," 58, 72
Strangelove, Michael, 38
striated space, 63–64, 69
studium, 56–57
sub for sub, 77, 92, 98
subject, 2, 5, 11, 24, 28, 52, 58, 65–67, 84, 96, 110, 124; and Barthes, 55; from singularities to tubers, 29–40. *See also* deoedipalized subject; oedipalized subject
subjectivity, 5, 8, 23, 24, 89, 105, 144; recast for electracy, 29–37, 41, 46–48, 141; as singularity, 46–47

Tarantino, Quentin, 124–28
TEGWAR, 83, 85
Teletheory (book), 2, 4, 11–12, 14, 17–18, 58–59, 88, 101, 123, 132, 145
teletheory (as precursor to electracy), 11–12, 14
television, 11–12, 92, 127, 134
territorialization, 32; as de- and re-territorialization, 33, 35, 65
text, 24, 44, 47–48, 55, 58, 105; as comments, 13, 18; as a "felt," 113; as a text-based status update, 48
Thebald, Jean-Loup. See *Just Gaming*
theory hope, 108–9, 143
THOMPSON, 34, 36–37, 39, 41
Thousand Plateaus, A (Deleuze and Guattari), 36, 64, 67, 70, 73, 90, 114

"Three Countertheses: or, A Critical In(ter)vention into Composition and Pedagogies," 23–25, 109–10, 144; and the first counterthesis, 51, 71; and the second counterthesis, 81–82; and the third counterthesis, 101, 103–4, 106
Tofts, Darren, 4
totality, 37, 51, 144
tourist, 16, 83, 88, 132
trace, 6–7, 48, 51, 62, 124, 132; as traces, 6, 21–22, 46, 61–62, 72, 91, 98, 107, 112, 117
tracing, 61–62, 144
"Transformational Grammars: Virtual Exiles and MyStory," 123–31
trauma, 24, 106, 128
Trimbur, John, 31
tubes, 71–73, 88
tubers, 71, 73, 79, 86, 90–92, 95, 97–98; as subjects, 29, 31, 33, 37, 141
tubing, 39, 71, 78, 89, 91–92, 98, 115–17, 132
Tumblr, 19

Ulmer, Gregory, ix, 1–2, 4–8, 27–28, 45, 59, 63, 70, 87–88, 101, 115, 137, 141–42; his appropriation of Roland Barthes, 54–55, 57–58; and chora, 60–62, 65–66, 68; and choragraphy, 25–26, 49–51, 66, 72; and the MEmorial, 17, 120–23, 130–32; and the MyStory and the popcycle, 14–17; in students' examples 123–24, 130–33, 136; and the subject, 34–37; and theory/practice 111–18, 144, 145; and videocy, 10–14, 18, 119
unconscious, 14, 32, 65, 73, 142

video culture, 2, 18, 26–27, 50, 65, 77–78, 81, 83–84, 86, 89–91, 98, 100, 106, 111, 119, 121, 132, 137, 143–44; and electracy, 4–5, 8, 10, 25, 41; and the idiocy of videocy, 13; and

mood, 113; and proairesis, 59–60; and "speaking as a listener," 79, 82; and subjectivity, 30, 32, 34, 36, 39, 45; and YouTube, 19–20, 22–23, 115
videocy, 1, 4, 10–14, 17–18, 27, 119, 132, 141; and electracy, 21, 45, 123. *See also* idiocy
video-remix, 74
video sharing, 1, 5, 7, 18–21, 43, 50, 58, 71, 77
Vimeo, 19
Vitanza, Victor, ix, 23–28, 39, 63, 142, 144–45; and chora, 65; in the first counterthesis, 49, 51, 53, 71; in the second counterthesis, 79–86; in the third counterthesis, 101–2, 104–6, 109–11, 113–14, 120
vloggers, 23, 47–48, 89, 91–92
vlogging, 22, 46–48, 92, 97

Wallace, Alexandra, 13
Walter, E. V., 35, 61–62, 65–68, 72, 88
Weinberger, Dave, 71

What is *x*?, 49, 51, 53–54
Wong, Jimmy, 13
Worsham, Lynn, 37, 79, 141–42, 144
wound, 56–57, 89, 90
Wysocki, Anne Frances, 3

Yarbrough, Stephen, 81, 83–88, 143–44
You3b, 117
YouCube, 117
YouTube, 23, 33, 36, 37, 74, 86, 88, 100; according to Alexandra Juhasz, 19–21, 29, 41–45, 69, 73; as a cultural site, 22; as an exemplar for choric invention, 26, 50, 58, 69, 71–73, 80; and hating, 90–94, 97; as a site for participatory pedagogy, 115, 117, 119–20, 125, 133–34; as a social network, 21; as the YouTube community, 22, 46, 77–78; and vlogging, 46–47, 89, 92, 97
YouTubers, 20–23, 30, 77–78

Zizek, Slavoj, 33

Sarah J. Arroyo is an associate professor of English at California State University, Long Beach, where she teaches courses ranging from composition and critical theory to digital rhetoric and multimedia composition. She has published articles in *JAC*, *Composition Forum*, *Kairos*, *Enculturation*, *Computers and Composition*, and edited collections.